I'm a Christian - What Next?

Growing in the Christian Faith

By

GERALD BOWERMAN

RB
Rossendale Books

Published by Lulu Enterprises Inc.
3101 Hillsborough Street
Suite 210
Raleigh, NC 27607-5436
United States of America

Published in paperback 2014
Category: Christianity
Copyright Gerald Bowerman © 2014

ISBN : 978-1-326-03996-7

Dedication & Acknowledgements

I would like to say thank you to my wife Ann without whose help this book would not have been written. I would also like to thank my children for the encouragement they have given me

Contents

Introduction

The purpose in writing this book is to help believers on the road to maturity. It is essential that Christians of all ages grow and reach the goal of their faith.

The 'Sermon on the Mount' concludes with the parable of the wise and the foolish builders. «Therefore everyone who hears these words of mine and puts them into practice is like a wise man who built his house on a rock. The rain came down, the streams rose, and the winds blew and beat against that house; yet it did not fall because it had it's foundation on the rock. But everyone who hears these words of mine and does not put them into practice is like a foolish man who built his house on sand. The rain came down, the streams rose, and the wind blew and beat against that house, and it fell with a great crash» (Matthew 7:24-27)

Jesus is saying that we must build our lives on a firm foundation, on His teaching. A life that is so based will be able to stand firm in the midst of the storms of life. A life constructed on the shifting sands of public opinion and the latest ideas is likely to be swept away by adverse circumstances and every calamity that may suddenly strike! Similarly if our behaviour is built on the morality of our changing culture it is likely to lead to disaster.

PART ONE: BUILDING ON A FIRM FOUNDATION

The first part of this book is written to help all who are attracted to Jesus Christ to build their lives on the firm foundation of His life and teaching. As we trust in Jesus as our Saviour and Lord and love Him with all our hearts and minds, we begin to build on that firm foundation. In the following chapters we will see what it means to become a follower of Jesus. We will explore the meaning of Baptism and how to prepare for it. We will identify with Jesus and look at how he dealt with temptation and testing and learn how to apply that to our own lives. We shall discover how to progress in the Christian life and faith towards maturity. All our lives are different, we have different experiences in our journey of faith but with Christ at the centre and as the foundation we can construct our lives on that firm rock, leaving the old life behind and becoming a new person.

PART TWO: BUILDING A HOUSE THAT WILL STAND

The second part of the book is written to help us 'live out' our Christianity. We are concerned in these chapters with the more practical challenges and demands laid upon us as followers of Jesus. The beginning of this section concentrates on the person of the Holy Spirit, who he is and how to receive Him into our lives. We learn about the 'fruit of the Spirit' and how to cultivate that fruit. We discover that God has given each one of us 'Gifts' to use in the building up and witness of the Church. We will look at the significance of participating in the Lord's supper, engaging in worship, reading the Bible and praying. There are chapters on how to be a witness, a faithful servant and a generous giver, and on living out our Christian faith in the community where we live and showing Christ's love to those around us. May God bless you as you read this book and may you be drawn closer to Jesus, and learn to love Him more. To God be all the glory.
Yours in Christ Jesus

Gerald Bowerman
Spring 2014

PART ONE

BUILDING ON A FIRM FOUNDATION

Chapter 1 - A New Beginning

In your imagination join me driving through the night in a convey of lorries. It is very dark and the country road we are following is quite narrow. There's another lorry in front of us and for some miles we follow it and benefit from its headlights illuminating the way ahead. The lead lorry signals for us to overtake him and we take a turn in leading the way through the darkness. As time goes by the sky on the horizon begins to change. It becomes a little brighter and some of the stars begin to fade but one star in particular shines more brightly, it is the « Morning Star ». The planet Venus heralding the dawn of a new day. Soon dawn breaks, everything looks different, the countryside is bathed in light Gradually the sun rises and a new day begins. When a person accepts Jesus into his/her life it is the dawn of a new day. The light of God's presence shines in and through the believer and all darkness is driven away. Life begins anew, the world seems to be a different place and nothing will ever be the same again. Wow!

The apostle John in his account of the life of Jesus writes about the time when a leader of the Jews called Nicodemus, came to question Jesus about the Kingdom of God. Jesus answered him saying « I tell you the truth, unless a man is born of water and the Spirit, he cannot enter the Kingdom of God. » (John 3:5) Jesus taught that entering the Kingdom of God, believing in Him, was the beginning of a new life in the Spirit. All of us enter human life through birth, equally all who follow Jesus enter the life he gives by being reborn. We are never the same again. Paul writes to the Church at Corinth, at a time when they were falling back into paganism, to remind them that in following Jesus they became new creations. « So from now on we regard no one from a worldly point of view. Though we once regarded Christ in this way, we do so no longer. Therefore if any one is in Christ, he is a new creation; the old has gone, the new has come! » (2 Corinthians 5:16-17) Brothers and sisters in Christ never forget that you are all new creations and no longer what you once were. You have made a new beginning and are living a new life. A new day has dawned for each of you!

Every human birth is different. All of us are born in different circumstances. The time and the place will not be the same and all of us begin our **spiritual** journey by becoming new creations but each one's path to this new birth will be different. In the New Testament we read that people came to Jesus for many different reasons and entered into a life changing relationship with Him. Saul was an intellectual Jewish leader, a Pharisee. He was opposed to those people who believed in Jesus of Nazareth. In the city of Jerusalem on the day that Stephen, a disciple of Jesus was stoned to death a great persecution against the Church broke out. We read in the New Testament that « All except the apostles were scattered throughout Judea and Samaria; godly men buried Stephen and mourned deeply for him. But Saul began to destroy the church. Going from house to house, he dragged off men and woman and put them in prison. » (Acts 8:1-3). Saul did not only persecute the church in Jerusalem but such was his hatred for those who believed in Jesus that he sought permission from the Jewish leaders to go to Damascus and arrest those who followed Jesus and bring them to Jerusalem. But Saul who persecuted the Christians, became Paul the missionary leader of the early church, his story is one of the most dramatic and well known conversions in the whole history of Christianity.

This is how it happened. We read in the 'Acts of the apostles' that as Saul neared Damascus « Suddenly a light from heaven flashed around him. He fell to the ground and heard a voice say to him, 'Saul, Saul, why do you persecute me?' 'Who are you Lord?' Saul asked. 'I am Jesus whom you are persecuting' he replied 'Now get up and go into the city, and you will be told what you must do' The men travelling with Saul stood there speechless; they heard the sound but did not see anyone. Saul got up from the ground, but when he opened his eyes he could see nothing. So they led him by the hand into Damascus. For three days he was blind, and did not eat or drink anything. » (Acts 9 :3-9). Proud Saul was humbled as he lay in the dust. The Lord he was persecuting spoke directly to him. Helpless and blind he was taken to the house of Judas on Straight street. Meanwhile the Lord had spoken in a vision to a disciple in Damascus called Ananias. We know very little about Ananias except that he was told by the Lord to go and minister to Saul and lay his hands on him. Ananias protested at first having heard many reports of all the harm that Saul had done to the Saints in Jerusalem and how he had come to Damascus with authority to arrest all who called on the name of Jesus. « The Lord said to Ananias 'Go! This man is my chosen instrument to carry my name before the Gentiles and their kings and before the people of Israel. I will show him how much he must suffer for my name'. Then Ananias went to the house and entered it. Placing his hands on Saul, he said 'Brother Saul, the Lord - Jesus, who appeared to you on the road as you were coming here - has sent me so that you may see again and be filled with the Holy Spirit', immediately something like scales fell from Saul's eyes and he could see again. He got up and was baptized, and after taking some food, he regained his strength. » (Acts 9:13-18)

Immediately after his conversion Saul began to preach in the local synagogues that Jesus is the Son of God! (Acts 9:20). Saul whose name was changed to Paul became the apostle to the Gentiles and it is through his ministry that the commission of the Lord began to be fulfilled. The Risen Lord Jesus had said to his disciples « All authority in heaven and on earth has been given to me. Therefore go and make disciples of all nations, baptizing them in the Name of the Father and of the Son and of the Holy Spirit, and teaching them to obey everything I have commanded you and surely I will be with you always, to the very end of the age. » (Matthew 28:18-20) What a dramatic change had taken place in the life of Saul. He had become a brand new person, a new creation, with a new name, and a new purpose for his life. After he met the Lord in such a dramatic way and had received ministry from the disciple Ananias. He was filled with the Holy Spirit and baptized in water. Immediately **he**

publicly shared his faith in Christ. We learn from this account of the conversion of Saint Paul that no person is beyond the love of God. God can reveal himself to those who oppose Him! Jesus can melt the hardest heart. We learn also that God can use those who believe in Jesus to impart the Holy Spirit to any person, whose heart is open, through the laying on of hands.

Not all conversions are dramatic like Paul's. There are many others in the New Testament such as Peter James and John who left their fishing boats to follow Jesus and start a new life.(Matthew 4:18-22) Matthew a tax gatherer disliked by many, left his tax booth behind, so as to follow the Lord. (Matthew 9:9-12) In later years as a leader of the church he wrote his account of the life of Jesus. Zacchaeus who was also a collector of taxes, came down from a tree to welcome Jesus into his home. He repaid four times over what he had dishonestly overcharged and gave away half his possessions to the poor! (Luke 19:1-9) All encountered Jesus. All the encounters were different! All made a new beginning. All were in Christ and became new creations. All made different spiritual journeys. In Acts chapter 16 we learn about Lydia.

Lydia was a dealer in purple cloth and was from the city of Thyatira which was famous for its dyeing processes. She sold purple-dyed goods which she had brought to Philippi from Thyatira, whose guild of dyers was well known. She was apparently well-to-do as a considerable amount of capital was needed to trade in such articles. The city of Philippi was situated in Macedonia but is today in Greece. Philippi was a Roman colony and of strategic importance. In the city Rome maintained an army of veterans who spoke the Roman language and wore Roman dress. Lydia seems to have been a successful business woman selling her purple cloth to Roman families. She was so successful that she owned her own house in Philippi. She was probably a Jewess who worshipped God. How did such a prominent woman meet up with Paul? Paul was in Philippi as result of a vision he had received.(Acts 16:9-10) Luke who was an eye witness to what happened writes in the Acts of the apostles « On the Sabbath we went outside the city gate to the river, where we expected to find a place of prayer. We sat down and began to speak to the woman who had gathered there. One of those listening was a woman named Lydia , a dealer in purple cloth from the city of Thyatira, who was a worshipper of God. The Lord opened her heart to respond to Paul's message. When she and the members of her household were baptized, she invited us to her home. 'If you consider me a believer in the Lord' she said, 'Come and stay at my house' and she persuaded us. » (Acts 16:13-15) Why did Paul expect to find a place of prayer? At the time of the exile in Babylon the Jewish people had no Temple or Synagogue so they gathered together on the Sabbath to Worship God by a river. Psalm 137 speaks of that time « By the rivers of Babylon we sat down and wept when we remembered Zion » To form a Jewish synagogue it was necessary for there to be ten men present. It seems that there was a group of woman wanting to worship God but not the necessary number of men! The woman followed the tradition stemming from the time of the exile and went down to the river to pray.

This beautiful story of how Lydia came to believe in Jesus is the complete opposite to what happened to Paul himself! No blinding light or voice from heaven, but simply the 'Lord opened her heart'. There is no indication of how long it took for her and her household to ask for baptism. I imagine that over a period of time and reflection, perhaps for several days, the Lord revealed himself to her so that she was sure that she believed that Jesus was the Son of God. She became a new creation. She provided hospitality for Paul and his friends and continued to support them as they continued the work of the Lord in other places. Paul did not have to rely on money earned by tent making because of the generosity of the church at Philippi. We know from Paul's other letters that he accepted gifts from the church at Philippi when he was at other churches. (2 Corinthians 11:8) (Philippians 4:16) Paul's letter to the Philippians reveals his special love for their church. (Philippians 1:3-8, 2:12,15-16, 4:1, 15, 16, 18,) I have no doubt that Lydia's help must have been one of the reasons for the special relationship Paul had with the Church he established at Philippi.

Today people of every race and culture become Christians. Each person is different and will have had a different experience of God working in their lives. Dramatic conversions do happen but many times the Lord works in a person's life over a period of time. This was my experience which I would like to share with you. It is by looking back one sees how the Lord draws people to himself. The time was just after the end of the second world war and we were living in the city of Bristol. Many buildings had been bombed and lives lost. My mother and father decided to send me to a boarding school in the country about twelve miles away from where we were living. The school had been evacuated from London and after my first term, much to my parents chagrin, I returned home for the holidays with a « cockney » accent! I was eight or nine years of age when I took the first steps of my spiritual journey. The mother of the principle of the school was an elderly retired missionary, who invited a group of us before bedtime, to come to her room. We sat on the floor in our pyjamas while she told us stories and read to us the brave exploits of missionaries in Africa. The one that has remained firmly in my mind down the years was the life story of Mary Slessor. She sailed for the coast of West Africa in 1888 and became known as «The White Queen of Calabar». Africa at that time was an unknown continent and a dangerous place for the white man. It was a land of disease, wild animals, slave markets, human sacrifice and cannibalism. In a land of death she brought a lesson of life. Her story made such a deep an impression on us that we played « church » in the woods. This consisted of constructing an altar in a clearing and decorating it. We picked a large quantity of bluebells which we placed in a 'Horlicks' tin full of water and carefully put them on the altar. We also buried several dead birds that we found and placed a suitable stone on top of the grave to mark the place!

I have to admit that I was not happy at boarding school and missed my mother and father a great deal. I vividly remember one evening going to a master's room to talk with him. He spoke to me about Jesus and asked me if I wanted Him to come into my life. Kneeling down I asked Jesus to come into my life and committed my young life to Him. The master prayed with me and gave me a Christian book. I sincerely believe at that moment the Lord entered into my life and although in later years I was to turn my back on Him and deny His existence, the Lord never left me.

I had a good voice and after being tested I joined the village church choir. My memories were mainly that of church services that seemed never ending and of the vicar getting worked up and banging his fist on the side of the pulpit as he tried to emphasise an important point in his sermon! I have no recollection of what he preached. Most of the boys in the choir were from the village and the tradition was that new boys were baptised under the water tap in the grave yard. I was duly baptised by an older boy! It was worth getting wet and having a pencil waved up and down in my mouth by the choir master, as I received payment at the end of the term for all my choir duties! So my spiritual journey began at boarding school in the country. It continued when after failing exams at the age of 11 and 13, I was accepted at a Church of England boarding school in Bristol. It was at this school that I was confirmed in the faith, the Bishop of Malmesbury laying his hands on my head! I felt nervous but nothing else! History was my best subject at school and I also opted to take Religious knowledge as one of my subjects for the 'school certificate.' I did not pass the exam but won the school Divinity Prize! At this stage of my spiritual journey I had been confirmed by the Church of England won the senior divinity prize, joined the school prayer guild (To be a member of the guild you had to promise to pray every day) but did not have a relationship with the living Lord Jesus. Academically I did not do very well at secondary school and was classed as a late developer. I had obtained two O levels and a belief in the Anglican church.

The two years after I left school at sixteen were very busy. I started work in a public analyst, dealing with food and drink. Most of my time I was engaged in the chemical and biological analysis of water and studying to obtain more O levels. We had moved house and having been at boarding school I had few friends, and those I did have my father thought were unsuitable for me to mix with! I think it was loneliness that led me to the local Anglican church. The vicar needed an Altar boy. Soon I was dressed again in cassock and surplus serving at the Altar assisting with the sacrament of Holy Communion. It was during this time that I was sent as a delegate to one of the first ecumenical gatherings of young people. I met Christians of different traditions and found myself deep in discussion with a group of Baptists. I was much impressed by their living faith which contrasted strongly with my church traditions. I saw something in them that I did not possess! Their religion was real, sadly mine was not! At this time there was another landmark on my spiritual journey. Close to our home was a river and some woods. One day I was walking down a path towards the river looking for some friends who had built a canoe, when I saw a young man whom I vaguely knew sitting on a park bench reading a bible. He engaged me in conversation and spoke to me about the bible. The bible for me at that time was just a big black book that people read at Church on a Sunday. He tried, I realise now, to lead me to the Saviour. I later discovered that he belonged to the local Brethren Assembly. I realised that this young man and those young people at the conference were different and had something that I wanted.

At the age of eighteen my spiritual journey hit the buffers! I was living in London and working for a drug manufacturing company. My chief interest was football and going out with the lads on a Saturday night. I was what was called in the fifties an « Angry Young man ». I was rebelling against my parents, society, and the God I no longer believed in. I got involved in left wing politics, CND ban the bomb marches, and protests of various kinds. The night that America and Cuba were on the brink of war I was protesting outside both the American and Cuban embassies and outside ten Downing street calling for a general strike! On reflection I think that it was this night in particular led me to the conclusion that political protests changed very little. I was I suppose living the normal secular life of a twenty year old boy away from home (Music, dancing, sport, drink and chasing girls!). Even now looking back with some nostalgia I can still feel the pain of loneliness, unhappiness and of being unsatisfied and unfulfilled. The company I worked for sent me to a conference the aim of which was to broaden the knowledge of the arts for those who worked in a laboratory. There was much discussion on many topics but the thing I remember most vividly was an Irish boy getting to his feet in the middle of a debate saying « What about the man who came back from the dead? » - he was of course referring to the death and resurrection of Jesus. The courage of this boy who was ridiculed by most of the others made a lasting impression on me and filled me with admiration.

I left the firm I was working for and went to college full time to study Analytical Chemistry. In another attempt to impart culture to would be scientists a liberal studies period was inserted into the time table. This was led by a retired business man who had worked for ICI, a large company that manufactured Chemicals. It was during one of these sessions which involved filling in a form about our belief in God that I stood up and declared in public that I did not believe in God! A strange thing happened. I felt a deep peace enter my being. It was a fresh start. The problem for me was that my understanding of Christianity was tied up with church and all the trappings of religion. All the activities of the churches were swept away and I was free! This denial of the existence of God was the first step in my discovering the possibility of a living relationship with Him. Good bye religion! Now comes relationship!

The amazing fact is that from that moment on God seemed to meet with me at every turn. I just could not get away from Him. The next weekend I went to stay at the house of a college friend who lived at Southampton. He was older than me and had been a RAF officer serving in Germany after the war. We had been at college together for well over a year and I had no idea that he was a Christian. During the weekend he began to talk about Christianity. I later discovered he had been part of an Evangelical church. In our conversation he challenged me saying « Gerald you do not even know what a Christian is. » I was a bit cross but replied that «a Christian was someone who helped other people» and added

« someone who helped old ladies to cross the road or gave up their seat on the bus! ». My friend told me that I had no idea but did not share his faith with me. This incident led me to look more deeply into Christianity. I bought a copy of JB Philips « Letters to the Churches ». I read it and decided to get a copy of « The Young Church in Action » by the same author . This book did make a deep impression on me but I was still in a spiritual fog. On another occasion I went into a second hand book shop on Uxbridge High Street. On the shelf was a book by Billy Graham entitled « Peace with God » I bought the book walked to the railway station to wait for the train. I sat on one of the seats on the platform and began to read. God spoke to me through that book and the fog began to clear. I still did not know the Lord!

I finished at college and returned to Bristol where I got a job as chief laboratory technician at a grammar school. I had two colleagues working as my assistants. One of these was a young lady of about thirty years of age. Every day at lunch time we ate our sandwiches in my office. Every day she brought up the subject of church. She was a member of a nearby Baptist Church. She spoke in glowing terms of what she had been doing as part of the church and for God. We discussed Christianity, Jesus, and eternal life. Many times I argued about God, Jesus and the church. Many times I think I won the arguments but there was something special about that young woman. I realised almost immediately she had that something that I was searching for. Now over fifty years on I realise that the presence of the Lord shone from her face. She made a profound impression on my life and although we have not met since, she was instrumental in me becoming a Christian and serving the Lord as a minister of the gospel. She does not know the effect her testimony had on my life. Her name was Mrs Angel! She was indeed God's messenger.

That was the pivotal point the rest of the story flowed from that event. My Grandmother died in my arms and I really felt a peace that her spirit had left her body and gone to be with the Lord. We moved to my Grandmother's house in Weston-Super-Mare. The local Congregational Church leafleted the area inviting people to come to the Church. My father and mother and my two brothers started to go to the church on Sunday. My two brothers were soon going to the youth club but I the oldest son did not go. I was after all a confirmed Anglican. Each Sunday I went to a different Church of England. None of the churches seemed very friendly towards strangers and they seemed to be completely out of touch with the real world! My father said one Sunday « Why don't you come with us to the local Congregational church? They have a minister your own age and I am sure that you will get on well with him. » It was in the Congregational Church that I came to faith in the living God.

Very soon having recommitted my life to Jesus I was asked to serve as a deacon by the minister and soon I was busy serving the Lord in the fellowship of the Church. The fog was dispersed and the light of Christ gradually began to shine on me. It was a gradual process that can be compared with the switching on of an eco- friendly light bulb! The dim light gradually grew brighter. Every spiritual journey is different with events on route that change a person's destiny. No two conversions are the same but always there is a time when you do not believe and a time when you know that you do believe. It can be described in all sorts of ways, crossing a line, seeing the light, or being born again. The important thing is that we make a new beginning and enter into the fullness of life that God gives to us when we give our life to Him.

I have heard it said that when a person becomes a Christian all problems cease! You must be kidding! In fact life and relationships can become more difficult. Being a follower of Jesus is not the most easy life but it can be the most exciting! Many people have described the differences they experienced after accepting Jesus into their life. I listened to the testimony of Kathryn Kulmann whose ministry of healing is acknowledged throughout the U SA and in other parts of the world. She said that after she had given her heart to Jesus her world seemed a different place! Life was no longer in black and white but in glorious Technicolor! She also described how on the Sunday she gave her life to Jesus she left the local chapel, and went skipping down the street speaking to everybody she met! Every conversion experience will vary but the signs of becoming a brand new creature are often similar. For example when I talked with people who came to faith through attending a ten week « Alpha course » nearly all spoke of a new peace in their lives. Many were set free from fears and anxieties. Some spoke of a new appreciation of the beauty of nature and all that which God has created. This new relationship with God, and the experience of being forgiven not only led to inner peace but to great joy. Other people in the group said they had been able to forgive others who had harmed them and forget old differences. Some had made a conscious effort to put right something that had happened many years ago much to the amazement of other members of their family! Nearly everyone in the group said that they had become aware of their sinfulness and of their need of cleansing. Behaviour and attitudes had begun to change. Their lives were moving in a new direction.

Not everybody after they have been converted are destined to be missionaries like the apostle Paul! Not all are called to be preachers, pastors or leaders of the Church but all are called to be disciples in the place where God has put them. Zacchaeus the chief tax collector of Jericho, had his life transformed by contact with Jesus (Luke 19:1-10) He was an important person, being the official responsible for the tax collectors of the district. Jericho the city of Palms and an oasis in the desert was the gateway to Judea's eastern trade route. Herod the Great, who was a murderous dictator, made Jericho his winter capital. He built a luxurious palace there. The question that fascinates me is what happened to Zacchaeus after he was converted? I suspect that he carried on working as chief tax collector. He had radically repented and made restitution. Those people he had cheated whether they were businessmen or tax collecting colleagues must have been amazed when he stood up and said to the Lord « Look, Lord! Here and now I give half of my possessions to the poor, and if I have cheated anybody out of anything, I will pay back four times the amount. » (Luke 19:8) What a change had taken place in his heart. His new beginning started by helping the poor of whom there were a great number, and making restitution for all the money he had taken unjustly. Wanting to put things right is often a result of conversion and one can read stories of people who have tried to do just that. There is the story of a person who had not paid the correct rail fare and went back to the station ten years later and tried to pay back what he owed! I have also heard of people who had fiddled their income tax return and later tried to put it right. There are those people who have « borrowed » something from their place of work who after receiving Jesus into their lives have returned the said article! Zachaeus' heart was melted by the gospel and he gave away half of his possessions to the poor. Many new converts have set up, or become active supporters of charities, making new beginnings in their attitude and helping other human beings. Their morals and their behaviour change. They become new creations.

A sure sign of a person becoming a new creation is the desire to serve others. Service in the context of church or community flows naturally from following Jesus.

Dorcas is described in the New Testament as a disciple of Jesus. She lived in Joppa and was full of charitable works. She made clothing for many people. She fell sick, died, and was raised from the dead by Peter after he had been urgently summoned from Lydda, nine miles distant. (Acts 9:36-42). Her death left widows weeping because of all her good works but her raising from the dead led to many people being converted; « This became known all over Joppa, and many people believed in the Lord. » (Acts 9:41) Even today there are women's groups called Dorcas' Societies who are devoted to good works. Her life has inspired many people to serve God in the community in a practical way. Today many Christians run food banks and do soup runs, helping the poor and hungry. There is an old Christian slogan, « Saved to Serve » When we make our new beginning, we will desire to serve God. The way that countless Christians have done this is by denying- self and serving others. A new day has dawned. Welcome to the first day of the rest of your life.

Chapter 2 - Counting the Cost

We live in a society dominated by consumerism. Many people are constantly looking for low prices, I have a friend who spends all his time looking for bargains. If he sees a bargain whether he needs it or not he buys it! Today many people do not want to pay the full price for anything. In contrast we need to be aware that it costs every thing to be a disciple of Jesus. Two of the parables that Jesus taught about the kingdom of God emphasise this point. He said «The kingdom of heaven is like treasure hidden in a field. When a man found it, he hid it again, and then in his joy went and sold all he had and bought that field. Again the kingdom of heaven is like a merchant looking for fine pearls. When he found one of great value, he went away and sold everything he had and bought it.» (Matthew 13:44-46) Matthew, uses the term kingdom of heaven synonymously with the term kingdom of God. They are interchangeable. The basic meaning in the bible of the kingdom of God is that of the kingly rule or sovereignty of God. To be a disciple of Jesus means being a subject of His kingdom. He is the King we are His obedient subjects. The parables teach us that it costs us everything to be part of the kingdom and one of his disciples. The treasure in the field was there because in an age with no secure banks and many thieves the safest place for money and most precious possessions was buried in the ground! The man stumbled on the treasure by accident and spent everything he had to obtain it. Similarly the pearl merchant after looking for many years finds the priceless pearl and he sacrifices everything to obtain it. I find it interesting that the merchant was looking for fine pearls that was his life's work. This search was the most important thing in his life. No matter how we discover Jesus and the kingdom of God it will cost us everything.

Dietrich Bonhoeffer was a German Lutheran pastor and theologian, who opposed Hitler and the Nazis'. He was a founding member of the confessing Church in Germany and was imprisoned for his faith and finally executed at Flosenburg concentration camp in April 1945. He coined the phrase 'cheap grace.' This he wrote was the greatest enemy of the Christian faith and the Church as a whole in his generation. Seventy five years on it still is a great enemy. Bonhoeffer in his book « The Cost of Discipleship » (1937), called Christians to be more faithful and obedient to Christ. He severely rebuked comfortable Christianity . He wrote «Cheap grace is preaching forgiveness without requiring repentance, baptism without church discipline, taking Holy Communion without confession. Cheap grace is grace without discipleship, grace without the cross, grace without Jesus Christ, living incarnate ». There are people in our churches who profess to be Christians and yet reject that they are sinners and need salvation. They by-pass the cross of Jesus. Theirs is a cross-less Christianity. There are those in the church who only emphasise the love of God and reject that He is judge of both the living and the dead. A coin has two sides, so also has the God of the Bible. We find in both the old and new Testaments God's love for his people but also his judgement on their behaviour. Another illustration of « Cheap Grace » is seen in those who preach a God of prosperity, and lose sight of Jesus' sacrifice for the sin of the world by dying on a cross. Yes God does prosper his people but he also calls for self sacrifice and consecration of our lives to Him. There is no such thing as a cross-less or cost less Christianity.

Immediately after Simon Peter had confessed that he believed that Jesus was «The Christ, the Son of the living God » Jesus spoke to his disciples concerning what following Him would cost. He made clear the conditions of discipleship. « Then Jesus said to his disciples, 'If anyone would come after me, he must deny himself and take up his cross and follow me. For whoever wants to save his life will lose it, but whoever loses his life for me will find it.' » (Matthew 16:24-25) **All discipleship begins with the confession of faith, « Jesus is the son of the living God » and with the acceptance of the conditions that Jesus laid down**. Until there is a personal surrender to Jesus Christ with its consequent peace of mind and cleansing of motive, there can be no real discipleship.

The mark of the true disciple of Jesus is that he wishes to be like his Master. If we really desire to be like Him, then Christ tells us, that it will cost us everything. On another occasion when large crowds were travelling with Him Jesus turned to them and said «If anyone comes to me and does not hate his father and mother, his wife and children - yes even his own life - he cannot be my disciple. And anyone who does not carry his cross and follow me cannot be my disciple » (Luke 14:25-27) At that time Jesus was probably at the peak of his popularity. As he travelled from one place to another many people were following him. The tradition was that the pupils of a Jewish Rabbi walked behind their master and listened to his teaching. Jesus knew that all these people who wanted to be his followers were not aware of what that would mean! His words must have hit them very hard as they do us today. Family life was important in those days just as it is today, but Jesus and his kingdom must be more important to his disciples than their families.

That crowd may have been stunned by the demands Jesus was making on them concerning their family relationships but that was only the beginning. Self denial was essential if they would follow Him. This self denial, death of self, Jesus compared with a prisoner carrying his cross to the place of execution! The prisoner has been condemned and is going to die an agonising death. The disciple of Jesus not only makes his master number one in his/her life but every day dies to his/her selfish nature.

Having made very clear what it will mean to be one of his followers Jesus, asks them to count the cost before becoming a disciple. He does this by two illustrations from daily life. There are many references to vineyards in the Bible. In those days there were many people who would steal produce. It is interesting to note the many references to thieves and robbers in the new Testament! Most vineyards had their watchtowers so that the grapes or vines would not be stolen. Jesus said to the crowds who were following Him « Suppose one of you wants to build a tower. Will he not first sit down and estimate the cost to see if he has enough money to complete it? For if he lays the foundation and is not able to finish it, everyone who sees it will ridicule Him saying 'This fellow began to build and was not able to finish.' » (Luke 14:28-30) Recently some relatives of mine built an extension to their house. The first thing they did was to get several estimates of how much it was going to cost. The second thing was to ask themselves if they had enough money for it. The third thing was in the light of their financial situation to give the go ahead for the extension to be built. **Any person wanting to become a disciple of Jesus must realise that it is going to cost them and be prepared to meet that cost.**

The second illustration Jesus used was of a king going to war. « Or suppose a king is about to go to war against another king. Will he not first sit down and consider whether he is able with ten thousand men to oppose the one coming against him with twenty thousand? If he is not able, he will send a delegation while the other is still a long way off and will ask for terms of peace; » (Luke14:31-32) This second illustration is a good reminder that Christians are involved in Spiritual warfare. We do go to war against evil both in ourselves and in our society. The Lord recruited people to be part of his army. Every soldier must be committed to the cause and obedient to his superiors. It is the same for the disciple. If we are looking for a life of ease we cannot be true disciples of Jesus. All soldiers know that they may have to give their life for their country. Today there are many who are being killed for their faith. The Church is persecuted in many parts of the world by people of other faiths or no faith at all. In many countries of the world the Christian Church receives no protection from political leaders. The cost of being a follower of Jesus can be very high indeed! In the parable that Jesus told we are encouraged to estimate the strength of the opposition that we face. Sometimes that opposition can appear to be very great but we also know that we will ultimately be victorious. Christ's kingdom cannot fail. Battles may be lost but final victory is certain. If we are on the Lord's side we will face many battles and the cost may be high but the victory is ours. Jesus concludes by challenging the crowd who were following him « In the same way, anyone of you who does not give up everything he has, cannot be my disciple » (Luke 14:33)

God does not call all of us to renounce wealth and position like Saint Francis of Assisi the founder of the Franciscan order in the Roman Catholic Church. Francis was born in in Italy 1181 and was renowned for drinking and partying in his youth. He fought in a battle between Assisi and Perugia and was taken prisoner. Whilst in prison he began receiving visions from God. God told him « To repair the Christian Church and live a life of poverty. » He abandoned his life of luxury, followed Christ teaching literally, putting it into practice in his life. We cannot all be like Mother Teresa the winner of the Nobel prize for peace in 1979. Born in Albania, called by God to help the poor whist living among them in Calcutta, India, Mother Teresa and her helpers built homes for orphans, nursing home for lepers, and hospices for the terminally ill. We cannot all be like Saint Francis or Mother Theresa but we can be wholehearted disciples called by the Lord to serve in the place he has put us. We are warned that we cannot be half hearted disciples of Jesus. Jesus knowing that soon he was to be betrayed and executed resolutely set out for Jerusalem. As «they were walking along the road, a man said to him 'I will follow you wherever you go' Jesus replied 'Foxes have holes and birds of the air have nests, but the Son of Man has no place to lay his head' » (Luke 9:57-58). That good man volunteered to become a disciple of Jesus but when Jesus spoke of the possibility of homelessness we read no more of him! This reply of Jesus challenges us regarding home comforts. Jesus wants us to follow him even if we have to sacrifice our security! Those who obey find a deeper security in Jesus! Many of the Lord's servants have allowed their homes to be open to all in need, to be places where all may receive a welcome. This incident is also a warning against volunteering too hastily to follow Jesus! **The call of God on a person's life has to be more than the desire to volunteer.**

Jesus did call the next person he encountered on the road. He said to another man, « 'Follow me' but the man replied, 'Lord, first let me go and bury my father' Jesus said to him 'Let the dead bury their own dead, but you go and proclaim the kingdom of God' » (Luke

9:59-60). The words that Jesus spoke to this would be follower seem rather harsh to our western ears. In all probability the man's father was not dead or dying. The man was using an eastern expression that most likely meant 'I will follow
you after my father has died'. He probably felt attracted to Jesus but was afraid of his father's displeasure. I remember a young man of fifteen who was persuaded by his family to join them at a service of infant baptism. His heart was stirred by the simple gospel message. Afterwards he came to me and said 'I would love to come to church but all my school friends would laugh at me. I will come when I leave school next year!' He never came back. Like the man in the story he missed the moment. **The story teaches us that if a person misses the moment when God is calling him, he is likely to miss out altogether!** We must be careful when we feel God's call not to allow our emotions to become a substitute for actions. That man and my young friend both missed the moment. They put off until tomorrow what should have been acted on right away.

Whilst I was staying in a hotel just outside Jerusalem, I looked out of my window where I saw a man ploughing using a donkey to pull a hand guide implement. The ground was very stony and uneven and he had to look ahead and really concentrate all his efforts for had he even looked back for a second the plough would have been knocked off course and the work spoilt. I was amazed at the sight in 20th century Jerusalem, a wonderful visual re-enactment of what Jesus was no doubt referring to in (Luke 9:61-62) « Still another said, 'I will follow you, Lord ;but first let me go back and say good-by to my family.' Jesus replied 'No one who puts his hand to the plough and looks back is fit for service in the Kingdom of God » Perhaps we might find Jesus' words to that man rather harsh too, but I think Jesus had summed him up and knew that the possibility of family pressures would be likely to knock him off course although he might well start off as a disciple.
I think Jesus is emphasising here that once a person agrees to be a disciple of Jesus it is for life. In our present society with more opportunities to pursue sports, hobbies, and leisure activities than

any previous age, people are often inclined to take up a sport or a hobby for a short length of time and then move on to something else! We cannot be a follower of Jesus for six months and then move on to something else! When we decide to be his disciple it is a commitment for life and eternity! We cannot 'blow hot' one moment and 'cold' the next! Weston-super-mare where I lived for several years has the motto « Ever Forward ». The Christian is to be ever looking forward not looking back. To the man in the story Jesus did not say « Follow » or « Return! » He said in effect « I accept no lukewarm service » and left the man to make his own decision. When we make that decision we want to say with S. Sundar Singh who based the lyrics of this song on (Luke 9:57)

I have decided to follow Jesus
No turning back, no turning back.
The cross before me, the world behind me,
No turning back, no turning back.

This is a life long commitment

We have been challenged by the words of Jesus to count the cost of discipleship before committing ourselves to Him. Here are some conditions of discipleship that we find in the gospels and in the letters of Paul.

1. The disciples are promised that they will be rewarded. In response to the heart felt cry of Peter « 'We have left all we have to follow you!' 'I tell you the truth' Jesus said to them 'No one who has left home or wife or brothers or parents or children for the sake of the kingdom of God will fail to receive many times as much in this age and in the age to come, eternal life'» (Luke 18:29-30) This is the experience of countless Christians. A life with Jesus is the best life of all. There may be hard times for all of us but through them all there is a peace that the world cannot give, or take away from us and a joy that the world does not know. **To love and be loved and receive the reward for all our labours gives our life purpose and meaning and points the way to heaven.**
2. Paul is prepared to renounce everything for his relationship

with Christ. He is prepared to consecrate himself completely to his Lord. Paul writes « But whatever was to my profit I now consider loss for the sake of Christ. What is more, I consider everything a loss compared to the surpassing greatness of knowing Christ Jesus my Lord, for whose sake I have lost all things; I consider them rubbish, that I may gain Christ and be found in Him, not having a righteousness of my own that comes from the law, but that which is through faith in Christ - the righteousness that comes from God and is by faith » (Philippians 3:7-9) Nothing else on earth mattered but Paul's relationship with Christ Jesus which was by faith in Him. He is prepared to renounce everything, time, possessions, security, self righteousness, in fact everything for the surpassing greatness of knowing Christ his Lord. Everything pales into insignificance in the light of Christ. It's just rubbish. **Renunciation and consecration are conditions of being a follower of Jesus**.

3. Renunciation and self-control are conditions of discipleship
Towards the end of his ministry Jesus warns his disciples concerning worldliness. In the context of the old age passing away and the coming of his kingdom Jesus said « Be careful, or your hearts will be weighed down with dissipation, drunkenness, and the anxieties of life, and that day will close on you unexpectedly like a trap. » (Luke 21:34) In an age when most people seem to have difficulty saying NO the Christian must be different. Of the nine fruit of the Spirit Paul writes about, self-control is the least evident in our generation! (Galatians 5:23) We must be able to say no to certain attitudes and behaviour.

4 Subduing Lusts is the hallmark of the man of God. Dealing with our natural instincts was as much a problem when Paul lived as it is today. Paul writes « And do this, understanding the present time. The hour has come for you to wake up from your slumber, because our salvation is nearer now than when we first believed. The night is nearly over; the day is almost here. So let us put aside the deeds of darkness and put on the armour of light. Let us behave decently, as in the daytime, not in orgies and drunkenness, nor in sexual immorality and debauchery, not in division and

30

jealousy. Rather clothe yourself with the Lord Jesus Christ, and do not think about how to gratify the desires of the sinful nature » (Romans 13:11-14) Many Christians have difficulty with one or more of the things that Paul lists here! We need to understand the morality of our present age. What is good and what is bad. What is right and what is wrong. We are to wake up and see things as they really are! We must not close our eyes to what is going on around us. We cannot escape from our Christian responsibility in the world. Paul gives us some clues as to how we can deal personally with our own sinful human nature. We are to put on the armour of light and clothe ourselves with the Lord Jesus Christ. How can we do this? One day while I was praying about this very thing the Lord began to show me how sinful I really was. He gave me a picture of myself dressed in filthy dirty clothes, torn and smelly. Then He reassured me that Jesus had died on the cross for my sins and the sins of the world. He had taken upon himself my filthy rags and given me a brand new white shining robe. He was clothing me with himself. He had taken **my** sins and given me **his** purity. It is important for us to see ourselves clothed in Christ Jesus. He can and will do this for anyone who seeks Him, by his Holy Spirit's power. Paul wrote « So I say live by the Spirit and you will not gratify the desires of the sinful nature. » (Galatians 5:16) It is the spirit filled Christian that can overcome the desires of the flesh. **The spirit can act within us like a mighty cleansing fire!** A fire that burns away our evil desires. He writes « Those who belong to Christ Jesus have crucified the sinful nature with its passions and desires » (Galatians 5:24) Notice the past tense. By faith in the finished work of Christ on the cross, our sinful nature has been crucified, it is dead or dying. Paul continues « Since we live by the Spirit let us keep in step with the Spirit » **Each day we need to be filled afresh with the Holy Spirit.**(Ephesians 5:18)

The cost of following Jesus could not be higher. I am sure the words of Jesus that we have been considering have challenged you as they have me. Perhaps this is a time of self questioning « Am I truly his disciple or have I been deceiving myself? » Maybe now is the time to find a quiet place and talk to your heavenly Father about your commitment. Christ Jesus demands loyalty to his person and to his mission. He desires us to be in a deep relationship with Him. To love Him and those He came to save, to be loyal to Him even if it results in a cross. A true follower cannot be just a « bit religious. »

What is required of us? To put **Jesus first, and to deny self.** We have seen how difficult that is in practice, to combat our desire for ease and comfort, our lusts and self indulgence. Without a deeper understanding of what it means to take up the cross and walk in the Spirit it is impossible. One sure sign that one is denying oneself is to live for Christ and the expression of it will be found in the fact that we are living for and serving others. This is one of the demands that the Lord makes upon us. Throughout the history of the Christian Church countless people have given themselves to right wrongs, to fight against injustice, and make life better for their fellow human beings. In the Victorian era of British history there are many illustrations of how Christians denied themselves in order to serve others and so change the society in which they lived. Elizabeth Fry worked tirelessly to reform prisons, which at that time were hellish places without hope. On the streets of London there were many homeless people especially children. Doctor Barnardo made it his life's work to rescue those children and care for them. His work still continues today through the Christian organisation he founded. William Wilberforce fought hard and succeeded in abolishing slavery, the cruel trading of African men women and children for financial gain. Lord Shaftesbury worked tirelessly to stop the exploitation of child labour. His work resulted in the removal of young children from working in coal mines. More recently there have been Christians such as the Baptist pastor, Martin Luther King who gave his life to change the situation of millions of black people in the USA. There are millions of ordinary people who never make the new's headlines who have denied themselves in the name of Christ and served others despite what it has cost them.

Christ demands loyalty. Even if loyalty ends with a cross. Many nuns in enclosed orders consider themselves to be « Brides of

Christ ». All disciple of Jesus are spiritually married to Jesus. In a sense we make a promise to follow Jesus for better or for worse. In a marriage between a man and a woman sacrifices are made. In our marriage with Jesus he has made the supreme sacrifice by dying on a cross once and for all so that we might enter a loving relationship with Him. We play our part by loving and serving him in the way we make sacrifices to serve other people. Jesus reminds us in the parable he told, about judgement for our actions. The parable tells of sheep and goats, and their separation. At the end of time we shall all stand before the judgement seat of Christ «Then the King will say to those on his right, 'Come, you who are blessed by my Father: take your inheritance, the kingdom prepared for you since the creation of the world. For I was hungry and you gave me something to eat, I was thirsty and you gave me something to drink, I was a stranger and you invited me in, I needed clothes and you clothed me, I was sick and you looked after me, I was in prison and you came to visit me'. Then the righteous will answer Him, 'Lord, when did we see you hungry and feed you, or thirsty and give you something to drink? When did we see you a stranger and invite you in, or needing clothes and clothe you ? When did we see you sick or in prison and go to visit you? The King will reply, 'I tell you the truth, whatever you did for one of the least of these brothers of mine, you did it for Me' » (Matthew 25:34-40)

John Bunyan was imprisoned for his faith in Bedford jail and during that time he wrote the spiritual classic « Pilgrim's progress » as a result of a vision he had. Through the ages people have taken time out to go on pilgrimages. They make a journey to a sacred place to improve themselves spiritually and increase their chances of going to heaven. The spiritual place is of religious importance geographically, or more often than not, the site where a Holy relic is to be found! The journey or pilgrimage he had in his vision was the journey that a person makes in becoming a Christian, facing the trials of living out the Christian faith in this world and eventually arriving in heaven. **To arrive at one's destination on our spiritual journey will mean endurance, perseverance and loyalty to Jesus. It costs us everything and therefore cannot be entered**

upon lightly. An inspirational hymn attributed to John Bunyan has the following verse -

Who would true valour see
Let him come hither
One here will constant be
Come wind come weather;
There's no discouragement
Shall make him once relent
His first avowed intent
To be a pilgrim
John Bunyan, 1628-1688)

David Livingstone was perhaps one of the most popular heroes of the late 19th century in Victorian Britain. At the time of writing this book the 200th anniversary of his birth approaches. He was born on the 19th of March 1813 in the mill town of Blantyre, Lanarkshire Scotland. My father left me a book, that had belonged to his elder brother who had received it as a prize in 1912, for morning and afternoon attendance at Sunday School. The book entitled « David Livingstone » had the-sub title «The weaver boy who became a missionary » by H.G.Adams. David Livingstone had an almost mythical status, « That of Protestant missionary martyr, that of 'rags' to riches' an inspirational story, that of scientific investigator and explorer, that of imperial reformer, anti-slavery crusader, and advocate of commercial empire. » He was a member of the Scottish Congregational Church, trained as a doctor, and was commissioned as a pioneer medical missionary by the London Missionary society to work in Africa. He trudged through the fever-infested jungle to bring the 'Good News' of Christ to Africans. He died on his knees, worn out and yet triumphant Whatever secular historians and political commentators may write about him the fact is that he was incredibly brave and totally committed in his service for his saviour, the Lord Jesus Christ. In 2003 and 2005 I visited Zambia to help with the training of pastors and evangelists in the indigenous Church there. CCAP (Christian Church of Central Africa) This Church was in fact founded by David Livingstone and still flourishes today. When we read his story and what he did we are humbled and inspired to serve the Lord, knowing that it cost him dearly, a price that David Livingstone was prepared to pay.

The apostle Paul in prison towards the end of his life wrote-« I have fought a good fight - I have finished the race, I have kept the faith » (2 Timothy 4:7) He had suffered beatings, shipwrecks, and imprisonment for Christ. He kept going faithfully until he was taken to glory. Anyone of us can only meet the cost of discipleship when Christ lives in us, and his presence is with us. Remember Jesus promised « Lo I am with you always to the very end of the age» (Matthew 28:20) He will be with us as we serve.

Chapter 3 - Becoming a Disciple

Well how do we become not just new converts but disciples. The Greek word for disciple is « *mathetes* » which means « one who learns instruction from another. » **A disciple is a learner who is under instruction**. He is not only a pupil but an adherent who imitates and follows his teacher's example. Jesus called twelve men to be his first disciples. They spent three years with Him, they were his followers. Besides the twelve there were many other disciples. In fact every Christian is called to be a disciple of Jesus. Each one will desire to learn from Him, and live according to His example. It is at this stage that many would be disciples lose their way. Many sincere people have made real commitments to Jesus Christ but sadly have not progressed to become disciples, eventually falling away from the faith altogether. The Church has a responsibility to nurture new converts and help them become disciples. Sadly many churches fail in this. Converts are lost in the first few months because they find it difficult to become part of the local Church. They never become disciples. They are like the seed sown on stony ground that did not take root. « Some fell on rocky places, where it did not have much soil. It sprang up quickly, because the soil was shallow. But when the sun came up, the plants were scorched, and they withered because they had no root » (Matthew 13:1-9) Just as a new baby is helpless and needs to be fed and cared for so the new Christian, needs to be guided and encouraged to participate in a « discipleship course » and to attend a caring « house group » and there to be fed and nurtured. It is also important for the new Christian to have a 'father or mother in God' who will help to nurture growth. If a new believer is left with no direction he or she will be weak, will not grow and will struggle to survive.

Many Churches have a course in Christian Discipleship that leads to baptism or confirmation. The book of Hebrews in the New Testament speaks of leaving behind the elementary teaching and going on to maturity; « Therefore let us leave the elementary teachings about Christ and go on to maturity, not laying again the foundation of repentance from acts that lead to death, and of faith in God, instructions about baptisms, the laying on of hands, the resurrection of the dead and eternal judgement » (Hebrews Ch 6 vs. 1-3) . This passage emphasises seven elementary subjects that were taught to new converts to the faith.

The first is repentance The new convert receives the forgiveness after an act of repentance. To repent means not just to say sorry for sins, but to turn away from them and to redirect life towards the Lord. Repentance from sins, also means to **forsake** the sins that have been forgiven, not to do the same thing again! Each individual will have different sins to repent of, which could be anything from sexual immorality, stealing, or adultery to having been involved in occult practices. Often it may also mean reconciliation and restitution.

The second subject is faith. Without faith it is impossible to please God. Faith grows through reading the word of God and developing a prayer life. Faith also grows when we listen to the word of God proclaimed in the fellowship of the Church. We are urged to encourage one another and build each other up in the faith. This can happen in large gatherings when believers come together to Worship God and listen to the proclamation of His word, or in the intimate atmosphere of a house group or Bible Study group. Faith grows by hearing the word of God.

The third subject is instruction concerning Baptisms. The Church in it's early days had a small problem of two understandings of baptism. There was John's baptism as a sign of repentance to prepare one to receive the Messiah, and there was baptism as the entry into Christ and his Church. We shall consider Christian Baptism and what it means in a separate paragraph.

The fourth area of instruction concerns the laying on of hands. This often followed conversion to impart the Holy Spirit. In practice it seems that often when a person was baptised immediately afterwards hands were laid on him/her and the Holy Spirit was received The laying on of hands by elders in the Church was also for healing. The work of the Holy Spirit will be dealt with more fully in the chapter entitled «Receiving the Holy Spirit ». People were also set aside for a particular act of service or missionary endeavour by the laying on of hands.

The fifth area of instruction for new Christians was concerning the resurrection of the dead. The belief in the resurrection of Jesus was part of the basic confession that all new believers made. The fact that Jesus rose from the dead, proved that the claim He had made to be the Messiah was true. Without the resurrection of Jesus there would have been no Christian faith and no Christian Church! Christians believe that because Jesus overcame death, they will also. Belief in the resurrection of Jesus was right at the heart of the gospel preached by the Apostles. They believed that because Jesus was alive they would also live. He has returned to be with the Father and we will go to be with Him when we die.

The sixth area of the teaching is that we shall all stand before the judgement seat of Christ If we have lived our lives on this earth in accordance with the way Christ has instructed us, we shall inherit everlasting life. All of us without exception will give an account of our lives before the judge of all the earth. The Christian who passes over from death to life eternal should have no fear of meeting with his/her maker

The seventh subject of the elementary teaching that is mentioned in these verses is the word of God. Those who have « tasted the goodness of the word of God and the powers of the coming age » (Hebrews Ch 6 vs. 5) should not fall away from the faith. When mention is made of the word of God in the New Testament the writer is referring to the books of the Old

Testament. Many times we find verses from the Old Testament quoted in the New as fulfilled prophecies concerning Jesus as the 'The one who was waited for' and about His death and resurrection. We experience the « powers of the age to come » when the Kingdom of God is proclaimed. The Holy Spirit is moving among people; the eyes of faith are being opened, those in Satan's grip are being delivered and the sick are being healed.

The first letter of Peter contains instruction for those who are going to be baptised. It has been suggested that this part of the letter has been taken from an address given by the apostle Peter to new converts prior to their baptism. Reference is made to « the baptism that saves us » (1 Peter Ch 3 vs. 21) and the advice given to slaves, wives and husbands would have be entirely appropriate for those who had formerly been pagans and were now entering the Christian Church .The whole theme of the letter is about leaving an old way of life behind and entering a new way of living. The letter is concerned with how a new Christian works out his/her salvation in a practical way. It starts with holiness of life. « Therefore, prepare your minds for action; be self controlled; set your hope fully on the grace to be given you when Jesus Christ is to be revealed. As obedient children, do not conform to the evil desires you had when you lived in ignorance. But just as He who called you is holy, so be holy in all you do; for it is written « 'Be holy, because I am holy' » (1 Peter1:.13 -16); New converts should have a desire to grow spiritually. « like new born babies crave pure spiritual milk, so that by it you may grow up in your salvation now that you have tasted that the Lord is good » (I Peter Ch 2 vs. 2) The one thing that a new born baby needs is milk. Feeding is the central activity of a new born baby's life. Regular feeding with good milk leads to growth. It is the same with the newly born Christian. He/she must feed on the word of God regularly and seek to grow towards maturity.

Peter in his letter now turns his attention to the new believer's place within the Church of Jesus Christ, he uses the beautiful analogy of living stones being built into a spiritual house. Together we become a holy priesthood offering spiritual sacrifices acceptable to God through Jesus Christ (1 Peter 2: 4-8) Our relationship with the Lord is of great importance but so is our relationship with each other in the Christian community. It is as part of the Church that we worship, learn, witness, and serve the Lord. It is of paramount importance that we relate well with our brothers and sisters where God has placed us in the fellowship of His Church. The new convert is to work out practically his/her salvation, in the context of love for one another. « Live as free men, but do not use your freedom as a cover up for evil; live as servants of God. Show proper respect to everyone; love the brotherhood of believers, fear God honour the king » (1 Peter 2: 16-17 & 1 Peter 4:8). We are also to work out our salvation by witnessing to Christ. Often when we tell others about Jesus our own faith increases. The act of baptism is a witness to the world that a person belongs to Christ. Normally when a person is baptised he or she testifies as to how he or she came to believe in the Lord. At the time when this letter was written the Christian church was enduring severe persecution, it was probably written from Rome not long before the Emperor Nero crucified Peter and had Paul beheaded. Persecution and suffering were a normal part of being a follower of Jesus in those times so Peter gives them warning. Finally the newly baptised convert is to live his life to bring glory to God. He is to use every opportunity that comes his way to live the Christian life to the full because Christ may return at any time. His life should be humble, free from anxiety, self - controlled, alert, full of love and service, standing firm in the faith at all times and in all circumstances. (1 Peter 5:6-11)

These two passages of instructions help us to see how vital it is that believers learn and grow. You will not make progress in the Christian life if you are not willing to learn! I have visited many churches and in some I have found people who do not want to listen to sermons or be part of a bible study group. Their love for the Lord has grown cold and often the Church is weak and has lost its way. In other churches one finds people who cannot get enough of the « Word of God » whether it be through sermons, conferences, bible study groups or reading the bible in private. In the second group of churches Christians are growing and maturing in the faith. The Church is alive, making disciples and experiencing God given growth. The nurturing and maturing of new believers is absolutely vital if a Church is to grow. You may have become a Christian suddenly but you can only learn gradually. The Church where I served in France baptises people by total immersion on confession of faith. Each candidate for baptism completes a Discipleship Course.

The course we use « Living for Jesus » by Vincent Esterman covers the following 15 subjects
1) Being saved
2) Baptism in water
3) The power of the word of God
4) Important elements of construction
5) Baptism in the Holy Spirit
6) Discovering Jesus Christ
7) Build a good life of prayer
8) The Church
9) A growing faith
10) Worship
11)Testimony
12) God's healing
13) Giving to God's work
14) The gifts of the Holy Spirit
15) Why do Christians share the bread and wine?
16) Spiritual growth

This course is only one of many available and the content of each discipleship course will vary but the aim is the same, to help converts move forward to become disciples.

Becoming a Disciple is not an option it is an obligation. Jesus personally calls a person to become his disciple. He calls them primarily to Himself and not just to His teaching. He expects total obedience. He taught them how to serve and warned them that they would suffer. We become disciples today when we begin to realise that we are chosen, called, and commissioned by Christ.. It is a very serious business. Why is it is essential for converts to become disciples? Here are four reasons..

Firstly, Jesus made it his first priority to choose and **train** twelve men during the three and a half years of His public ministry on earth. He taught them by word and example. He also sent them out to put into practice what they had learned.

Secondly, Jesus commissioned all His followers to train disciples. « All authority in heaven and on earth has been given to me. Therefore go and **make disciples** of all nations, baptizing them in the name of the Father and of the Son and of the Holy Spirit, and teaching them to obey everything I have commanded you. And surely I will be with you always, to the very end of the age » (Matthew Ch 28 vs. 16-20)

Thirdly discipleship is the best method to reach the world for God. The impact that Jesus' eleven disciples and Paul had on the world show us this. A small number of committed disciples who are well trained will achieve far more for God than large numbers of converts who lack spiritual depth. Discipleship is God's chosen strategy to reach the world

Fourthly, the end result of discipleship is spiritually mature Christians. Immature Christians can cause great problems in a church! Maturity does not come automatically with increase in age, knowledge or experience. It is the result of a gradual spiritual growth on the basis of obedience to Christ Jesus and His Word.

There is an old legend which tells how Jesus, after his death and resurrection, returned to heaven. One of the angels met Him and saw the nail marks in his hands and the wound in his side. The angel said « You must have suffered terribly for men down there in the world? » Jesus answered « I did ».
« Do all men know how you loved them and suffered for them » said the angel. « No » said Jesus.

« Well then » said the angel. « What have you done about letting all people know about it? »

Jesus said « I have asked Peter, James and John, and the others to tell others, and others to tell yet others and still others, until all people will know »

Now the angel knew human beings and was very doubtful. « Yes » he said, « but what if James and John and Peter forget? What if the others fail in their task?

What if the years go on and men do not tell others about you and your sacrifice?

What then? Have you made other plans? »

Jesus replied «*I HAVE NOT MADE ANY OTHER PLANS; I'm counting on them* »

Think about this, if one disciple led just one other person to Christ and devoted a whole year to training him, and the following year these two disciples made two new disciples each, and the next year those four made four more (one each) in less than 40 years the whole world's population would be saved - according to plain mathematics!

Discipleship is not only a very serious business but a very costly one too. John in his gospel tells of an occasion when the followers of Jesus faced opposition from the religious authorities. He writes « From this time many of His followers turned back and no longer followed Him » Jesus asked the twelve disciples « You, do not want to leave too - do you? » Simon Peter answered Him « Lord, to whom shall we go? You have the words of eternal life. We believe and we know that you are the Holy One of God »

(John 6:66-69)

Not long after I met Ann who was to become my wife I was alarmed when she informed me that she was going away to a missionary conference as a delegate from our local Church. I did everything in my power to dissuade her but to no avail. I was so afraid I was going to lose her! I so much wanted to marry her I could not bear the thought that she might be called to be a missionary. (However God had other plans. We married a year later and during our second year of married life God called me to be a minister) She remembers me saying at that time « It seems to me that this Christianity demands a person's entire life! » In truth it does

The first essential for being a disciple is that God must come first. Jesus must be number one. The disciple seeks in all things and at all times to please God. We pray in the lord's Prayer « Thy will be done ». The disciple seeks God's will, accepts God's will but above all aligns his/her will with His. The disciple takes up the Cross daily and follows Jesus (Luke Ch 14 vs. 27). That means dying to self which is easy to say, but very hard to do. It means giving our whole lives and everything we have to God, for Him to use as He wants. We cannot do it in our own strength and determination but only by the grace of God. The Holy Spirit helps us to die to our selfishness and live for God. We become temples, dwelling places, where Christ lives in us in the power of the Holy Spirit. We need to remind ourselves that Jesus only ended up with a few deeply committed followers BUT those were enough to change the world! When we enter into God's plan for our lives, we are enriched and blessed beyond measure by Him.

To be a disciple is to be a learner in the school of Christ. Whether we are converted when we are young, in middle age or later, we must have a teachable attitude. There is always more to learn. We do not finish or graduate from the school of Christ until we have risen with Him and reign with Him. All through this life we learn more and more about Him and His will for our lives. When I was young, some Christians I knew wore tee shirts with the words «Be patient God has not finished with me yet:» If we are spiritually hungry and desire more and more of God and we feed on His word the Bible, we will continue to grow, but if we close our minds and stop hungering after God we stop growing and this can be fatal. Jesus warns the Church at Ephesus about this very thing, he says « I know your deeds, your hard work and your perseverance. I know that you cannot tolerate wicked men, that you have tested those who claim to be apostles and are not, and have found them false, you have persevered and endured hardship for my name, and have not grown weary. » (Revelation 2:3-5) What a great Church full of hard working, persevering, enduring, and discerning believers! However He adds «Yet I have this against you: you have forsaken your first love. Remember the height from which you have fallen! Repent and do the things you did at first » The love of the people in that Church had grown cold. Love for the Lord and for each other and for the lost people around them. If we cease to grow spiritually, and will not be taught in the school of Christ we are in danger of losing our first love for Christ and we will stop seeking His Kingdom and righteousness.

In Matthew's account of the life of Jesus we read that Jesus taught his disciples, and the crowd that had gathered around Him. We call this teaching the « Sermon on the mount ». It is good for every new convert to read chapters 5-7 of Matthew's Gospel. Here are just a few pointers. Be humble and receive the Kingdom of God. Comfort those who mourn. Seek always to be just, good and fair in the way you treat others. Be kind and always have mercy. Keep your heart pure so that your motives will be pure. Strive for peace. Suffer persecution for being good. Just as salt is used to preserve food and make it good, so be an influence for good. Be good witnesses for the Kingdom of God. Avoid adultery, lust, telling lies, revenge, anger. Don't resist violence. Don't do good to impress others. Love your enemies, always seek reconciliation. Keep praying, keep forgiving others. Give to those in need. Do not love money and make it your God. Stop worrying about essentials, instead trust your Heavenly Father. Stop Judging and criticising others. Look at your own life first! Ask, seek and knock. Father God is always there. God listens to His children. Jesus finishes His teaching by using the example of two men building their homes. One was a wise builder the other foolish. (Matthew Ch 7 vs. 24-29) One built his house on the rock the other on sand. When the flood came the house on the sand collapsed because it was not on a firm foundation. In the same way our lives must be on a firm foundation. Jesus said « Therefore everyone who hears these words of mine **and puts them into**

practice is like a wise man who built his house on a rock » Build on this firm foundation throughout your lives, apply the words of Jesus to everyday situations.

We live in what is called a celebrity culture. In most people there is a hidden desire to be recognised and be famous. We all have our heroes, and our impossible dreams. Sadly the quest for power can ruin a life and the lives of others. Being ambitious is essential for living and is not wrong but to desire power for power's sake is wrong. Many people want to be in control not only of their own lives but the lives of others! Much damage is caused by those people who have to control others, or put others down, so as to build up their own self esteem. As the saying goes « Don't blow out my candle to light yours » Don't build your life on seeking fame, power, or controlling others. Such a life will not result in satisfaction and peace.

Jesus taught his disciples and those in the crowd, if you want to stand firm in times of trouble, put into practice what I teach you and when trouble comes you will not fall. If you are completely self- seeking you are heading for disaster when the storms of life come and streams rise so that you drown in self pity. If you want to walk in faith and victory your life must be built on the sure foundation of Jesus and His teaching. Read and reread The sermon on the Mount and make the teaching part of your life. If you build your life on the sands of intellectualism, paganism, hedonism, (search for pleasure) or religiosity; on the shifting sands of other people's opinion, or your own self worth, you will surely tumble when trouble comes. The Christian's life is built on a personal relationship with Jesus Christ. He is the rock on which a Christian's life is built.

(1 Corinthians 3 :10 - 15) The life built on the « Rock » Christ Jesus is the best life of all. A life that has repented of sin and received forgiveness. A life that has made a new beginning with God. A life that has heard the call to follow Jesus. Such a life has purpose and satisfies completely. It is full of contentment and inner peace. Peace

with God and reconciliation with other human beings. A life of responding to a challenge; a life of sacrifice and service to other people. A life lived under the shadow of the cross and in the power of the resurrection (Luke Ch 9 vs. 23 - 26) A life filled with the Holy Spirit a life that lasts for eternity. (Romans Ch 8 vs. 15-17)

Chapter 4 - Be Baptised

The next step for the new believer is to ask to be baptized. The great commission was to « Go and make disciples of all nations baptizing them in the name of the Father and of the Son and of the Holy Spirit » (Matthew 28:19) Being baptised is not an optional extra for the believer but follows naturally as a new Christian becomes a disciple.

On the day of the feast of Pentecost the Holy Spirit was poured out on the believers. There was a great crowd of people in Jerusalem celebrating this feast. They were mainly Jews who came from many different countries throughout the Roman Empire. They heard these disciples of Jesus declaring the wonders of God in their own tongue! « Amazed and perplexed, they asked one another, 'What does this mean?' Some, however, made fun of them and said 'They have had too much wine' » (Acts 2:12-13) Peter addressed the crowd and told them that the prophecy made by Joel was being fulfilled. He went on to tell the crowd about Jesus the Messiah, his death and their responsibility for it. « When the people heard this they were cut to the heart and said to Peter and the other apostles, 'What shall we do?' Peter replied **'Repent and be baptized, every one of you in the name of Jesus Christ** so that your sins may be forgiven. And you will receive the gift of the Holy Spirit. The promise is for you and your children and for all who are far off - for all whom the Lord our God will call' With many other words he warned them, 'Save yourself from this corrupt generation.' Those who accepted his message were baptized, and about three thousand were added to their number that day. » (Acts 2:37-41)

The Christian Church was born on that day. By being baptized the people became part of the Christian community, the Church.

Baptism is the way of entry into the Church.

Where were the **three thousand** people baptized in Jerusalem is a question that many have asked? Maybe as they were near the Temple they would have used the pools closeby that were used for washing the sacrificial lambs! Another question is who baptized whom? Possibly they baptized one another. We read that after they were baptised they met daily in the Temple and in each other's homes. In (Acts 8:26-40) we are given a clear picture of the baptism of an Ethiopian eunuch, a government official who was seeking for a deeper relationship with God. Philip was guided by an angel and the Holy Spirit to approach the chariot, in which he was riding. The official was perplexed by what he was reading in the scroll which contained the words of Isaiah the prophet. Maybe he had bought the scroll recently in Jerusalem. It would have cost a lot of money! He did not understand what he was reading until Philip joined him and explained. « Philip began with that very passage of Scripture and told him the good news about Jesus. As they travelled along the road, they came to some water and the eunuch said, 'Look, here is water. Why shouldn't I be baptized?' And he ordered the chariot to stop. Then both Philip and the eunuch went down into the water and Philip baptised him. When they came up out of the water, the Spirit of the Lord suddenly took Philip away, and the eunuch did not see him again, but went on his way rejoicing » (Acts 8:35-39). This account seems to suggest that the Ethiopian was baptised by total immersion.

Many who come to faith, have already been baptised as babies as a result of their parent's wishes. When infants are baptized the parents make promises to bring their child up in the Christian faith. At the same time they confess **their** faith. This is not the same as being baptised on confession of your own faith. The new believer chooses to go forward for baptism because he/she is convinced that the commitment which has been made should be sealed so to enter fully into the church The amount of water is not important but the sincerity of the believer is. By being baptised the new believer makes a public confession of faith telling all the world that he/she is dedicated to Jesus Christ. This public witness is very important as it is impossible to be a secret follower of Christ Jesus. Jesus himself said « I tell you, whoever acknowledges me before men, the Son of Man will also acknowledge him before the angels of God. But he who disowns me before men will be disowned before the angels of God! »

How did the practice of infant baptism come about and do we find reference to it in the New Testament? In (Acts 16:5) we read that after her conversion Lydia the seller of purple dye was baptised along with her whole family. Then « When she and the members of her household were baptized, she invited us to her home » (Acts 16:15). Whether that family included infants and young children has been the subject of much speculation. Similarly when Paul was at Philippi the converted jailer's whole family was baptized. Paul and Silas had been beaten publicly, thrown into jail and the ground had been shaken by an earthquake. The jailer came to Paul and Silas and asked « 'Sirs what must I do to be saved? Paul and Silas replied 'Believe in the Lord Jesus and you will be saved - you and your household.' Then they spoke the word of the Lord to him and to all the others in his house. At that hour of the night the jailer took them and washed their wounds, then immediately he and all his family were baptized. » (Acts 16:30-33) No doubt whole families were baptised but whether they included babies and very young children is open to debate, children were deemed to be of very little importance at that time and their lives were of little consequence! I have travelled extensively in Israel and seen the sites of early Christian church buildings that have been excavated. At Bethshan recent excavations revealed a first century church building which contained a baptistery. The baptizing of infants and young children seems to have become a common practice two centuries after the death of Christ. The main reason seems to have been that believers wanted their children to go to heaven when they died. The life expectancy of a baby at that time was very short indeed. Today in many maternity hospitals if a baby is sick and about to die a clergy person is often called to come and baptize that baby immediately.

Near the entrance of many church buildings, or even just outside the door, a font can be found. This symbolizes that it is by baptism that we enter the Church of Jesus Christ. The issue of how and at what age people are to be baptised is a divisive one.

People have strong views about it. Christians who advocate baptism of believers on confession of faith often have a service of thanksgiving or dedication for their new born baby. The child grows and comes to a living faith, confesses that faith and is baptised either by total immersion or by pouring/sprinkling water on his head at the font. There is a case made for those who are baptised as children arriving spiritually at the same place as those who have been baptised as believers. In this instance when they grow to maturity they make their own profession of faith and are confirmed publicly by the laying on of hands. At that moment the Holy Spirit is received. Most often the person who lays hands on the new believer is a leader in the Church. It is a time of rejoicing for the parents who have kept the promises they made at their son/daughter's christening, to bring them up in the knowledge of the faith and to encourage them in their Christian walk.

Imagine the surprise of a group of canoeist who on rounding the bend in the river Dourbie came face to face with two pastors waist deep in water in the process of baptising new converts. On a sunny August day its not the usual thing a holiday maker expects to find! The smiling singing Christians on the river bank were also witnesses to this special act and confession of faith. Truly this baptism was a very public confession of faith. The new converts declared in public that they would follow Jesus for the rest of their lives. It is a very important day for the person being baptised and for the Church. I have baptised people in rivers, the sea, as well as in Church baptisteries. It makes no difference where a person is baptised or the amount of water! Baptism is always accompanied by a confession or declaration of faith in Jesus as the Son of God and is done in the **Name** of the Father the Son and the Holy Spirit. To baptise a person who has never become a true Christian is like dressing a man in uniform and declaring him to be a soldier when he has never enlisted in the army! **A person is not baptised to make him a Christian but rather to show that he is a Christian.**

Being present at the baptism of a believer is inspiring. Very often after baptism hands are laid on the believer to impart God's blessing on their lives. We read how Jesus blessed the children. (Matthew 19 :13-15)(Mark 10 :13-16) At this very important time in the new believer's life, how wonderful to receive God's blessing! All believers are called to live the Spirit filled life. Each day we are to be filled with the Holy Sprit.(Ephesians5:5) The way that the Holy Spirit was often imparted to believers was by the 'laying on of hands.' In the New Testament, believers in general, as well as leaders, were involved in imparting the Baptism of the Holy Spirit.(Acts 8 : 14-24) (Acts 9 :10-17) (Acts 19 : 6). (More will be written about the work of the Holy Spirit in a later chapter.) When a person is baptised often they are received into the membership of the local Church. It is very important that every Christian plays their full part in the life and work of the local Church. The recently baptised believer makes specific promises to be faithful in public worship, be part of the fellowship of the Church, and to share in its witness and service.

What does Baptism signify?

a) Baptism is a visible sign of God's grace and Salvation. It is an outward sign of an inward change. It is one of the first steps in the believer's life and the way of entry into the church. **Baptism is a sign of being forgiven.** To come to the cross where Jesus was crucified and understand that He took the punishment we deserved for our sins is to experience the joy of salvation. Baptism is a sign that we have been forgiven. Just as washing in water makes a person clean so being baptized is a symbol of being cleansed of sin.
In the words of Henry Frances Lyte's Hymn, « Ransomed, healed, restored, forgiven, who like thee His praise should sing? »
Hallelujah the burden of sin has been taken away at the cross! Symbolically we have been washed clean and are making a new beginning. Baptism is a sign to the world that the believers' sins have been forgiven, and that the believer is being transformed into a new creation. Sin is no longer master.

b) Baptism is a sign that the believer has been born again.
Peter also promised that those who repented would receive the gift
of the Holy Spirit.(Acts 2:8) Every person who becomes a Christian
is given the Holy Spirit. To try to live the Christian life without the
Holy Spirit is like trying to drive a car without any fuel in the tank!
It will not go anywhere. We cannot make any progress without the
Holy Spirit. Paul writes to Titus declaring that « He saved us
through the washing of rebirth and renewal by the Holy Spirit »
(Titus Ch 3 vs. 3-5) Baptism is a sign of being born again by the
Holy Spirit.(John Ch 3 vs. 5). A sign of a new beginning, of
transformation, and of being a new creation living in a world seen
through new eyes!
(2 Corinthians Ch 5 vs. 17)

c) Baptism is a sign of being identified with Christ. John the
Baptist, baptised all those who repented in response to his
preaching The gospels tell us that Jesus himself asked to be
Baptised by John. At first John refused because he knew that Jesus
was without sin but Jesus insisted and was baptised.. Jesus was
baptised by John in the Jordan identifying himself with sinful
humanity. He went down into the water to stand in our place. He
identified with all of us. It was the same with His baptism on the
cross (Luke Ch 12 vs. 50). Jesus by dying on the cross was
immersed in suffering as He bore God's judgement on man's sins.
Jesus who was sinless took the place of those who were sinful. He
took the punishment that we deserved. The words of the following
Hymn by Philipp Bliss express how Jesus identified with fallen
humanity.
  « Bearing shame and scoffing rude,
  In my place condemned He stood,
  Sealed my pardon with His blood,
  Hallelujah! What a saviour! »

d) Baptism is a seal of ownership. Paul compares Baptism to the
Jewish rite of circumcision. The Jew understood that circumcision
of the flesh was a sign that he belonged to God. Paul understands
the circumcision of Abraham as both a sign and seal of his faith

« And he (Abraham) received the sign of circumcision, a seal of the righteousness that he had by faith. » (Romans 4:11) Baptism for the believer is a seal of ownership, a sign that we are in a covenant relationship with God and that we belong to Him. He redeemed us by the sacrifice of His Son Jesus. By identifying ourselves with the death and resurrection of Jesus we are sealed (signed up) for eternity.

e) Baptism is a means of grace. Imagine the grace of God flowing down an invisible pipe into the believer's heart! God's grace enables us to « put off the old self and put on the new » (Galatians Ch 3 vs. 26-29). The believer is clothed with Christ. In baptism the believer is united with Christ and with other believers. As Paul puts it, we are « One in Christ Jesus ».Our nationality, our age or the colour of our skin, our gender or social standing does not matter, for we are all one in Christ Jesus. When a girl is given an engagement ring by the one she loves it is a visible sign that indicates to others that her life is now linked with her fiancé's. We are engaged to be the Lord's. We desire to worship the Lord and to serve Him in the Church and in the world. We want to do His will. Baptism is a sign that we are engaged to the Lord and by His grace we will live our lives to please Him.

The believer is baptised into Christ Jesus. His death, His burial, and His resurrection. We go down into the water signifying his death. Our few seconds under the water signifies the burial. Then our emergence from the water symbolises being resurrected with Him. (Romans Ch 6 vs. 5-14) Baptism is a sign to all the world that your sins have been forgiven, that you are being transformed into a new creation, and that you have identified yourself with Jesus.

Chapter 5 - Temptation: Facing the Enemy in Times of Testing

All of us who are followers of Jesus remember how we were converted, for some of us it happened very quickly for others it took place over a period of time. Then came the most important day of our lives, we were baptized into Christ and His Church.

An emotional time of peace, joy and love in our innermost being! Will our lives now be free of all troubles! We have to be aware that we will share in carrying the burden that Christ had to bear. He was tempted, persecuted, misunderstood by his family, sneered at by religious people who did not accept his claim to be their Messiah. He was betrayed by one of his disciples, and deserted by those closest to him. They forsook Him and fled. He was arrested, falsely accused, unjustly condemned, flogged and tortured, and finally put to death by crucifixion. He suffered for us and we should be found worthy of suffering for him! We have the great privilege of being His children and joint heirs with Him. It is important that we should understand from the beginning the cost of following Jesus. It will help us to rejoice in many a dark hour and not to give up in despair. We do not become Christians for the purpose of having ecstatic joy but to become followers of Jesus. This is the highest plain of living. We must also understand that we will never reach a stage in this present life where we can hope to be free of temptation. Just as Jesus underwent temptation so will we.

Immediately after Jesus had been baptised in the Jordon by John the Baptist he was « led by the Spirit into the desert to be tempted by the devil » (Matthew Ch 4 vs. 1). When a believer **has accepted Jesus** into his life in most cases in the following days he comes under spiritual attack. In a similar way after being **baptised**, that person nearly always comes under attack from the devil. All believers need to be able to recognise these attacks and learn how to defend themselves. The apostle Paul writes to the Christians at Corinth « We are not unaware of Satan's schemes » (2 Corinthians 2:11) The more we become mature in the faith the more we are able to recognise the attacks of the enemy. The newly Baptised believer may not detect the wiles of Satan, or be aware that they will be engaged in spiritual warfare from the moment they give their life to Jesus and transfer out of the Kingdom of darkness into the Kingdom of light, from Satan's Kingdom to Christ's Kingdom. Satan does not let go of fallen man easily and will try every device to regain the person he has lost. He is the author of confusion, always lying and using every form of temptation; beguiling new Christians into doubting their salvation.

In popular usage today the word temptation has the meaning of being seduced into evil. We remember that Eve was tempted by the serpent in the Garden of Eden to take and eat the forbidden fruit which was « good to eat and pleasing to the eye. » (Genesis 3:6) The devil is always tempting us to disobey God. We speak of being tempted to do something we should not do for our own good. When faced with a plate of delicious chocolate cakes we may be tempted to eat more than is good for us! This use of the word has the sense of being attracted to something. We often say that we are tempted to buy something, in other words our desire for that certain thing has been aroused! The Greek word for temptation in the Bible is better translated as testing. Just as at the beginning of His public ministry Jesus was tested, so every believer is tested. The gospel of Mark makes the plain statement concerning the temptation of Jesus whilst the gospels of Matthew and Luke elaborate on it. Satan tries to tempt Jesus to doubt that he is God the Father's son and hence destroy His whole mission. Satan does the same thing to the newly baptised, sowing seeds of doubt about his/her conversion, and commitment. In the football world cup competition of 2010 a new kind of ball was used. The makers said that it was thoroughly tested before it came to be used. The ball became a problem for the players because it swerved and bobbled and was difficult to control, for although the ball had been tested it was not tested at the altitude where the games were to be played. Christians are tested so that they become stronger and they will be tested in the conditions, and circumstances where they are called to serve the Lord! In the Old Testament we read the story of how God tested the loyalty of his servant Abraham by demanding that he sacrifice his son Isaac (Genesis 22:1) The word here does not mean to seduce him into sin, something that God would never do, but to test Abraham's faith, submission, obedience and loyalty. God tests us to know what is in our hearts, and if we will keep His commandments! Remember God's testing is always for our own good, exposing loyalty and disloyalty, faith and unbelief, it is never to seduce us into sin.

The new Christian must be clear in his mind that temptation is not the same as sin.

God's word records « For we do not have a high priest who is unable to sympathize with our weakness, but we have one who has been tempted in every way, just as we are - yet was without sin. » (Hebrews 4:15). Because Christ himself was tempted he is able to sympathize with us. He was the sinless Son of God yet he was approached by every temptation that approaches us. Sin begins when we encourage temptation. When we are tempted we begin to understand something of the sufferings of Jesus which were caused by temptation assailing His sinless nature and absolute purity. Temptation tests us and purifies us. The prophet Isaiah wrote of Israel « See, I have refined you, though not as silver: I have tested you in the furnace of affliction. » (Isaiah 48:10) The testing of God's people is to refine them as silver is refined. Peter uses the same analogy for Christians going through times of testing and persecution. « Praise be to the God and Father of our Lord Jesus Christ! In his great mercy he has given us new birth into a living hope through the resurrection of Jesus Christ from the dead and into an inheritance that can never perish spoil or fade kept in heaven for you, who through faith are shielded by God's power until the coming of the salvation that is ready to be revealed in the last time. In this you greatly rejoice, though for a little while you may have to suffer grief in **all kinds of trials.** These have come so that your faith - of greater worth than gold, which perishes even though **refined by fire - may prove genuine** and may result in praise, glory and honour when Jesus Christ is revealed » (1 Peter 1:5-7).So we see that trials and temptations can increase our faith.

Until recently I have been living in France where I served a Church in the town of Millau. The town has a long history dating back to Roman times - but more recently it has become famous for it's new viaduct; the highest in the world. The viaduct, which was constructed as part of the A 75 Motorway is a magnificent feat of engineering and in my opinion very beautiful. It took several years to build and at each point in its construction it was tested. Before it was finally opened to the public a large number of heavy lorries were employed to drive slowly across it to see whether it could take their weight! Fortunately it could! Temptation is designed to test us and make us better servants of our master, not designed to make us sinners but to make us stronger Christians. It is designed to make us better able to take the strain of living for Jesus in this fallen world. Each one has to be tested before being able to be used by God.

Throughout the history of the Christian Church there has been persecution. Even today we read of the horrendous persecution of Christians in China, North Korea, India, Iran and many other parts of the world. Jesus warned us that if we followed Him we would undergo persecution in one form or another. Many Christians fear that they will not be able to stand firm in the faith during times of persecution. However, if we remain faithful to the Lord in little things we will most likely remain faithful in big things. We are tested in times of persecution. Peter was tested and found wanting. He denied that he even knew Jesus. You can read about this in (Mark 14) Are we willing to be known as followers of Jesus. We can deny the Lord by our silence. Years later Peter wrote «Dear friends, do not be surprised at the painful trial you are suffering, as though something strange was happening to you; But rejoice that you participate in the sufferings of Christ, so that you may be overjoyed when His glory is revealed. If you are insulted because of the name of Christ, you are blessed, for the Spirit of glory rests on you » (1 Peter 4:12-1) Encouraging words written by the man who denied Jesus and was lovingly restored to be the leader of the first Christian Church! If we begin to understand temptation in terms of testing to make us more like Jesus, the words of the Lord's prayer « Lead us not into temptation » (Matthew 6:13) make better sense. It is not God the Father who leads us into temptation but the circumstances that He permits.

The devil uses many wiles to bring about our downfall. As a teenager I occasionally went fishing. I learnt to put bait on the hook so that the fish would see the bait and not the hook. Often when faced with temptation we do not consider the possible consequences of our actions. Like the fish we take the bait. Again in the garden of Eden, Eve did not consider the consequences of eating the forbidden fruit offered her by the devil. Eating it led to death. (Genesis 3) The satanic voice suggested to her that no harm would come from eating the forbidden fruit. Remember « the devil was a murderer from the beginning, not holding to the truth, for there is no truth in him. When he lies he speaks his native language for he is a liar and the father of lies » (John 8:44)

He also comes tempting us into sexual sins. Israel's greatest King was David. His early life was full of courage, hardship and bravery. He was God's man for the hour; The Psalms he wrote express love, devotion and obedience to God. He was a man of integrity, a leader and a man after God's own heart but he fell into Satan's trap.2 Samuel chapters 11&12 tells the whole sorry story which starts with lust - follows with adultery - which in turn leads to murder, and eventually punishment by the death, of David's infant son. David deeply regretted these actions as have many who have fallen when tempted by an attractive member of the opposite sex!

Temptation often comes when our human powers of resistance have been broken down. Satan attacks us when we are tired, disappointed and complacent, always at our weakest points. Often with men it is in the misuse of sex, or an illicit sexual relationship, which can leave a man or woman open to Satanic attack, when they are tempted into making unsuitable relationships. Many a Christian has been seduced by the world , the things of this world and sometimes by loneliness. At such times we must remind ourselves that Satan has authority in the world for a limited time, only because the all powerful God allows it. The devil has been defeated by the blood of Jesus at the cross and we share in that victory by faith in Christ's finished work. The devil for a time is roaming the earth seeking to destroy human beings and keep them in captivity. He is the master of deception and can masquerade as an angel of light so that even those mature in the faith can be deceived. (2 Corinthians 11:14) The spiritual gift of discernment helps us to distinguish between what is of the flesh, what is of the world and what is of the devil. Seek to be filled with the Holy Spirit each day and so combat the devil's tricks. (Ephesians 5:18)

Another trick of the devil is to make sin look respectable. We overlook the sin of covetousness in our consumer based society and call it good business, distorting the truth. We excuse ourselves with little white lies. When faced with world poverty we do not acknowledge our gluttony, we 'borrow' from our workplace and think we are clever, not admitting even to ourselves that we have stolen these goods. We gamble to gain money to feed our covetousness, deceiving ourselves that the money we make will give us an easy time. We like to take the way of least resistance without recognising that the devil is luring us by his lies. To be a Christian we have to be different. We need to resist his temptations to sin, however small he tells us those sins are.

Often we do not take sin seriously. Satan uses this to trip us up. He makes people believe that there is a scale of sin! We think of big sins and little sins. We speak of a little pride, a little lie, a little anger, a little mistake, but how ever small or inconsequential we may reckon a sin to be, the Bible makes it clear that sin is sin and destroys our relationship with God. If a ship has a hole in it, what ever size, it will sink! My brother Peter was working by the side of a large moat and he managed to get himself stuck in the mud. Slowly he began to sink deeper and deeper into the mire. First he was knee deep in the mud, and then thigh deep and soon the mud was up to his waist. He was absolutely stuck and the more he struggled the more he sank. At this point he began to shout for help at the top of his voice and luckily for him a colleague heard him and with planks and ropes he was rescued! Sin like that mud drags us down, but when we repent and call out to Jesus for help he rescues us, and our broken relationship with the Lord is restored.

Satan uses every trick possible to drag us down. Many young Christians are tempted by the attractions of the world. I was very sad when an eighteen year old member at our Church youth club was pulled back into the world and lost her faith. She had accepted the Lord and appeared to be progressing well. She had nearly always been present at Worship and mid week activities. She was missing for several Sundays. We discovered that she was going with several of her non Christian friends to a night club on Sunday evenings, looking for excitement and a boy friend! She was being pulled away from the Lord. She came occasionally to the Church but gradually the pull of the world was stronger! The Christian cannot be on both sides at once. Satan is a master of compromise. The compromising Christian is not really happy in the world, neither is he truly happy with God and His people. We cannot have a foot in both camps. I remember a holiday when my two younger brothers and I hired a boat on the river Avon. We wanted to take it in turns to row. We decided to steer the boat towards the bank so that we could change places without capsizing. My brother David caught hold of a small tree stump on the river bank and tried to pull the boat in but the boat was gradually taken downstream by the current so that his feet were in the boat, but his body was stretched across the water as he held onto the tree stump. Of course he landed up in the river! When we follow Christ we have to make choices and stick with those choices. As the Hymn, by Frances Ridley Havergal puts it

«Who is on the Lord's side?
Who will serve the King?

Who will be His helpers
Other lives to bring?
Who will leave the worlds side?
Who will face the foe? ».
Who is on the Lord's side?
Who for Him will go?
By Thy call of mercy,
By Thy grace divine,
We are on the Lord's side;
Saviour, we are Thine.

We have to choose to stay loyal to the King and with the help of the Holy Spirit resist the pull of the world.

One of the Devil's cleverest tricks is to make the suggestion to us that all religions lead to God. I have often heard people use an illustration of a mountain with different paths on different sides. One person takes one path and another person a different one. They travel from numerous starting points but reach the same destination, so conclude that all religions lead to God. The problem with this is that no account is taken of the contents and truth of the religion. The Bible claims that there is only one God the creator of all things. All other god's are false creations of human imagination. The true God is the Father of our Lord Jesus Christ and our Father. Jesus made it clear to his disciples that He had come from God and was returning to God his Father. Thomas one of his disciples said to Him « Lord we don't know where you are going so how can we know the way? » Jesus answered « I am the way the truth and the life. No one comes to the Father except through me » (John 14:5-6) Christianity claims that there is one God and one God only, the one revealed to us in the Bible. All other gods are false gods and the worship of them is idolatry. In our diminishing world and our multi faith culture it is easy to get drawn into this human idea that you can find God by different religions. This is one of Satan's most effective strategies at this time in the history of the world. People speak of the sincerity of those who embrace a different faith from Christianity. They may be sincere but they are sincerely wrong! All man made religions seek to find god by self effort. All these religions obey rules, take part in rituals, and follow customs and traditions. Christianity is unique as it is based on a relationship with God who has revealed himself to us in the person of Jesus Christ. We are not seeking to find God because God has found us! The one true God has visited this planet in the person of Jesus, and it is by faith in Him that we are in relationship with almighty God.

Temptation comes and disaster often follows through domestic relationships that are not the result of the guidance of God. Christians should be very careful and very prayerful when they are contemplating marriage. There is always conflict when a Christian falls in love with an unbeliever. Paul writes « Do not be yoked together with unbelievers.» (2 Corinthians 6:14-17) He continues by asking the question « What does a believer have in common with an unbeliever? »   If you go ahead with such a relationship you are playing a dangerous game. God's word makes it very plain that we should not be yoked with an unbeliever. You may feel that everything will be all right and you will be able to lead your unbelieving spouse to the Lord. Conversion of the unbeliever can happen but many times it does not. You will have different values, different priorities and any children you have will cause tension between you, as you consider how to bring them up. King Solomon provides us with a classic example of starting life upholding the faith of his father David but in the latter days of his life, due to marrying heathen woman, he ended his life under a spiritual cloud. Many a union between Christian and non Christian ends in heart-break and disillusionment. Bitterness often follows and guilt that one has grieved the heart of God.

We are never more open to temptation than when we are on a « spiritual high » The Holy Spirit is moving in a marvellous way, converts are being won, miracles are being seen and many people are being carried away by emotion. In such situations good people, even Church leaders are tempted to exaggerate, and even to tell lies! They will claim that they have done certain things for God which they have never done at all. They are seeking their own glory in the situation. Many an evangelist has inflated the figure for the number of people, attending his meeting or the number of people who have been led to the Lord! Temptation comes even to those who are close to Jesus. Judas Iscariot who betrayed our Lord was one of his twelve disciples! Judas lived with Jesus and joined with the other disciples in hearing his teaching and receiving His blessing, but he fell into temptation and sold his Master for thirty pieces of silver! Demas was with Paul on his missionary journeys but deserted through temptation. He was pulled back by the devil into the world. It is important to watch and pray at all times but especially when on a « spiritual high.» We are often disturbed when we are trying to have a time of prayer or reading our Bible! The devil is the master of distraction. Jesus taught his disciples how to pray saying « When you pray, go into your room close the door and pray to your Father » (Matthew 6:6) The instructions to close the door seems to imply that you must get away from any thing that is likely to distract you! When harassed by Satan tell him to go in the name of Jesus. Turn your phone off and don't answer the door! Nothing is more important than talking to your heavenly Father! Satan wants to stop us praying because he is seeking to put out our spiritual fire, for he knows a person on fire for Christ is a threat to his Kingdom.

Satan likes to attack us at our weakest point. He knows our weaknesses, so it's important that we know our weaknesses too and are on our guard. Often a temper which explodes like a steam engine, can lead us into actions and words we regret and the evil one has a foothold. Paul writes to the Ephesians « In your anger do not sin. Do not let the sun go down while you are still angry, and do not give the devil a foothold. » (Ephesians 4:26-27) Our attitude to money and possessions is another area where we can come under attack. Jesus taught his disciples a great deal about money and possessions. Paul writes to Timothy warning him about the love of money « for the love of money is a root of all kinds of evil. Some people eager for money, have wandered from the faith and pierced themselves with many griefs » (1 Timothy 6:10) Sometimes people who give large sums of money to the Church cannot freely give it;

they want to be in control of how it is used. It is not the money that causes problems but the power it generates, which can be directly opposed to the Kingdom of God. Money of itself is not evil but when it takes over a person's life the devil will exploit the situation.

So how then can we resist Satan's wiles? How does the believer react when tempted? During the religious wars in France many Protestant pastors were executed, other leaders were sent to the galleys or imprisoned. In the town of Aigues Mortes, situated four kilometres from the Mediterranean sea, is the Tower of Constance, where many woman were imprisoned, because of their faith. A young woman Marie Durand was held prisoner for thirty eight years because she would not renounce her faith. She became the spiritual leader of a group of woman who were « abandoned by every one, prey to vermin, stripped of clothing, resembling skeletons, breathing only as much as necessary so that they would not be thought dead » If you visit this grim prison you will see, scratched, on one of the stones the word **resist.** We must resist. Resist when tempted. « Submit yourselves then to God. Resist the devil and he will flee from you. Come near to God and he will come near to you » (James 4:7-8) We must stand firm and give the devil no foothold in our lives. Peter the apostle writes « Your enemy the devil prowls around like a roaring lion looking for someone to devour. Resist him, standing firm in the faith » (1 Peter 5:8)

If we look at how Jesus dealt with temptation it will help us resist Satan. We have already noted in Mark's gospel that after His Baptism Jesus was sent out into the desert by the Spirit to be tempted by the devil. The accounts of the temptation of Jesus by Matthew and Luke give us the details of how the evil one was defeated. Every time Jesus was tempted by the devil, He answered by quoting from the Bible the word of God. He refuted Satan's suggestions by direct quotes from Scripture. The tempter said to him when he was hungry «**If** you are the son of God tell these stones to become bread. » Jesus answered « It is written that man does not live on bread alone, but on every word that comes from the mouth of God. » The reply that Jesus gave can be found in Deuteronomy 8:3. Then the devil took him to the Holy city and had him stand on the highest point of the Temple. « **If** you are the son of God, throw yourself down. For it is written: he will command his angels concerning you and they will lift you up in their hands, so that you will not strike your foot against a stone. » Here we have an example of the devil using Scripture to tempt Jesus. Satan quotes to Jesus some words from Psalm 91:11-12. Jesus replies « It is also written do not put the Lord your God to the test. » This again is a direct quotation from the Bible, Deuteronomy 6 :16. In refuting the third temptation Jesus again quotes directly from the book of Deuteronomy. The devil took him to a very high mountain and showed him all the Kingdoms of the world and their splendour. « All this I will give you he said » he said « If you will bow down and worship me » Jesus said to him away from me Satan! For it is written 'Worship the Lord your God and serve him only' » (Deuteronomy 6:13). Then the devil left him, and angels came and attended him. As you can see the most powerful way to combat temptation by the evil one is to quote out loud the word of God. The new Christian must learn this quickly.

Rejoice in persecution. Even rejoice when you are tempted. James, one of the leaders in the early Church writes about being tempted. He says that we should « consider it pure joy » when we face trials of any kind. When our faith is tested we learn to persevere and become mature not lacking in anything. (James1:2-4). James understood that trials and temptations lead to Christian maturity. As we go on with the Lord we should expect our faith to be tested so that it becomes stronger. Steel that is strong is produced by smelting iron in a furnace. A Christian becomes strong after being tempted in the 'furnace' of affliction. A little later on in the same letter James writes « Blessed is the man who perseveres under trial, because when he has stood the test, he will receive the crown of life that God has promised to those who love him. » (James 1:12) If we would receive the crown of life we will undergo trials. We should expect and be prepared for them, for the person who meets trials and temptations, in the right way, there is joy here and in the hereafter. Weaknesses of character are eradicated and faults are cleansed away so that the believer becomes stronger and purer in this life. In the life to come he receives the « Crown of Life ». A crown of joy, life in all its fullness lasting through eternity. A crown of victory, in Christ we are more than conquerors in this life and we will reign with Him for ever and ever in life everlasting. The crown is a symbol of royalty and of authority. We are children of the King in this life and we will reign with our Lord in the life to come. James adds « When tempted, no one should say God is tempting me. For God cannot be tempted by evil, nor does he tempt anyone: but each one is tempted when, by his own evil desire he is dragged away and enticed. Then after desire has conceived, it gives birth to sin; and sin when it is full-grown gives birth to death. » (James 1:12-15) It is easy to find fault with God and blame Him for our circumstances. It is part of our fallen human nature to play the blame game which is as old as history itself. James teaches us that we cannot put the blame on God when we are tempted, we are personally responsible for the sins we commit. The doorway to temptation can be our own evil desires. If we have not been crucified with Christ and died to sin we will fall when tempted.

The book of Hebrews pictures Jesus, crucified and risen, ascended and glorified as our great High Priest who makes intercessions for us before the throne of God. We read that « Because he himself suffered when he was tempted, he is able to help those who are being tempted. » (Hebrews 2:18) We identify with him and he identifies with us during times of temptation. We have someone who helps us and pleads our cause with the Father. Further more because he was tempted he is able to sympathise with our struggles (Hebrews 4:15) When many people in the Church at Corinth were struggling with trials and temptations of various kinds the Apostle Paul encouraged them to stand firm with these words « No temptation has seized you except what is common to man. And God is faithful; he will not let you be tempted beyond what you can bear. But when you are tempted, he will provide a way out so that you can stand up under it. » (1 Corinthians 10:13)

When we are tempted we should turn to God in prayer, use the Word of God the **Bible in proclamation against the suggestions of the devil**, and with the help of the living presence of Christ, within us, in the power of the Holy Spirit we can resist the evil one. Proclamation is powerful and helps us withstand temptation. Here are a few proclamations that can be used to help us.

When God seems distant and our prayers do not seem to be getting through and we are being harassed by the evil one. Romans 8:37-39 **« for I am convinced that neither death or life, neither angels or demons, neither the present nor the future, nor any powers, neither height nor depth, nor anything else in all creation, will be able to separate us from the love of God that is in Christ Jesus our Lord. »** Nothing that Satan can do is able to separate us from the love of God. We have the victory in the name of Jesus.

« We are more than conquerors through him who loved us » (Romans 8:37)
Paul also reminds his readers « That if God is for us, who can be against us »
(Romans 8 :31);

When the tempter tells us we are no good and confronts us with past sin, declare **« Therefore if anyone is in Christ, he is a new creation the old is gone, the new has come and all this is from God »** (2 Corinthians 5:17)

There are times when we need to remind Satan and ourselves that we have been purchased by the Saviour's blood and we belong to him and he has given us his righteousness. **« You are not your own you were bought with a price »** the precious blood of Jesus shed for us has redeemed us on the cross (1 Corinthians 6:20)

We can stand tall because we have a righteousness before God not of our own making but from Christ Jesus **« God made him who** had no sin to be sin, so that in him we might become the righteousness of God » (2 Corinthians 5:21)

Jesus reassured his disciples of their eternal destiny. When Satan tempts us to doubt this, proclaim the words of Jesus **« Because I live you also will live »** (John14:19)

When Jesus began to talk about his suffering, Peter objected to the idea of Jesus suffering and took him aside to tell him not to talk like that. Jesus recognised that Satan was using Simon Peter. He turned and said to Peter **« Out of my sight Satan! You are a stumbling block to me. You do not have in mind the things of God but the things of men »** The literal translation of the Greek text for **« Out of my sight Satan »** is «Scram Satan » or « Satan get lost!»; When you are being tempted do not hesitate to tell Satan to get lost as Jesus did., saying « **In the name of Jesus** I command you to go Satan »

All of us are sinners, saved by the grace of God. In our own strength we are weak. With the Holy Spirit we are strong . All of us will be tempted and if we do not rely on the Holy Spirit to help us we will fall. It is easy to break a bamboo cane in half, but if you bind the cane to an iron bar, it is not possible to break it or even bend it in your hands. The cane is protected and strengthened by the iron bar! We are protected and strengthened by the Holy Spirit. It is impossible to resist temptation without the help of the Holy Spirit. If we should fall we must repent and seek God's forgiveness. **May God strengthen you and sanctify you, through testing and trials, so that you become useful servants, working for His Kingdom.**

Chapter 6 - Walking With Confidence

Most parents remember the first steps their children take. I remember kneeling down on the floor with my arms outstretched encouraging my little boy to take his first step. He took a very unsteady step towards me, then another, then his legs buckled he reached the safety of the floor and crawled away. The next time he managed a few more steps sometimes grasping hold of furniture to steady himself! The first faltering steps had been taken and very soon he was walking confidently. We all need to learn to walk, and it's the same with our Christian faith. We may begin falteringly even after our baptism, so this is where our instruction and teaching from a discipleship course really take on meaning. Most importantly we need to observe the daily discipline of Bible study and prayer, alongside worship and fellowship with other Christians. New Christians have a spiritual hunger, they want to be at Church with other Christians, they have a desire for more and more of God, they want to praise and worship Him, read his word avidly so that their knowledge of Him and his ways will grow. This is a time for taking notes, writing a prayer diary, memorising scriptures, getting closer to God, coming to know Jesus more fully. Try to build a relationship with one or two mature Christians of the same sex as you, so you can ask their help when you don't understand, or are in difficulty. Pray with them and for them out loud and ask them to pray for you, by doing this you will encourage one another in the faith, and build up an important relationship. If your Church has a discipleship group be sure to join it.

Just as a baby falls after having made a few faltering steps, there is a danger that the new believer will fall backwards and stop making progress in the Christian life. Whilst visiting my parents at a very anxious time. I drove my small van rapidly up the steep drive way, turned into the parking bay, got out of the van and ran towards the front door, unfortunately I had forgotten something. I had neglected to put the hand brake on, and the van began to roll slowly backward. I sprinted after the van and somehow managed to get in to the moving vehicle and put the brake on as it was about to hit the wall opposite the driveway! The van rolled backwards because I had neglected to put the brake on. Many new Christians fall back spiritually because they neglect their quiet time with God. They find themselves too busy to put aside time to read the Bible and pray. Their spiritual life becomes very superficial and the devil begins to rub his hands together and smile as he sees what is happening:- someone slowly slipping back into his kingdom of darkness! The next stage is a reluctance to be at church, often followed by self justification and criticism of the pastor, elders, or the music group. « I am not getting anything out of being at Church » says the young Christian to himself and now the devil is really happy. Beware of falling back through neglect.

When I was a young child of five or six, I used to spend hours playing in the garden. The second world war had just ended and their were many shortages of essential things. It was the time of ration books, and most families grew as much fruit and vegetables as they were able. To help conserve water, for the garden, my father installed a very large barrel to collect rain. The barrel had previously contained Vaseline. One day I climbed on the wall next to it and stood on its wooden cover The cover moved and suddenly I was in the barrel up to my waist in cold rain water! I tried desperately to climb out but to no avail, the inside was slippery because of the greasy Vaseline. There was no way I could get out. I began to shout at the top of my voice but my mother could not hear me as she was busy in the front of the house. Eventually she came looking for me in the garden and heard my shouts, and with the help of a neighbour pulled me out! I was expecting to be in big trouble. Fortunately for me, my parents were so relieved that I had not drowned, that I was not punished but was sent to take a warm bath and no more was said! I imagine my father put a stronger lid on that barrel! Spiritually there is the danger of slipping back into the ways of the world and getting stuck. Often the pull of the world is very strong. Maybe the biggest danger is leisure and pleasure. Watching TV at face value is a harmless occupation but there are people who have it on all the time regardless of the programme. This wastes time, influences our thinking, and can take over our lives. Consider how many hours you spend watching television compared with the time you spend with God and His word! The same can be said about electronic games, computers, and any sport or pastime. The problem is that the Lord is no longer central in the life of the new Christian, other things are taking His place. The devil is very happy to see a person, slipping back into his Kingdom, huffing and puffing but making no progress, trapped and not able to escape.

One of the things that hinders us when we walk is a stone in our shoe! It can be very painful. The only remedy is to stop, take the shoe off and shake out the stone. Unconfessed sin can be like that stone hindering our walk and slowing down our progress in the Christian faith. The Bible teaches us that all of us sin and fall short of what God wants us to be. (Romans 3: 23). In the letter of John writing to Christians we read « If we claim to be without sin, we deceive ourselves, and the truth is not in us » (1 John1:8). All sin is first and foremost rebellion against God. The Bible tells us how we can live our lives so as to please God. God sets the standard not man. The Bible teaches that all of us fall short of the glory of God. The Bible also teaches us that there is a remedy for sin. John writes in his letter « My dear children, I write this to you so that you will not sin. But if anybody does sin, we have one who speaks to the Father in our defence - Jesus Christ, the Righteous One. He is the atoning sacrifice for our sins, and not only ours but also for the sins of the whole world » (1 John 2:1-2) It is important that we repent of the sins that we have committed and receive the pardon of God. We must not only receive God's forgiveness through the blood shed by Jesus on the cross but try with the help of the Holy Spirit not to make the same mistake again. We find this helpful advice in (Hebrews 12:1-3). « Let us throw off everything that hinders and the sin that so easily entangles, and let us run with perseverance the race marked out for us. Let us fix our eyes on

Jesus, the author and finisher of our faith, who for the joy set before Him endured the cross, scorning it's shame, and sat down at the right hand of the throne of God. Consider Him who endured such opposition from sinful men, so that you will not grow weary and lose heart »

When we fail to make progress in our Christian walk because of sin we must sincerely repent. Sometimes it helps to make confession of sin in the presence of other Christians in a ministry situation. The confession is being made to God but by speaking it out its reality is underlined. As the above scripture makes it plain the only way to receive forgiveness of our sins is to look to Jesus. Jesus is the sin bearer whose blood was shed at the cross, the atoning sacrifice, that puts us right with God, by faith in what Jesus has done, His finished work, by this we receive the pardon for our sins. The slate is wiped clean, we are no longer under condemnation, we are forgiven and set free. The scripture also tells us to look to Jesus, not only to his death but to His living presence at the right hand of the throne of God. Jesus King of Kings and Lord of Lords is one with the Father. He lives, He reigns, and we are citizens of His Kingdom. If we look to the King and stay close to Him, we are less likely to commit the same sins again. In Christ we become more than conquerors. He who is living in us is greater than he who is in the world. It is by looking to the throne where Jesus is seated that we receive the Baptism in the Holy Spirit which is God's gift to every believer. You will not be able to walk in faith and victory without receiving the baptism in the Holy Spirit.

I myself needed to have a deeper understanding of faith and a deeper trust in God before I came into the fullness of the Holy Spirit. I am going to use an example based on the relationship between a father and his child. When my daughter was a little girl of six or seven, we used to play a game which she invented. She would climb up to the fifth step on our stair case and jump into my arms. She trusted me to catch her! After jumping two or three times off the fifth step she would do the same from the sixth step and then the seventh and finally the eighth step! All was well and I managed to catch her and she trusted me even though she became a little more excitedly fearful as she jumped from the higher steps. Unfortunately the game ended in tears one day when I slipped on the polished floor and failed to catch her! The lesson from this is that faith is trusting in God as we move from one level of faith to another, we can trust Him in all circumstances, and as we are human beings there are different levels of faith, but unlike a human father our heavenly Father will never let us fall. When we become Christians we believe in Christ Jesus, and Him alone for our salvation. Many times at the beginning of our Christian life we trust in Jesus for our salvation but in **ourselves** for day to day living! Many people have difficulty in trusting anyone, let alone God because of bad experiences with people who have let them down. People who have been rejected, abandoned, who have a bad self image, or have suffered a break down in relationships, often have difficulty trusting God or other human beings. To reach a new level of faith the new convert will sometimes need ministry for healing and deliverance. Like my daughter's progress up the stairs, the believer has to get to new levels of faith and trust. Even the disciples of Jesus said to Him « Increase our faith » (Luke17 :5)

Many times we read that Jesus was amazed by the disciples' lack of faith. We read in Matthew's gospel of the time when Simon Peter answered the call of Jesus to walk to him across the water. Peter got out of the boat and started to walk towards Jesus. When he took his eyes off Jesus and saw the wind and the waves he began to sink! He cried out, « Lord save me » Immediately Jesus reached out his hand and caught him. «You of little faith, » He said «Why did you doubt? » (Matthew 14:21).

In another incident on the sea of Galilee, Jesus was with His disciples, when a storm arose and waves began to break over the boat. Jesus was in the stern of the boat sleeping on a cushion. The disciples woke Him and said to Him, « Teacher don't you care if we drown ? » He got up, rebuked the wind and said to the waves, « Quiet! Be still » Then the wind died down and it was completely calm. He said to his disciples « Why are you so afraid, Do you still have no faith, » (Mark 4:40)

One day Jesus took Peter, James and John up a mountain with him. While they were gone a man approached the other disciples to ask for healing for his epileptic son. When Jesus and the three came down from the mountain, they found everyone in great consternation. The disciples had been unable to heal the boy. The father of the boy approached Jesus and knelt before Him, « Lord have mercy on my son » he said. « he is an epileptic and he is suffering greatly. He often falls into the fire or into the water. I brought him to your disciples but they could not heal him » « O unbelieving and perverse generation » Jesus replied. He cast out the demon and the boy was healed from that moment. Then the disciples came to Jesus in private and asked « Why could not we drive it out? Jesus replied « Because you have so little faith » (Matthew 17:19 -20)

Jesus also commended people for their bold faith. Two of these people were not even Jews, they were Gentiles! One was a Roman Centurion who came to Jesus to ask for healing for his servant who was sick some distance away. Jesus said « I tell you the truth, I have not found anyone in Israel with such great faith! » (Matthew 8 :10) The other was a pagan Canaanite woman, who came to Jesus because her daughter was sick and possessed by a demon. Jesus at first put her off but she persisted with great faith. Jesus said to her « Woman you have great faith! Your request is granted, » and her daughter was healed from that very hour. (Matthew 15:28). Different people are at different stages of Christian maturity. Some have more faith than others. When we are new converts we need to grow in faith. We need to reach a higher level. Trust and obedience are essential if our faith is to grow. When we accepted Jesus, we asked Him to come and live in us, and of course He did. Our baptism was an outward sign of Christ's presence in our lives. If we are to grow in faith and obedience we have to consciously hand over the control of our lives to the Lord. This is not always easy as most of us like being in control. If our faith is to grow our self must have less and less influence on our lives and the Lord more and more! When I started to teach my daughter to drive I handed over the controls of the car to her when we arrived at a place that I thought was suitable. I sat helplessly as she drove the car across a traffic roundabout! Unlike handing over control of my car to my daughter, handing over your life to the control of the Lord is the very best thing you can do. Walking with the Lord is the happiest, and most satisfying life of all.

Many of us know that we believe, but like the disciples we would like to know how to increase our faith. How does faith increase. Paul wrote « faith comes from hearing the message, and the message is heard through the word of Christ ». (Romans 10:17) The Bible is the word of God. God speaks to us through His word. The Bible is the only authority for the believer's faith and conduct. Our faith grows when we listen to Biblically based teaching and sermons. Faith grows when we take what the Bible says as the truth. Many people in the last two hundred years have tried to discredit the Bible but for the Christian it is the word of God and stands above all other books. Other people have made their Bibles slim by cutting out those stories, miracles, and even teaching that they don't agree with. They have studied it like any book written by human beings and have rejected its divine inspiration. Paul writes to Timothy his son in the faith, reminding him « All Scripture is God breathed, and is useful for teaching, rebuking, correcting and training in righteousness, so that the man of God may be thoroughly equipped for every good work! » (2 Timothy 3 :16)

How do we reach a higher level of faith? It is important to let go of our own thoughts, our own way of thinking, and take on God's thoughts, His way of thinking. We do this as we spend more and more time reading the Bible. A man gave this remarkable testimony concerning the Word.« Never compare this book with other books. Comparisons are dangerous. Never think or never say that this book **contains** the Word of God; **it is the** Word of God. It is supernatural in origin, eternal in duration, inexpressible in value, infinite in scope, regenerative in power, infallible in authority, universal in interest, personal in application, inspired in totality.

Read it through. Write it down. Pray it in. Work it out. And then pass it on. » These remarkable words were often quoted by Smith Wigglesworth who was well known as « The apostle of Faith ». He learnt to read by reading the Bible and was a man of «one book ». During his lifetime he performed many miracles of healing and deliverance. Even the dead were raised and countless people were saved. His great faith and powerful ministry were due to his feeding on the Word. Today if you desire to reach a new level of faith read the Bible, meditate on and memorise the Word of God. Just as when a child fails to eat he becomes weak and open to catch all sorts of illness so also the Christian who neglects to read his Bible will soon become weak and open to all sorts of errors. If you truly desire to walk in faith and victory you will need to spend much time listening to what God says in His Word.

The most important step a new Christian takes in learning to walk is receiving the Baptism in the Holy Spirit. After Jesus had risen from the dead, and whilst He was eating with his disciples, He gave them this command « Do not leave Jerusalem, but wait for the gift my Father promised, which you have heard me speak about. For John baptised with water, but in a few days you will be baptised with the Holy Spirit » (Acts 1: 4-5) Later they met together and asked Him « Lord are you at this time going to restore the Kingdom to Israel? » He said to them « It is not for you to know the times or dates the Father has set by His own authority. But you will receive power when the Holy Spirit comes on you, and you will be my witnesses in Jerusalem, and all Judea and Samaria, and to the end of the earth. »(Acts1:6-8) The risen Christ told His disciples to expect to receive God's power, the Holy Spirit, to enable them to witness for Him in all the world.

The Holy Spirit will come when a man is cleansed. I used to use as a preaching aid « Sam the Saucepan ». In preparation I would take a saucepan about the size of a human head, and put lots of spots of black shoe polish all over the inside of the pan! I put on the lid put a hat on top of the lid and a tie or scarf around the saucepan. I explained that Sam was ready to go to church I said « Sam looks very smart on the outside but what's he like inside ». At that point I would remove the lid and the people would see the black marks all over the inside of the saucepan. Then I would say « Oh dear look at what Sam has been doing, and point out a lot bad things that Sam had done. » Then I would list Sam's bad thoughts! Then taking a damp cloth or sponge with the word Jesus written on it, I would wipe away all the black marks and make Sam clean on the inside. I would stress that if we repent and confess our sins we can receive God's forgiveness and be made clean because of the sacrifice Jesus made on the cross. His shed blood washes all our sins away and we are made clean within. For the Holy Spirit to come there must be a washing away of the old life, that is the life we led before we came to Christ and entered His Kingdom. We must repent of everything that is wrong in our lives and then ask the Lord to fill us with the Holy Spirit. Jesus said to His disciples « Ask and it will be given to you, seek and you will find, knock and it will be opened unto you. For everyone who asks receives; he who seeks finds; and to him who knocks the door will be opened »

(Luke 11: 9-10) Jesus reassured them that what the Father gives is good and not bad and finished by saying « How much more will the Father give the Holy Spirit to them that ask Him » If we come to the Father with clean open hearts, having repented of our sins, and ask Him to fill us with the Holy Spirit He will do it! As somebody once said « If you don't ask you don't get! » This is true of the Holy Spirit, God's precious gift to the believer.

If you desire to be baptised in the Holy Spirit you must surrender your life to the Lord. The words of the old Hymn by Frances Ridley Havergal express this absolute surrender and we can use the words as a prayer.

« Take my life, and let it be consecrated Lord, to Thee.
Take my moments and my days, let them flow in ceaseless Praise.
Take my hands and let them move at the impulse of Thy love.
Take my feet, and let them be swift and beautiful for Thee.
Take my voice and let me sing always, only, for my King.
Take my lips, and let them be filled with messages from Thee.
Take my silver and my gold not a mite would I withhold.

Take my intellect, and use every power as Thou shalt choose.
Take my will and make it Thine; it shall be no longer mine.
Take my heart, it is Thine own, it shall be Thy royal throne.
Take my love, my Lord I pour at Thy feet it's treasure-store.
Take myself, and I will be ever, only, all for Thee »

The Lord will honour the prayer.

When we receive the Lord by faith, we receive Jesus into our lives. The Holy Spirit comes and dwells within us. All who truly believe are indwelt by the Holy Spirit. When we are **Baptised** in the Holy Spirit it is not that **we have the Holy Spirit** but that the **Holy Spirit has us.** When a person becomes a Christian the Holy Spirit comes and lives in that person. When a person is **Baptised in the Holy Spirit**, he/she is immersed **in** the Holy Spirit. That person is full of the Holy Spirit and is also consciously walking all the time in the Holy Spirit. Living life in the Holy Spirit is to live life in a completely different dimension. It is to live and move in the supernatural. The Bible gives us no fixed time table for this to happen. Paul received the Holy Spirit prior to being baptised others receive after being baptised. Some people receive the baptism in the Holy Spirit when they are converted and some as a separate experience after conversion. Indeed some many years after conversion. All who would receive the Baptism must repent, be cleansed, yield, ask and receive.

Let us think of our life as a house. We have a lodger living in the attic room. He does not bother us much. Sometimes we have a quick word as we leave for work in the morning and similarly when we return in the evening. On Sundays we pass an hour or so with him. It's all nice and friendly does not cost us anything, he's a nice enough chap. We just get on with our life. This is like being at Church on Sunday for an hour or two, saying a brief prayer morning and evening, but then forgetting about Jesus, for the rest of the time.

We read in the book of Revelation that Jesus stands at the door of our lives. He knocks and waits for us to open the door. If we do open the door He comes in « If anyone hears my voice and opens the door, I will come in and eat with Him, and he with me » (Revelation 3:21) Sharing hospitality with a guest, in the middle eastern culture of the time when Jesus lived, was to put what you had at your guest's disposal, so we can have Jesus living in our house as a guest. He is our friend and we share fellowship with Him. He is an honoured guest and we seek to make our guest happy. Having Jesus as a guest in our house is much better than having Him as a lodger! However when we have someone as a guest we don't expect that person to go poking about in the dark corners of our house. We keep our guest in the best room and do not allow him in the other rooms. Best of all we can have Jesus as the owner occupier of our house. The house in its entirety belongs to Him and he occupies it completely, we live in union with Him. When we allow our lives to be taken over by the Holy Spirit we receive the Baptism of the Holy Spirit. Jesus spoke too of a house being cleansed and set in order by the casting out of a demon but then being left empty. «When an evil spirit comes out of a man, it goes through arid places seeking rest and does not find it. Then he says 'I will return to the house I left' When it arrives, it finds the house swept clean and put in order. Then it goes and takes seven other spirits more wicked than itself, and they go in and live there. And the final condition of that man is worse than the first » (Luke 11:24-26) The warning Jesus gives us here is that if evil has been driven out of our lives and our house has been made clean it is essential that we are not left empty but are filled with the Holy Spirit!

Receiving the Baptism of the Holy Spirit is by faith. We believe and we receive! Each person will have a slightly different experience of how it happens and how it affects their lives. We hear testimonies and they all differ. Dwight L Moody the great American evangelist was challenged by two ladies praying for him. At the time he was a pastor and evangelist working in a church in Chicago. He was preaching at an out reach meeting and he saw these two ladies praying throughout his sermon. After the meeting he asked them if they were praying for the unconverted, they shook their heads and answered « no we were praying for you ». Moody was taken aback because he was a proud man. Soon after he met with God in a new way. He describes how he came to an end of himself and how God filled him with the Holy Spirit. It was immediately after his fresh encounter with God the Holy Spirit, that his international ministry began. He was a changed man and a great number of people in many parts of the world came to faith in the Lord Jesus Christ through his ministry. John Wesley the founder of the Methodist Church met afresh with God after his ministry in North America ended in failure. 'I went to convert the Indians' he cried out to God, but who will convert me!' On the way back from America his ship was caught in a storm and he was terrified. He heard singing and a group of Moravian Christians were praising the Lord in the midst of the storm! Their witness of faith was to change the rest of his life and ministry. Soon he was sharing fellowship with the Moravians in London and on the 24th May 1738 he went to say prayers at St Paul's cathedral, listened to a Psalm being sung, and went back to a room in Aldersgate street and met with other Christians. Whilst praying there he met with God the Holy Spirit. He felt that at last he really did believe and he was filled with the Holy Spirit. He wrote in his diary that « his heart was strangely warmed ». The « Evangelical Revival » in Britain had begun. The effects of his ministry are still being felt to this day.

Although there are many differing accounts of how people have had a life changing encounter with God the Holy Spirit, there are some features that are common to all. A person who is Baptised in The Holy Spirit, is aware of a change in their life and others notice this too. The Baptism in the Holy Spirit leads to a deeper assurance and greater sense of the presence of God, to a closer walk with God and a deeper cleansing of the soul. Each person in the body of Christ receives the gifts of the spirit, for the building up of the Church and for it's mission in the world. The Holy Spirit helps us to be more obedient and have a greater concern for those who do not know the Lord. God may also give different ministries and abilities to his servants through the Baptism. Most people receive the gift of tongues and the ability to pray and sing in the Spirit. The Holy

Spirit helps us to witness to the unbeliever by what we are, what we say and what we do. Our prayer life improves dramatically as does our ability to praise and thank the Lord in all circumstances.

Over a period of time the Lord brought me into contact with Christians who were Baptised in the Holy Spirit and were moving in the Spirit and using the gifts. After searching the Scriptures and underlining every reference to the Holy Spirit in the book of the Acts of the Apostles I realised that the first Christians were **empowered** by the Spirit and that the mission of the Church was **accomplished** by the Spirit and that the lives of those first Christians were **led** by the Holy Spirit. I took note that this was **normal** Christian living and that supernatural happenings were common place and that the believers were conscious of the Lord working with them. I looked at much of contemporary Christianity and realised that it was « man-centred, not Christ centred ». It became more and more clear to me that I needed to be Baptised in the Holy Spirit.

The more time I spent with Spirit filled Christians the more I wanted to have what they had. I had sensed God's presence powerfully in several meetings, and decided to ask for prayer from a friend of mine who was a Church of England vicar. One afternoon I knocked on the vicarage door and my friend Eric shared with me the passage of Scripture that tells of Peter getting out of the boat to walk on the water towards Jesus.(Matthew 14:25-31) He asked me by faith to get out of my boat, to rely on Jesus by faith, and accept the Holy Spirit as he placed his hands on my head and prayed over me in tongues. I was very nervous and not relaxed. I was not quite sure what would happen and I knelt on the floor for quite some time. Eric then asked me to praise and thank the Lord which I did. I felt an inner peace and sensed the presence of the Lord. I was expecting to start speaking in tongues and thought that I would have no control over my voice. But this did not happen and I made my way home feeling a great peace. The next Sunday I preached as normal. When the service came to an end I was approached by a saintly lady who was a member of the Church. She said to me « Gerald what ever has happened to you! Your preaching has changed. There is a new power present » This lady had recognised that I was filled with the Holy Spirit in a powerful way and that God was speaking through me. Praise the Lord!

In learning to walk with the Lord the new Christian must learn to receive forgiveness and to forgive others. Jesus made it plain that those whom God has forgiven are expected to forgive those who sin against them! In the Lord's prayer we find the words « Forgive us our debts (sins) as we have forgiven our debtors (those who have sinned against us) » The next verse is interesting it says « For if you forgive men when they sin against you, your heavenly Father will also forgive you. But if you do not forgive men their sins, your Father will not forgive your sins ».(Matthew 6:12-15) That is the condition God puts on our being forgiven. In learning to walk we will fall many times. When we sin we repent and confess to our heavenly Father that we have sinned and through the sacrifice Jesus made on the cross, by his shed blood we receive forgiveness and restoration. Two problems often arise. A person cannot receive the pardon from God because he/she is full of resentment and bitterness because she/he is unable to forgive someone who has hurt them or sinned against them. To receive total forgiveness it is important that you forgive that other person. Even if that other person does not accept your forgiveness, God knows about it and will pardon you. The second problem many people have is that they cannot forgive themselves. If God can forgive you, you must forgive yourself. If you cannot you are making yourself superior to God!

When you unconditionally forgive someone who has wronged you, healing power is set free in your life. Many times people carry a guilt they cannot get rid of because the person they injured is no longer alive. In such cases God can bring peace to a person's life when he/she asks Him for forgiveness for this past action. Unresolved guilt can destroy the strongest person. One day I received a telephone call from a stranger who requested an interview with me. I took one of the elders from the Church with me. We met with a strong, well built man, a soldier who had been serving in Northern Ireland. He patrolled the streets of Belfast at the height of the troubles. He began to tell his story. He was unable to sleep at night, he was moody and depressed and his wife was threatening to leave him. This tough looking soldier burst into tears as he spoke of the picture that haunted him day and night. He was on street patrol with the rest of his section when one of the section shouted « Behind you » He turned around and let fire with his automatic gun. A fair haired child was lifted off the ground by the bullet fire and killed instantly. That picture haunted the soldier day and night. The guilt had already destroyed his ability to serve in the armed forces. His health both mental and physical was being destroyed as also was his family. He was in danger of taking his own life. The elder, who had himself been a soldier in the war and had been taken prisoner in Burma, was able to help him. I led him to the Cross of Jesus Christ and after confession he received forgiveness, he left us to start a new life with the Lord. His guilt was taken away. Through his repentance and confession, God was able to heal and restore him, something he could not do for himself. I went to visit a sixteen year old girl who was in hospital suffering from severe headaches. The medical staff suspected that she had had a brain haemorrhage. I talked with her and she told me that she felt guilty and responsible for her mother's death. It seemed that she had persuaded her father against his will to take her out to the pictures. In fact she had thrown a tantrum and he had given in. When they returned to the house they found that her mother had had a severe brain haemorrhage and had died in their absence. The girl naturally felt that it was her fault - even that she had caused her mother's death. Only two weeks after this incident, she was admitted to hospital. Once this guilt was revealed I was able to pray with her for forgiveness. She received God's pardon, was healed and was discharged from hospital. How heavy a load is guilt. If it is not dealt with it can destroy believers and non believers.

As you begin to walk it is important to realise that God loves you and wants your life to be the best it can be. God's plan for your future is for the best. We trust our future into our Father's hands who cares even for the sparrow. How much more does He care for us. When we fall He is there to pick us up and put us back on the way.

Chapter 7 - Persevere or Perish

Memories of our schooldays can be good or bad! Some people would describe them as the happiest days of their life, others would remember them as the worst days they had endured! One vivid memory of my schooldays was taking part each term in a cross country race. I was only an average runner but there were those boys who were very good and others who gave up. It was not unusual to see the boys who had given up, sitting on the grass by the side of the route, calling out to others to give up also! It can be the same with Christians! Together we are running a race which is a marathon rather than a sprint, at times we feel like giving up. Perhaps living for Jesus has proved to be more difficult than we had imagined, some of our friends may be saying to us « Don't become too religious! » or « You have become a religious fanatic » (One person defined a religious fanatic as someone who believes more than you do!) Paul nearing the end of his life, writes to his protégé Timothy to encourage him in his ministry «I have fought the good fight, I have finished the race, I have kept the faith » (2 Timothy 4: 7). There are times when living for Jesus seems to be an unending struggle. We need to continue to battle, to fight the good fight, to keep going and finish the race, to remain faithful to the Lord and to keep the faith! We can sum this up in one word! **PERSEVERANCE.**

Very soon the new believer will encounter opposition, and maybe rejection from family and friends. Living for Christ in the work place can be very difficult indeed and those who do may be persecuted. The Christian swims against the current of popular culture, just as in the spring Salmon swim against the flow of the river to reach higher ground in order to spawn their young so Christians find themselves battling against the current of popular behaviour to reach the higher ground of the kingdom! At this point it is important that we realise that we are not on our own. The Lord is with us, as are our brothers and sisters in Christ. In the New Testament the emphasis is not on the individual believer so much as on the community of believers. In the words of the popular song by Paul McCartney « We all stand together »

« Win or lose, sink or swim,
One thing is certain we will never give in,
Side by side, hand in hand,
We all stand together »

Paul writes to believers at Philippi to encourage them to stand together against opposition so that others may hear the gospel and believe. « Whatever happens, conduct yourselves in a manner worthy of the gospel of Christ. Then whether I come and see you or only hear about you in my absence, I will know that you stand firm in one spirit, contending as one man for the faith of the gospel without being frightened in any way by those who oppose you. » (Philippians 1:27-28) The letter of Peter makes it clear that we must stand firm, he says « Make every effort to add to your faith goodness; and to goodness add knowledge; and to knowledge self control; and to self control perseverance …… » (2 Peter 1:6)

Christianity has its roots firmly planted in Judaism. Jesus was Jewish and so were most of his early disciples. Judaism is dominated by legalism, in other words you get right with God by obeying the law. Early in the history of the Jews, God gave them the law, the ten commandments. To these ten commandments in the course of time many other laws were added, perhaps as many as six hundred! During the life time of Jesus on earth you could hardly do anything without being in danger of disobeying one or more laws! It is no wonder the New Testament often speaks of the Jewish people being held in bondage by the law. The problem for the first Christian communities was that Jewish converts who continued keeping the law wanted Gentile converts to do the same. This caused division in the churches. Paul, particularly in his letters to the Romans and Galatians focused on this issue declaring that Christ had set the believer in Jesus free from the Jewish law. The council of Jerusalem which was made up of the apostles debated this and wrote to the Christians at Antioch « It seemed good to the Holy Spirit and to us not to burden you with anything beyond the following requirements: You are to abstain from food sacrificed to idols, from blood from the meat of strangled animals and from sexual immorality. You will do well to avoid these things. » (Acts 15:28-29) As legalism began to establish itself in the new Christian communities, Paul urges the churches to stand firm to persevere and not be enticed back into Judaism.« It is for freedom that Christ has set us free. Stand firm then and do not let yourselves be burdened again by a yoke of slavery » (Galatians 5:1) At this point you may be thinking 'What has this got to do with Christianity today?' It is still a big problem today, in some Churches, where people think that their salvation depends on amassing « Brownie points in heaven » by obeying rules and regulations! It is by faith in Jesus Christ that we have been saved. It is by grace that we have been saved. It is all of Him and nothing of us. Today we must be free from 'salvation by good works' and this may mean perseverance in the face of religious opposition. We do not follow the teaching of Jesus in order to gain salvation, rather our hearts are changed because He lives in us and we desire to be like Him.

Christians are also people who persevere in their fight against evil and injustice. Many are familiar with the name William Wilberforce. Two centuries or more ago the economy of Great Britain depended upon the slave trade. English traders sailed to West Africa and bought captured Africans for a pittance. They were held in irons on crowded ships and treated with unspeakable cruelty. They were then exchanged for sugar, cotton or other products in the plantations of the Southern states of America and the Caribbean. Many slave traders amassed vast fortunes in Great Britain. William Wilberforce and his fellow Christians called the « Clapham Sect » campaigned tirelessly for the abolition of slavery. The opposition was very great as the trade was making many people of influence very rich! William Wilberforce did not give up and eventually succeeded in his campaign to get the evil trade abolished, despite his failing health. Today evil and injustice abound on a world scale. Today the words of Peter are just as relevant as they were in New Testament times. He writes telling Christians to « Be self controlled and alert. Your enemy the devil prowls around like a roaring lion looking for someone to devour. Resist him, standing firm in the faith, because you know that your brothers throughout the world are undergoing the same kind of sufferings » (1 Peter 5:8-9) There are many Christians who are being persecuted for their faith in Muslim and Communist countries and they have need of our prayers and support. In Europe, also there is injustice, anti- Christian laws and increasing secularisation, so the need for perseverance and firmness in the faith is important. We resist the devil who is behind the evil in our world just as James advised « Submit yourselves, then to God. Resist the devil and he will flee from you. » (James 4:7)

Christian perseverance and endurance are inseparably linked. Jesus warns his twelve disciples as he sent them out to preach the good news of the kingdom that they would be opposed. « All men will hate you because of me, but he who stands firm to the end will be saved » (Matthew 10:22) It is natural to want to be loved and accepted by other people. Many want to be popular. Our self esteem may depend upon it, but Jesus warns us that we may be hated even by those who are close to us because we are His disciples. We are called to stand firm. The Holy Spirit Himself will strengthen us in our inner being. That's good news because we cannot operate in our own strength, that would lead to disaster! James writes « Blessed is the man who perseveres under trial, because when he has stood the test, he will receive the crown of life that God has promised to those who love Him » (James 1:12) There will be times when our faith is tried and tested, that is when with God's help we persevere and do not give up. Just as for Jesus the agony of the cross led to His being crowned King of kings and Lord of Lords, so if we persevere to the end we will receive the crown of life eternal. We shall be with Him in glory. « Endure hardship as discipline » writes the author of the book of Hebrews. He goes on to reassure those who are going through bad times and being tested « God is treating you as sons. For what son is not disciplined by his father? If you are not disciplined (and everyone undergoes discipline), then you are illegitimate children and not true sons » (Hebrews 12:7) We live at a time when discipline in general has been relaxed! Indeed it is often thought of being negative where freedom reigns. God is reminding us through the Bible that we shall be tried and disciplined because we are His precious children!

We have to keep going and not give up. « When the going gets tough, the tough get going » is a trite saying. It is a call for perseverance. Jesus commanded his disciples during the last supper to remain in his love, « As the Father has loved me so have I loved you. Now remain in my love » (John 15:9) To love Him is to obey His commands and to remain true. Those who do, are filled with inexplicable joy! We must keep going writes Paul « let us not become weary in doing good, for at the proper time we will reap a harvest if we do not give up » (Galatians 6:9) In the Churches I have served as a Pastor there have been times when Christians have grown weary and have come and said to me 'Gerald, I need a break, I do not want to go on serving the Lord in such and such a service;' People do become weary, bored even, with their service in the church. Sometimes they feel trapped, or they look at what others are doing or not doing and want to be released. The call is to run with perseverance and not give up. I began this chapter with an example from my school days running a cross country race where some gave up. The author of the book of Hebrews uses the same kind of imagery. « Therefore since we are surrounded by such a great cloud of witnesses, let us throw off everything that hinders and the sin that so easily entangles and let us run with perseverance the race marked out for us. Let us fix our eyes on Jesus the author and perfecter (finisher) of our faith » (Hebrews 12:1-2) When a person feels like giving up or becomes weary with doing good, what should that person do? He should fix his eyes on Jesus. The word fix means to gaze for a long time. To look and keep looking at Jesus who endured the agony of the cross for us, and maybe think again about giving up. Find a quiet place, tell the Lord all about that which is making you weary and wanting to give up. Remain in his presence fixing all your attention on Him. This will help you see everything in a different light. Your perspective will change, as the words of the old chorus say

Turn yours eyes upon Jesus
Look full in His wonderful face
And the things of the world will grow strangely dim
In the light of His glory and grace'

Sometimes if a person has been hurt by another Church member he/she gives up suddenly, or maybe slowly fades. Sylvia was gloriously converted. She served the Lord with great enthusiasm for a number of months. In fact there was never a service, activity or meeting in the Church that she did not attend! The danger signals of Christian burnout began to show. Slowly her enthusiasm waned, and her spirituality began to diminish. It was as if her light had been dimmed. Very soon she seemed to enter a spiritual wilderness and ceased to be part of the Church fellowship. Perhaps the novelty had worn off! I am sure you remember during your school days crazes that would sweep through the schools, such as hula hoops, solving Rubic's cube, or more recently scooters! Not only school children get obsessed but adults also. Certain dress or hair styles are all the fashion for a short time accentuating particular hair cuts or hem lines. As we have seen being a Christian is for life and eternity. It is a life long commitment not a craze, fashion or novelty that soon is forgotten. Some times people cool down spiritually when there is a change of circumstances. Many young people who were brought up in a Christian family, who accepted Jesus into their lives, and helped with Sunday school or in youth work stopped being practising Christians when they left home to go to college or to work elsewhere. The Oxford popular dictionary defines the word « backslide » to relapse into error or bad ways! In the Church the word backsliders is often used to describe Christians who have given up the faith and gone back to the life they lived before becoming Christians. When I attended a Church Sunday School in Kenya, East Africa, the leader was doing a series of lessons on backsliding! He was challenging all the participants. Why do people give up as Christians after having made a good start? I am suggesting to you four common reasons.

1) A person was not truly converted
They may in the words of the apostle Paul « Have a form of Godliness but denying its power » A person can be very religious without having a relationship with the Lord. The real meaning of Jesus' sacrifice for sins has not been properly understood, so He is not recognised as Saviour.

2) They have been hurt by other Christians
A few years ago a survey was taken of why people had given up on Christ and His church. It showed that they had lost the faith they once had not because of any crisis in theological understanding of God but because they had been hurt by their brothers and sisters in the church! Their hurt had festered and grown so that they distanced themselves from the whole church and from God Himself. This is so sad. We know that in family life people fall out with one another and so it is in the family of the church, but we must be slow to take offence and quick to forgive. At the centre of every Church activity is Jesus, we meet as his body knowing that we are forgiven, and that we are required to forgive anyone who has hurt us, and be reconciled to those whom we have hurt, any broken relationship of love is to be repaired.

3) The pull of the world
Many young people who come to know Christ at a young age often feel that they are missing out on fun. Maybe their non Christian friends seem to be having a wonderful time. They talk of parties and raves, girls and drugs and it all sounds so exciting. Their friends do not tell of the pain, the loneliness, the alienation, and the depth of dissatisfaction of their inner being, guilt instead of peace, lust instead of love, drift instead of purpose. The name Demas occurs several times in the New Testament. In Paul's letter to the Colossians his name appears alongside Luke «Our dear friend Luke, the doctor, and Demas send greetings » (Colossians 4:14) In Paul's personal letter to Philemon concerning his run away slave Onesimus he mentions Demas as one of his fellow workers alongside Mark, Aristarchus and Luke. (Philemon :24) Then a little

later on when Paul was imprisoned in Rome he wrote to Timothy asking him to come to him because Demas « In love with this present world » had deserted him and gone to Thessalonica. (2 Timothy 4:10). Our love for Jesus must be greater than our love for the world!

4) Persecution

Christians are becoming more aware of the persecution affecting millions of other Christians all over the world. Fear of persecution or persecution itself may cause some to give up their faith.

One secular example of great perseverance is the story of the Odone family and their struggle to find a cure for the rare disease *adrenoleukodystrophy* (ALD). The film « Lorenzo's oil » tells the true story of how Lorenzo the son of Michaela and Augusto Odone was diagnosed with the cerebral form of ALD, a progressive degenerative nervous system disorder for which there is no cure. The parents devastated by the diagnosis that Lorenzo will become totally disabled and die in a few years, decide to research ALD even though neither has a scientific or medical background. The Odones often worked at odds with sceptical doctors, scientists, and support groups. They spent endless hours in medical libraries reading articles in journals and talking to researchers and doctors. After persevering for a long, long time and after much hard work they helped develop a treatment for ALD made from olive and rapeseed which they name Lorenzo's oil. As the disease progressed Lorenzo becomes totally bedridden and disabled. He made a partial recovery however and the story ends on a positive note as several children with ALD are shown to have benefited from the oil.

In the Old Testament there are many stories of persevering people. Most of us will be familiar with the story of the flood and of Noah building an ark and rescuing the animals but have you ever thought of the courage and perseverance that the enterprise demanded. What did the people round about him, in a sun scorched country, think? That man Noah's gone crazy building a gigantic boat in the middle of a desert! It took a lot of perseverance to follow God's instructions.(Genesis6:14) Christians must persevere in prayer. We have the example how Abraham persevered in his prayer to save his nephew Lot and the people of Sodom. (Genesis 18:16-35) Job was a man who persevered in difficult circumstances. Job accepted God's will for him even though he believed that he was being unfairly treated! Moses persevered in persuading the Israelites to follow God's instructions for the construction of the Tabernacle and sacrifices. (Leviticus Ch 1-7 The prophet Daniel persevered in prayer to the Almighty even when it was forbidden by the king Darius! (Daniel ch6)

The church is to persevere when tried and not to give up in the face of persecution. The Church that Paul founded in Thessalonica was so heavily persecuted that Paul had to flee for his life. After his hurried departure those left behind continued to preach the gospel in the face of great opposition. Paul singles them out as an example of perseverance for other Churches to emulate. « Therefore among God's churches we boast about your perseverance and faith in all the persecutions and trials you are enduring. » (2 Thessalonians 1:4) One of the saddest evenings of my life was when I was asked to be at a meeting of church members to discuss the closure of their church. No they were not being persecuted but they had run out of energy and the light of their faith had become very dim. No one wanted to persevere and reach out to the community with the gospel. The Church at Ephesus is one of the seven Churches in the book of Revelation. We remember it as the church that had forsaken its first love, forsaken Jesus its living Lord. However they are commended for their perseverance. « I know your deeds, your hard work and your perseverance » and « You have persevered and endured hardship for my name and have not grown weary » (Revelation 2:2 -3) They had lost their love for Jesus but they were still persevering! Again the risen Lord speaks to another of the seven churches, the one at Thyatira. He commends them for their deeds, their love and faith, their service and perseverance, and the progress they are making. (Revelation 2:19) .

How do we keep going in all circumstances? What is the secret of the perseverance of the Saints? How do we nurture and develop perseverance when tempted to give up? Here are some pointers that might help.

1) Vision. Christians are visionaries.
All of us need to receive inspiration. Christians need to have a vision of where God is leading them. Paul writes of his own personal vision and the thorn in his flesh. (2 Corinthians 12: 1-10) The vision of Christ and his Kingdom helps us to persevere in times of difficulty. « Where there is no vision, the people perish » (Proverbs 29:18)

2) Expectation Believing that God is in control and that he is all knowing, helps us to persevere in times of difficulty. If we are puzzled by what is happening to us it may be because « God is doing a new thing in our lives » He is involved in our lives.

3) Aim Someone has written « If we do not aim at a target we are not likely to hit it! »
Christians and Churches must have aims. If we know where we are going we are much more likely to persevere and get there. We are drawn towards the finishing line.

4) Encouragement Again I want to emphasise how important it is to realise that we do not live our Christian lives in isolation. We are related to one another in Christ just as the many parts of our human body are related and have their own distinctive function. When a person is being tempted to give up, a word of encouragement from another brother or sister can be so important! We must learn to encourage one another! It is often easier to criticise people when things are going wrong than to encourage them. Encouragement breeds perseverance!

5) Worshipping together
Ever since that Sunday when the risen Lord Jesus appeared to his disciples Christians have gathered together for worship. No matter the dangers or the risk of being arrested Christians worship the

Lord on Sunday. All disciples worship the Lord it is not optional. It is a time to receive strength from the Lord so as to keep persevering together with our brothers and sisters in times of difficulty.

6) Reward

Jesus taught his followers that they would receive their reward in heaven for being his servants on earth. The parable of the talents uses the idea of a master giving his servants money to use each according to his ability. To one he gave five talents, to another, two and to a third, one. Then the master went on a long journey. When he returned he settled accounts with them. The man who was given five talents brought five more and the man who had been given two brought two more but the man with one talent just returned what he had been given without gaining any interest. He was condemned as a wicked and lazy servant, but the others received their reward.« His master replied 'Well done, good and faithful servant! You have been faithful with a few things. I will put you in charge of many things. Come share your master's happiness! » (Matthew 25:23)

Jesus taught his disciples to be generous and they would receive their reward « Love your enemies, do good to them, and lend to them without expecting to get anything back. Then your reward will be great, and you will be sons of the Most High, because he is kind to the ungrateful and wicked. (Luke 6:35) Jesus taught that when Christians were insulted and persecuted they would receive a reward in heaven « Blessed are you when people insult you, persecute you, and falsely say all kinds of evil against you because of me. Rejoice and be glad, because great is your reward in heaven, for in the same way they persecuted the prophets who were before you » (Matthew 5:11-12) Paul encourages Timothy to persevere « If we endure, we will also reign with Him. If we disown Him he will also disown us. » (2 Timothy 2:12) In many schools one of the big events of the year is the annual prize giving. Pupils are rewarded for what they have achieved. We shall all be rewarded for our faithfulness and service for the master. The day of judgement for the Christian will be like an award ceremony when we shall receive our « Oscars »!

All Christians face challenges. Many times we shall let Jesus down. What does Jesus require of us? I believe it is to be faithful to Him and keep going till we complete our earthly race. As we get older we will like the wise athlete need to pace ourselves, maybe slow down a bit, but we must never give up, for it is by enduring to the end that we receive the crown of life.

Chapter 8 - The King and the Kingdom

In the city of Liverpool there is a superb modern Cathedral built in the shape of a very large crown! It is dedicated to « Christ the King » The coming of God's Kingdom is announced in the opening of Mark's gospel with the words of Jesus .« The time has come. The Kingdom of God is near. Repent and believe the good news!' » (Mark 1:14-15) Matthew commences his gospel with an account of the birth of Jesus. The mysterious travellers, Magi, Kings, came from the east in search of a new king. They arrived at Jerusalem and asked « Where is the one who has been born king of the Jews? » When Herod who was himself King of the Jews heard this he was not happy. He consulted the religious leaders who told him that the prophets had foretold that a messianic king would be born in Bethlehem. Herod, believing that a rival king had been born, ordered all male children of two years or younger living in the vicinity of Bethlehem to be killed. In John's gospel we read that when Jesus entered Jerusalem a crowd gathered « took palm branches and went out to meet him shouting 'Hosanna ! Blessed is he who comes in the name of the Lord! Blessed is the King of Israel.' » (John 12:13) Messiah mania was in vogue and all the people of Israel were looking for a king like David who would defeat the occupying Romans. They were hoping for the restoration of Israel. David had been Israel's greatest king, a shepherd boy who became a mighty warrior, conquering and ruling over the nations nearby. The people were waiting for the promised Messiah to come who would be powerful and all conquering as King David had been. Luke tells us how Jesus was unjustly tried. The council of the elders of the people accused him before the governor Pontius Pilate « We have found this man subverting our nation. He opposes payment of taxes to Caesar and claims to be Christ a king. So Pilate asked Jesus 'Are you the king of the Jews?' 'Yes it is as you say » Jesus replied. (Luke 23:2-3). The gospels tell us that the soldiers mocked Jesus putting a crown of thorns upon his head. Pilate ordered « a written notice to be nailed above him which read :THIS IS THE KING OF THE JEWS. (Luke 23:38) » In each of the four gospels then Jesus is described as a King either at his birth or at his death.

The Christian Church celebrates four great festivals every year, Christmas the birth of Jesus, Easter His resurrection, Ascension His return to the Father in heaven and Pentecost the gift of the Holy Spirit and the birth of the Church. Today most Churches celebrate Christmas, Easter and Pentecost with enthusiasm but do not always celebrate the Ascension of Christ. The Ascension has become the forgotten festival of the modern Church! It was not like this among the first Christians. The Ascension into heaven was of the utmost importance. Just as here on earth a selected person ascends to a throne to become king or queen, so Jesus the Christ ascended to the throne to be crowned King. No longer limited to human form, the Bible declares that Jesus is King of Kings, and Lord of Lords. His kingdom has no end. To fully understand the teaching of Jesus about the Kingdom of God we must recognise Him as our everlasting King in heaven. This perception is very important. It clears away some of the fuzziness about our understanding of the nature of God's Kingdom in heaven and on earth. No King no kingdom! Every kingdom has to have a King.

In our present day many people struggle with the idea of Jesus visibly ascending into heaven. For those who say « you don't really believe that Jesus ascended into heaven like a rocket entering into space! », all I can do is point them to the biblical accounts and say that I believe the words, the testimonies, of those who were there. Just as the resurrection of Jesus from the dead was a 'one off' happening in the history of mankind so was the ascension. Luke, the historian describes the event in his gospel and again in the Acts of the Apostles. « When Jesus had lead them out to the vicinity of Bethany, he lifted up his hands and blessed them. While he was blessing them he left them and was taken up into heaven. Then they worshipped him and returned to Jerusalem with great joy. And they stayed continually at the temple, praising God » (Luke 24:50-53)

This happening is of supreme importance. This account is the ending of Luke's portrayal of the life of Jesus. Luke was the one who declared that « Since I myself have carefully investigated everything from the beginning, it seemed good also to me to write an orderly account for you, most excellent Theophilus, so that you may know the certainty of the things you have been taught » (Luke 1:3-4) Quite simply we read that he « was taken up into heaven ». He left the human arena to enter the spiritual one. He was now one with God transcendent over the world. Christ's enthronement after His ascension, expresses the finality of His victory over sin and death. Now all things on heaven and on the earth are under Christ's control. The baptised believer of every age shares in God's victory Baptism signifies being united with Christ. Those who are willing to die by saying NO to self, sin, the world system, and the devil's control over them, consider themselves to have been spiritually crucified with Christ. The believer having died with Christ shares in His resurrection. Just as God raised Jesus from the dead the believer shares in Christ's victory and receives the gift of eternal life becoming immortal. The disciples were overjoyed when Jesus finally left them. Normally we are sad when a friend we love leaves us! They accepted that He had moved beyond human existence and had embraced eternal life. The Christian is able to see life from a different perspective. Christ is King of the universe, the gift of the Holy Spirit is received, and the Church, with all its human weaknesses is nothing less than a supernatural society!

The last book of the Bible, the revelation of John is not easy to understand. John was as part of the persecuted church in prison for his faith, on the Isle of Patmos. He suffered much hardship being incarcerated with many notorious criminals. The prison on the Isle of Patmos had a notorious reputation! It was in these difficult circumstances that John received his vision. He wrote it down as instructed by the voice in his vision (Revelation 1:10-11) It has been of inestimable value to Christians in every age. It was as if a curtain had been drawn aside and John could see beyond his earthly abode into heaven and the mysteries of the life to come. Some of the language is metaphorical and in code so that people outside the persecuted Church would not understand it. One of the most important parts of the apocalypse ie revelation is the vision of God's throne and its surroundings. At this point it would be good to read carefully the whole of chapter four. John saw « before him a throne in heaven with someone sitting on it! » (Revelation 4:2) Then follows a description of the ascended Christ. The Lord Jesus is now Christ the King seated on His throne. The four living creatures are the writers of the gospels who tell the story of Jesus who came from His Father in heaven, was born on earth, crucified, risen, ascended into heaven, and enthroned as Christ the King. « The first living creature was like a lion, the second was like an ox, the third had a face like a man, the fourth was like a flying eagle. » (Revelation 4:7) Matthew's gospel is represented by a lion, because in it Jesus is depicted as the Lion of Judah, the one in whom all the expectations of the prophets came true. Mark's is represented by the man because it is the most factual report of the human life of Jesus. Luke's is represented by the ox, as it depicts Jesus as the sacrifice for all human beings regardless of race, class or sex. John's is represented by the eagle, because of all birds it flies highest and is said to be the only living creature that can look directly at the sun. John's gospel reaches the highest point of human thought.

When we begin to grasp the truth that Christ is King in heaven, we begin to understand that the Jesus rejected and crucified by his own people is in charge of the universe. Wow! He was with the Father at the creation of the world. He helped fling the stars into space and design everything on planet earth. Being one with the Father he knows all, sees all, and is concerned even if a sparrow falls to the ground! « Are not two sparrows sold for a penny? Yet not one of them will fall to the ground apart from the will of your Father; And even the very hairs of your head are all numbered. So don't be afraid you are worth more than many sparrows » (Matthew 10:29-31) This is perhaps one of the most revealing verses in the Bible. God is all knowing, all seeing, and all powerful. Jesus has returned to the Father and reigns with Him eternally. I had in my congregation a not too honest businessman who attended Church to please his mother. His life was transformed after discovering that

God was all powerful and knew all about him. It happened this way. He met a young lady who invited him to a Bible Study house group. The small group of believers were studying Psalm 139. As he read the psalm, verses jumped out from the page, as if God was talking directly to him. The following phrases in particular spoke to his heart and led him to a new understanding of the greatness of God. « O Lord you have searched me and you know me » « You perceive my thoughts from afar » « you are familiar with all my ways » « Where can I flee from your presence » He realised that there was no escape from the presence of God. God was both omnipresent and omnipotent, the sovereign King of the universe who had created all things. Reading on through the psalm he came to realise that his days on earth were numbered and were determined by that same king! « All the days ordained for me were written in your book before one of them came to be » Wow! « How precious to me are your thoughts O God! How vast is the sum of them. Were I to count them they would outnumber the grains of sand. » My friend's understanding of the greatness of God and the Kingship of Jesus led him to ask Christ to come into his life. He soon became a changed man! When we take on board that « God is King of all the earth » (Psalm 47:7) and such a King demands obedience from his subjects we want to please and obey him.

Jesus came to announce the coming of His Kingdom. « Jesus went throughout Galilee, teaching in their synagogues, preaching the good news of the Kingdom, and healing every disease and sickness among the people » (Matthew 4:23). The Kingdom of God was right at the centre of the message that Jesus proclaimed. It was of the first importance that all people should enter His Kingdom He told his followers not to worry about food and clothing on this earth «For your Father knows that you have need of them but seek first his Kingdom and his righteousness, and all these things will be given to you as well. Therefore do not worry about tomorrow. For tomorrow will worry about itself. Each day has enough trouble of its own. » (Matthew 6:33-34). His followers were to be Kingdom seekers. What did Jesus mean? The Jewish people were familiar with the concept that God was their King and they were his chosen people. The God revealed in the law and the prophets was a heavenly King, and they were His subjects. Throughout their history they had acknowledged this but on many occasions they had disobeyed God their King and replaced him with pagan idols! In the book of Daniel in the Old Testament we read that « The God of heaven will set up a kingdom that will never be destroyed. (Daniel 2:44) And again we read « How great are his signs, how mighty his wonders! His Kingdom is an eternal Kingdom: his dominion endures from generation to generation. » (Daniel 4:3) and again « then the sovereignty, power and greatness of the kingdoms under the whole heaven » (earthly kingdoms) « will be handed over to the saints, the people of the Most High. His kingdom will be an everlasting kingdom and all rulers will worship and obey him.» (Daniel 7:27). Jewish people were looking out for the coming of that King, the Messiah, the anointed one who would establish his kingdom on earth.

When John the Baptist came on the scene many flocked to the desert to hear his message about the Kingdom of God. They were expecting a King to come, John announced to all that he was not that King but had come to prepare the way for his coming. « In those days John the Baptist came, preaching in the Desert of Judea and saying 'Repent, for the Kingdom of Heaven is near' This is he who was spoken of through the prophet Isaiah:
'A voice of one calling in the desert, Prepare the way for the Lord, make straight paths for him' » (Matthew 3:1-3) John announced that Jesus was coming to bring into being the Kingdom the people were waiting for. The big question was what would this kingdom be like and would Israel be liberated so that they were no longer governed by the Romans. There was a party called the Zealots who were willing to fight the Romans to bring about the establishment of this kingdom. All they needed was the right leader and they would follow him. During the early life time of Jesus there had been several rebellions ruthlessly put down by the Romans. The nature of the Kingdom of God that Jesus announced and began to bring into being was very different from their expectations. Jesus taught about the Kingdom in many of his parables and the miracles he

performed were signs that the Kingdom of God had come. In his trial before Pontius Pilate the governor asked him « 'Are you the King of the Jews?' 'Yes, it is as you say', Jesus replied » (Matthew 27:11) In John's gospel Jesus before Pilate declares « My kingdom is not of this world. If it were, my servants would fight to prevent my arrest by the Jews. But now my Kingdom is from another place. » (John 18:36) There is a sense that the Kingdom begins to come into being in this world through the ministry of Jesus. One might describe the kingdom being present as the interface between heaven and earth. The kingdom is seen when light penetrates darkness and eternity, breaks into the temporal and the supernatural, and impinges on the natural order of things. Where is the Kingdom of God where God reigns supreme? In heaven of course but also on earth where Christ reigns in the believer's life. The Kingdom is not just about individuals but also it is where believers live together in a community which obeys God. We are, as followers of Christ, to be light, in darkness. Satan's kingdom is one of darkness whereas Christ's is one of light. The two kingdoms are in constant opposition. Where the Gospel is preached in the power of the Holy Spirit and miraculous signs follow that preaching, God's Kingdom is present. Just as light dispels darkness, the Kingdom of God overcomes the world's sinful systems which are part of Satan's kingdom.

To understand the nature of the Kingdom that Jesus announced and brought into being by the miracles he performed we turn to chapter13 in the gospel of Matthew . Jesus speaks of a common rural scene where a man is sowing seed. Some of it is scattered on a path and the birds swoop down and consume it. Other seeds fall on ground where there is very little soil, begin to grow but as they have no proper roots the young plants are scorched by the sun and die. Seeds that fall on seemingly fertile ground, grow up but are choked by the weeds which grow with them. Some of the seeds however fall on good soil and go on to produce a crop of. - a hundred, sixty, or thirty times what was sown. (Matthew 13:1-9). Jesus explains to his disciples the meaning of the parable at their request; « Listen then to what the parable means. When anyone hears the message about the Kingdom and does not understand it, the evil one comes and snatches away what was sown in his heart. This is the seed sown along the path. What was sown on rocky places is the man who hears the word and at once receives it with joy. But since he has no root, he lasts only a short time. When trouble and persecution comes because of the word, he quickly falls away. What was sown among the thorns is the man who hears the word, but the worries of this life, and the deceitfulness of wealth choke it, making it unfruitful. But what was sown on good soil is the man who hears the word and understands it. He produces a crop yielding a hundred, sixty, or thirty times what was sown. » (Matthew 13:19-23) What does this tell us about the nature of the Kingdom. It tells us how it comes into being. The message about the Kingdom is preached, people hear it and respond in different ways. It is interesting that the word must be heard and understood for the Kingdom to come into being. The different soil stands for the different experiences people have in responding to the word. Some people do not understand and Satan takes the message away from them. Others start off well but when circumstances change and life becomes difficult because of persecution or hardship they fall away. The opposite is true for those who have plenty, their concerns about holding onto their wealth cause them to reject the message of the Kingdom. Those who accept the word, and go on to maturity in the faith produce fruit in plenty albeit in different quantities.

The second of the parables in chapter 13 is one about opposition to the Kingdom. « The kingdom of heaven is like a man who sowed good seed in his field. But while everyone was sleeping, his enemy came and sowed weeds among the wheat, and went away. When the wheat sprouted and formed heads, then the weeds also appeared. The owner's servants came to him and said 'Sir, didn't you sow good seed in your field? Where then did the weeds come from? ' 'An enemy did this' He replied. The servants asked him 'Do you want us to go and pull them up?' 'No' he answered 'because while you are pulling the weeds, you may root up the wheat with them. Let both grow together until the harvest. At that time I will tell the harvesters, first collect the weeds and tie them in bundles to be burned, then gather the wheat and bring it into my barn » (Matthew:13:24-30) The parable was spoken to a large crowd but afterwards his disciples came to him and said « Explain to us the parable of the weeds in the field. He answered 'The one who sowed the good seed is the Son of Man. The field is the world, and the good seed stands for the sons of the Kingdom. The weeds are the sons of the evil one, and the enemy who sows them is the devil. The harvest is the end of the age, and the harvesters are the angels. As the weeds are pulled up and burned in the fire, so it will be at the end of the age. The Son of Man will send out his angels, and they will weed out of his Kingdom everything that causes sin and all who do evil. They will throw them into the fiery furnace, where there will be weeping and gnashing of teeth; Then the righteous will shine like the sun in the Kingdom of their Father; he who has ears, let him hear.' » (Matthew 13:36-43). The parable shows us that there will always be opposition to the message of the Kingdom of God. Satan is always reluctant to relinquish his hold on people who wish to enter the Kingdom of light. We also realise that God's Kingdom and Satan's kingdom will exist on earth, side by side, until the coming of the King on the day of Christ's return. All who have engaged actively in preaching the gospel are aware of opposition. Jesus also teaches that there will be separation from and destruction of evil at His return with those who responded to his message receiving eternal life: abundant life in this world and everlasting life in the world to come.

The Kingdom of God will begin in a small way and grow and grow. « The Kingdom of heaven is like a mustard seed, which a man took and planted in his field; though it is the smallest of all your seeds, yet when it grows, it is the largest of garden plants and becomes a tree, so that the birds of the air come and perch in its branches » (Matthew 13:31-34) The Kingdom might not look much compared with the kingdom of Rome but it will replace it and indeed surpass it! I think that is what those who heard Jesus tell the parable would have concluded! This had begun to happen with the demise of the Roman empire, but we still wait for God's kingdom to come on earth. The next parable emphasizes not only the growth of the

Kingdom but that its influence will penetrate all levels of society. « The Kingdom of heaven is like yeast that a woman took and mixed into a large amount of flour until it worked all through the dough. » (Matthew 13:33)

The next two parables emphasize how precious the Kingdom is and how costly it is to enter it. « The Kingdom of heaven is like treasure hidden in a field. When a man found it, he hid it again, and then in his joy went and sold all he had and bought that field. » (Matthew 13:44). In ancient Israel people used to bury all their money and precious possessions in the ground so that they would not be robbed! Sometimes people forgot the exact spot where they had buried their treasure, or maybe they would die without passing on information of its whereabouts and someone else would find it. The man who found the treasure wanted the treasure so much that he sold everything he had to buy that field. To be part of God's Kingdom it is worth giving up everything to obtain it. In the next parable « A merchant is looking for fine pearls. When he found one of great value, he went away and sold everything he had and bought it. » (Matthew 13:45). Precious pearls were greatly sought after at the time when Jesus lived on earth. The pearl was a thing of beauty and was to be found in the waters of the Red Sea. It was for many the loveliest thing in all the world and people went to great lengths to obtain one for themselves. The Kingdom of God is the loveliest thing in the world. To be in the Kingdom is to accept and to do the will of God. The Christian life is the loveliest life of all. In the parable the merchant compared pearls. No other life can compare with the life of the Kingdom. There is only one way to find peace, joy and beauty in this life and that is to enter the Kingdom of God. We notice that unlike the man in the previous parable who stumbled on the hidden treasure the merchant here was actively seeking, looking for, the fine pearl. In each case the cost is the same. It costs everything to be part of God's Kingdom

The final parable of the Kingdom in Matthew 13 describes a very familiar scene from daily life, fishing. « Once again the Kingdom of heaven is like a net that was let down into the lake and caught all kinds of fish. When it was full, the fishermen pulled it up on the shore. Then they sat down and collected the good fish in baskets, but threw the bad away. This is how it will be at the end of the age. The angels will come and separate the wicked from the righteous and throw them into the fiery furnace, where there will be weeping and gnashing of teeth 'Have you understood all these things?' Jesus asked, 'Yes they replied' » (Matthew 13:47-51) The church is made up a mixture of people, young and old, good and bad, rich and poor, from different nationalities. The church is an instrument of God's Kingdom on earth. It follows that all sorts of people will be drawn into the Kingdom. We are taught not to judge others. God is the judge and he will separate the good from the bad when His Kingdom comes in all its fullness. This parable speaks of the universality of the Kingdom and of judgement and separation when King Jesus returns.

What have we discovered so far about the nature of the Kingdom? It is a universal Kingdom for all people. It comes about through the preaching of the message. People will respond to it in a variety of ways. Some will fall away due to persecution others due to plenty. The Kingdom of God will exist alongside Satan's kingdom. Separation will come at the end of time. The Kingdom will begin in a small way and keep growing. It will penetrate every part of society. It will bring about change in our world. The Kingdom of God is precious and hidden but when found it takes our all, to be part of it. Some people find the Kingdom after a long search and are prepared to sacrifice everything for it. The Kingdom of God consists of people who obey the King and seek to do what he tells them to do. Jesus came to announce and bring into being the Kingdom of God. He performed many miracles that acted like a magnet drawing people to Himself. He was full of compassion for people, the blind, the paralysed, the deaf, the dumb and lepers who were outcasts, and he healed many but the main object of his ministry was the announcement of the Kingdom. When John the Baptist sent two of his disciples to ask Jesus « Are you the one who was to come, or should we expect someone else. Jesus replied to the messengers 'Go back and report to John what you have seen and heard. The blind receive sight, the lame walk, those who have leprosy are cured, the deaf hear, the dead are raised, and the good news is preached to the poor. Blessed is the man who does not fall away on account of me.' » (Luke 7:18-23) The miracles that Jesus did showed that he was the Messiah, the King and were signs that the Kingdom of God had arrived. The future reign of God was breaking into the present age. This was a foretaste of what was to come at the end of the age.

Not only do we find mention of the Kingdom of God in the gospels, but also in the Epistles. If we look carefully at Paul's letters which reflect the life of the first Christian communities, the teaching about the Kingdom of God is clearly to be seen. Paul writing to Timothy about Christ Jesus coming to save sinners finishes with a prayer. « Now to the King eternal, immortal, invisible, the only God be honour and glory for ever and ever. Amen » (1 Timothy 1:17). Again Paul writes « God, the blessed and only Ruler, King of Kings and Lord of Lords, who alone is immortal and who lives in unapproachable light, whom no one has seen or can see. To Him be honour and might forever. Amen » (1 Timothy 6:14-16) For Paul God is King and Jesus Christ is one with Him.

In the life of the early Church we read of miracles done in the name of Jesus Christ; Peter healing a crippled beggar at the Temple gate was a notable one.(Acts 3) We read « The apostles performed many miraculous signs and wonders among the people. » (Acts 5:12). We even read that people were healed when Peter's shadow fell upon them! « People brought the sick into the streets and laid them on beds and mats so that at least Peter's shadow might fall on some of them as he passed by. » (Acts 5:15) People being healed was a sure sign that the Kingdom of God that Jesus had taught about, was present after his resurrection and ascension to the right hand of God in heaven. All these miracles were evidence that the Kingdom of God was continuing to grow. Paul writes that « the Kingdom of God is not a matter of talk but of power » (1 Corinthians 4:20).

Paul wrote about the morality associated with the Kingdom of God. « Do you not know that the wicked will not inherit the Kingdom of God? Do not be deceived : neither the sexually immoral nor idolaters nor adulterers nor male prostitutes nor homosexual offenders nor thieves nor the greedy nor drunkards nor slanderers nor swindlers will inherit the Kingdom of God. And that is what some of you were. But you were washed , you were sanctified you were justified in the name of the Lord Jesus Christ and by the Spirit of our God. » (1 Corinthians 6:9-11) Behaviour is of the greatest importance for those who belong to the Kingdom. Through the sacrifice of Jesus on the cross and the work of the Holy Spirit in our lives we are cleansed of the sins of our past lives and enter into the Kingdom of God. We read in Paul's letter to the Galatians that the Holy Spirit produces fruit in the believer's life, but we often fail to take notice that the acts of the sinful nature will exclude us from inheriting the Kingdom of God. « So I say live by the Spirit and you will not gratify the desires of the sinful nature; for the sinful nature desires what is contrary to the Spirit, and the Spirit what is contrary to the sinful nature. They are in conflict with each other, so that you do not do what you want. But if you are led by the Spirit, you are not under the law. The acts of the sinful nature are obvious: sexual immorality, impurity and debauchery; idolatry and witchcraft: hatred, discord, jealousy, fits of rage, selfish ambition, dissensions, factions and envy; drunkenness, orgies and the like. I warn you, as I did before, that those who live like this will not inherit the Kingdom of God. » (Galatians 5:16-21). Paul writes to the Ephesians in similar vein « But among you there must not be even a hint of sexual immorality, or any kind of impurity, or of greed because these are improper for God's holy people. Nor should there be obscenity, foolish talk or coarse joking, which are out of place, but rather thanksgiving. For of this you can be sure: No immoral, impure or greedy person - such a man is an idolater - has any inheritance in the Kingdom of Christ and of God. » (Ephesians 5:3-5) We neglect the moral demands of the Kingdom of God at our own risk!

Paul also talks about the Kingdom in terms of a fruitful life. He wrote to the Church at Colosse, a fellowship with which he was unfamiliar, never having visited it himself. « For this reason, since the day we heard about you, we have not stopped praying for you and asking God to fill you with the knowledge of his will through all spiritual wisdom and understanding. And we pray this in order that you may live a life worthy of the Lord and may please him in every way: bearing fruit in every good work, growing in the knowledge of God, being strengthened with all power according to his glorious might so that you may have great endurance and patience, and joyfully giving thanks to the Father, who has qualified you to share in the inheritance of the saints in the Kingdom of light. For he has rescued us from the dominion of darkness and brought us into the Kingdom of the Son he loves, in whom we have redemption, the forgiveness of sins. » (Colossians 1:9-14) His prayer reveals his understanding of Kingdom living. Those who live the Kingdom life, know God's will. They have spiritual wisdom and understanding; they live lives worthy of the Lord Himself. Such a life is fruitful, full of good works, and continually growing in the Knowledge of God. Endurance, patience, and inner strength from God, result in joyful thanksgiving. Such a life qualifies the believer to share with other believers in the Kingdom of God. Paul ends this letter with a reference to Aristarchus, Mark, and Jesus called Justus listing them « among his fellow workers for the Kingdom of God » (Colossians 4:11) To say as some have said that Paul did not proclaim the Kingdom of God is clearly unacceptable. His letters show that he lived the Kingdom life and sought to bring others into it.

There are those who manage to muddle up the Kingdom of God with the Church. One cynic has said « Jesus preached the Kingdom but ended up with a Church » This person was very aware of the weakness of the modern Church! I think it is better to think of the Kingdom of God as being the agent of the Church. Where is the Kingdom of God to be found today? The simple answer is where the King is honoured and obeyed. Many pray daily as Jesus taught his disciples to do. « Your Kingdom come, your will be done on earth as it is in heaven. » (Matthew 6:10) Jesus is saying that The Kingdom is present when God's will is being done here on earth! The Kingdom comes into being when the gospel is preached in the power of the Spirit, people respond and are born again spiritually and enter the Kingdom. Today we see many signs of the presence of the Kingdom. The Kingdom is present when people are being saved, healed, delivered and set free. Miracles happen when the power of the world to come, breaks into our daily life on earth. When we are at the interface between heaven and earth!

We can say that yes the Kingdom is present but will not come in all its fullness until Jesus returns in glory. When we pray « Your Kingdom come », we are not only praying that we might experience more of its presence on earth but we are equally praying for the return of our Lord Jesus Christ! We look forward to his coming with the angelic host. At that time every eye will see him and every knee will bow. Those who belong to him will rejoice and receive their reward and hear « Well done thou good and faithful servant! » He will come in Glory as King of Kings to judge both the living and the dead. He will establish His Kingdom and the final destiny of believers and non believers. When will this take place? No one knows except our heavenly Father. Many have tried to work out when the world will end by using human understanding but it has been a futile exercise. Some people believe that an increase in the work of the Holy Spirit in our generation is a sign of the return of Christ. No one knows the hour or the day, but all believers need to be aware of Jesus' promise to return and need to be watching and waiting for that time, living as children of the light not of darkness. Those who belonged to the first Christian Church used to greet each other with the word Maranatha « Come Lord Jesus » (Revelation 22:20-21)

PART TWO

BUILDING A HOUSE THAT WILL STAND

Chapter 9 - Receiving the Holy Spirit

It is difficult to understand the person and work of the Holy Spirit. Much confusion has arisen because believers have attempted to limit the work of the Holy Spirit to their own understanding. He has been referred to as the « Forgotten person of the Trinity » Since the beginning of the last century more and more Christians have discovered the reality of the person and work of the Holy Spirit. Many people think of the Holy Spirit as just an influence for good. He certainly is an influence for good but they forget that He is the third person of the trinity. The God we believe in is, God the Father, God the Son Jesus Christ and God the Holy Spirit. One God expressed as three persons. Many theologians have tried to understand the Godhead and how the persons relate to one another. The new Christian would be wise not to get caught up in speculation but accept that our God is beyond all human understanding. The most clear understanding of God the Father, Son and Holy Spirit is revealed in the life, death, and resurrection of Jesus. In Him we get an understandable glimpse of what God is like. God reveals himself to those He wills. The Holy Spirit works in ways far beyond the limits of human reasoning. Jesus compares the Holy Spirit with the wind. «The wind blows wherever it pleases .You hear its sound, but you cannot tell where it comes from or where it is going.» (John 3:8) We experience the results of the wind whether it be as a gentle breeze or a mighty tornado! Similarly we experience the Holy Spirit at work in our lives as a gentle prompting or so powerfully we are knocked over! If we are to be fully equipped to serve the Lord we must be full of the Holy Spirit. I remind you that after I had made a sincere commitment to the Lord Jesus, and asked him to come into my life, I still lacked the **fullness** of the Spirit. As I said in part 1. all born again believers receive the Holy Spirit at the time of their incorporation into Christ through faith, they have the Spirit dwelling in them but are not necessarily filled with the Spirit or baptized in the Spirit.

A simple way to understand the difference between the Spirit dwelling in us and the baptism of the Spirit is to think of this illustration. Pick up an empty bottle and fill it with water. The water level rises as the bottle is filled. It can be nearly empty or full and overflowing! We can allow the Holy Spirit to fill us, so that we are only partially filled or full and overflowing. Now if we take that bottle full of water and plunge it in a lake, not only is the water in the bottle but the bottle is in the lake! When a person is baptised in the Holy Spirit he/she is immersed in the Holy Spirit. Not only is the Holy Spirit indwelling them, but the Holy Spirit has them, surrounds and holds onto them! This happens when we hand over all of our life to the Lord. It is as if we unconditionally surrender absolutely to Jesus Christ, so that he can use us in whatever way he wants to. If we are to learn more about the Holy Spirit we must turn to the Bible.

The Holy Spirit in the Old Testament
We read of the activity of the Holy Spirit in the Old Testament. In the beginning the « Spirit of God was hovering over the waters » (Genesis 1:2) God the Holy Spirit was present when the universe was created! He was with God's chosen race Israel, leading, guiding and protecting. The Spirit inspired Kings, rulers and prophets. The holy Spirit came on them but was not a permanent abiding presence. He inspired certain people to be prophets but came and went as they spoke the word of God. After Moses had led the Israelites out of Egypt, God gave him instructions about the Tabernacle, the Tent of meeting and the specific way He wanted it to be made. We read that God told Moses « see I have chosen Bezalel son of Uri, the son of Hur of the tribe of Judah and I have filled him with the Spirit of God, with skill, ability and knowledge in all kinds of crafts » (Exodus31:1-3). When Samuel anointed Saul as King he told him he would meet some prophets. He said « The Spirit of the Lord will come upon you in power and you will prophesy with them and you will be changed into a different person. (1 Samuel 10:6-7) Ezekiel was sent by God in the power of

the Spirit with a message for the house of Israel. « The Spirit then lifted me up and took me away and I went in bitterness and in anger of my spirit with the strong hand of the Lord upon me; I came to the exiles who lived at Tel Aviv near the Kebar river. » (Ezekiel 3:14-15). Warriors came to see David when he was an outcast. He asked them if they were for him or against him. « Then the Spirit came upon Amasai, chief of the thirty, and he said 'We are yours O David. We are with you Son of Jesse. Success, success to you and success to those who help you, for your God will help you!' So David received them and made them leaders of his raiding bands. » (1 Chronicles 12:18). On many occasions we read of the work of the Spirit in the Old Testament but we notice that it is only a temporary filling and sometimes in order to achieve specific God given tasks but the prophet Joel revealed that this was about to change (Joel 2:28-32). This prophecy was fulfilled when we turn to the New Testament and read about the coming of the Holy Spirit on the day of Pentecost in Jerusalem.

The Holy Spirit in the ministry of John the Baptist who prepared the way for Jesus
« So John came, baptizing in the desert region and preaching a baptism of repentance for the forgiveness of sins. The whole Judean countryside and all the people of Jerusalem went out to him. Confessing their sins, they were baptized by him in the Jordan river. John wore clothing made of camel's hair, with a leather belt around his waist, and he ate locusts and wild honey. And this was his message: 'After me will come one more powerful than I, the thongs of whose sandals I am not worthy to stoop down and untie. I baptise you with water, but he will baptise you with the Holy Spirit' » (Mark 1:4-8) In Matthew's gospel the word 'fire' is added. « He will baptise you with the Holy Spirit and with fire. » (Matthew 3:11) This fire was evident on the day of Pentecost when the Holy Spirit was poured out upon the 120 disciples. Jesus was baptised by John in the river Jordan and « as Jesus was coming up out of the water, he (John) saw heaven being torn open and the Spirit descending on him like a dove. And a voice came from heaven : You are my Son, whom I love; with you I am well pleased »

(Mark1:10-11) John was present when Jesus received confirmation that his ministry was to commence and that he was possessed by the Holy Spirit. Peter refers directly to the baptism of Jesus in his sermon at the house of Cornelius « This is the message God sent to the people of Israel, telling the good news of peace through Jesus Christ, who is Lord of all. You know what happened throughout Judea, beginning in Galilee after the baptism that John preached - how God anointed Jesus of Nazareth with the Holy Spirit and power, and how he went around doing good and healing all who were under the power of the devil, because God was with him. We are witnesses of everything he did in the country of the Jews and in Jerusalem. » (Acts 10:36-39) Here we see the change from temporary and partial Spirit possession in the Old Testament to the abiding presence in the life of Jesus. No longer is the Holy Spirit an impersonal force but rather a state of intimate personal union with God the Father. This union resulted in the continuing and enduring endowment of authority and power in the life of Jesus, the Spirit descends like a dove on Jesus. The disciples probably remembered Noah's dove in the Old Testament story of the flood. This covenant, or binding agreement, was the first one made between God and man. (Genesis 9:8-17) The Spirit descending upon Jesus in the form of a dove points to the new covenant that was to come into being.

The Holy Spirit and the birth and ministry of Jesus
The Holy Spirit was present from the moment of conception in Mary's womb. The angel Gabriel was sent to the town of Nazareth « to a virgin pledged to be married to a man named Joseph, a descendant of David. The virgin's name was Mary. The angel went to her and said 'Greetings you who are highly favoured! The Lord is with you.' Mary was greatly troubled at his words and wondered what kind of greeting this might be. But the angel said to her, 'Do not be afraid, Mary, you have found favour with God. You will be with child and give birth to a son, and you are to give him the name Jesus. He will be great and will be called the Son of the Most High. The Lord God will give him the throne of his father David, and he will reign over the house of Jacob forever; his kingdom will never

end' 'How will this be' Mary asked the angel 'since I am a virgin ?' The angel answered 'The Holy Spirit will come upon you, and the power of the Most High will overshadow you. So the holy one to be born will be called the Son of God.' » (Luke 1:26-35). The same Holy Spirit that was present at the creation of the universe came upon Mary. The all powerful presence of God overshadowed her so that the Holy one born to her was the Son of God.

The Holy Spirit was at the centre of the earthly ministry of Jesus making the Kingdom of God a present reality. The miracles that Jesus performed with power and authority were done through the agency of the Holy Spirit. The chief sign of this is the defeat and destruction of the demonic powers of evil. This is clearly demonstrated when Jesus delivered a blind and deaf man possessed by demons. Some of the onlookers were saying that he cast out demons by Beelzebub the prince of demons. Jesus pointed out that evil cannot overcome evil. « Every Kingdom divided against itself will be ruined, and every city or household divided against itself will not stand. If Satan drives out Satan, he is divided against himself. How then can his kingdom stand? And if I drive out demons by Beelzebub, by whom do your people drive them out? So then they will be your judges. But if I by the Spirit of God cast out demons, then the Kingdom of God has come upon you. » (Matthew 12:25-28) also a similar passage in (Luke 11:15-20). The Holy Spirit in the ministry of Jesus enabled him to defeat and destroy all the works of the evil one.

Jesus understood that His ministry was a result of the Spirit of The Lord being upon him. When the scroll was handed to him to read on the Sabbath day in his home town of Nazareth he chose to read the words written by the prophet Isaiah.« The Spirit of the Lord is on me, because he has anointed me to preach good news to the poor. He has sent me to proclaim freedom for the prisoners and recovery of sight for the blind, to release the oppressed, to proclaim the year of the Lord's favour. »(Luke 4:18-19) (Isaiah 61:1-2) The Holy Spirit was the energizing principle of the mighty works of Jesus. His ministry fulfilled the Old Testament prophecies.

The Holy Spirit and the believers in the first Christian communities, the early Church

After his death Jesus appeared to his disciples and promised them that they would be empowered by the Holy Spirit. « Then he (the risen Jesus) opened their minds so they could understand the Scriptures. He told them 'This is what is written: The Christ will suffer and rise from the dead on the third day, and repentance and forgiveness of sins will be preached in his name to all nations, beginning at Jerusalem. You are witnesses of these things. I am going to send you what my Father has promised: but stay in the city until you have been clothed with power from on high.' » (Luke 24:45 -49)

During forty days the risen Jesus appeared to his disciples, «On one occasion, while he was eating with them, he gave them this command: 'Do not leave Jerusalem, but wait for the gift my Father promised, which you have heard me speak about. For John baptised with water, but in a few days you will be baptised with the Holy Spirit.' » (Acts1:4-5) This promise of power was fulfilled in Jerusalem on the day of Pentecost. After the risen Lord Jesus had left his disciples and ascended into heaven, the Holy Spirit continued to be the link between Jesus the heavenly King and his disciples on earth. From the day of Pentecost onwards the disciples of Jesus were empowered by the Holy Spirit to witness that Jesus was the Son of God. His kingdom advanced as they preached the word and performed miracles, mighty works of power. They were commanded to take the good news that Jesus proclaimed to the ends of the earth. The holy Spirit is the dynamic principle of missionary enterprise. The Church was born and its members were possessed by the Spirit. We have a picture of the nature and activities of that Spirit possessed community in the second chapter of the Acts of the Apostles. (Acts 2:42-47) In chapter 12 « Belonging to the Church » this passage is considered in detail.

We can discover more about the work of the Holy Spirit as we look at some of His characteristics, titles and symbols in the Bible.

TITLES

1) Spirit of truth

Jesus talks about the Spirit of truth making it plain that spiritual truth is not the same as the truth spoken of in the world and that the Spirit of truth cannot be received by the world « The world cannot accept him because it neither sees him nor knows him. But you know him for he lives with you and will be in you. » (John: 14:16) Paul writes « We have not received the spirit of the world but the Spirit who is from God, that we may understand what God has freely given us. This is what we speak, not in words taught by human wisdom but in words taught by the Spirit, expressing spiritual truths in spiritual words. The man without the Spirit does not accept the things that come from the Spirit of God, for they are foolishness to him, and he cannot understand them, because they are spiritually discerned. » (1 Corinthians 2:14) In other words the natural man cannot accept things of the Spirit. The man of the world has knowledge in many areas but does not have knowledge of spiritual truth. Jesus himself said « I am the way, the truth and the life no one comes to the Father except through me » (John 14:6) Jesus is the truth, and He reveals the truth to those who believe in Him.

2) Spirit of Holiness

We must remember that the Spirit of God is Holy as God Himself is Holy. Paul writes to the Romans explaining that it is by this Spirit of Holiness that Christ Jesus was declared to be the Son of God in power. He writes « As to his human nature he was a descendant of David, and through the Spirit of holiness was declared with power to be the Son of God by his resurrection from the dead: Jesus Christ our Lord.» (Romans 1:3-4) In the Old Testament over and over again God reminds the children of Israel that He is a Holy God That His name is Holy. (Leviticus 22) « Tell Aaron and his sons to treat with respect the sacred offerings ------- so that they will not profane my holy name » God also tells them « I am the Lord who brought you up out of Egypt to be your God; therefore be holy because I am holy » (Leviticus 11:45) The word holiness essentially means separation, otherness, and moral perfection. It is an attribute of God and not of humankind. It was this Spirit in Christ Jesus that enabled him to live a perfect life on earth so demonstrating his divine nature. No one could prove that Jesus was guilty of sin (John 8:46) and in the book of Hebrews this is confirmed it states, « For we do not have a high priest who is unable to sympathise with our weakness, but we have one who has been tempted in every way, just as we are - yet was without sin. » (Hebrews 4:15) It is this Spirit that sanctifies us and helps us to consecrate our lives to the Lord. Peter in his first letter writes about the « sanctifying Spirit » that helps us to be obedient to our Lord. (1 Peter 1:2)

3) Spirit of Life
The Christian is forgiven for his sins and God keeps no score of wrongs! We are no longer under condemnation but have been set free by the Spirit of life. « Therefore there is now no condemnation for those who are in Christ Jesus the law of the Spirit of life set me free from the law of sin and death. » (Romans 8:1-2) The Holy Spirit is the Spirit who gives us life so that we are no longer in bondage to sin and death. Jesus reaffirms to his grumbling disciples « The Spirit gives life the flesh counts for nothing. » (John 6:63)
This life that the Spirit gives is one of overflowing abundance. It has been designated 'Life with a capital L'

4) Spirit of Adoption
It is always difficult for a parent to tell their unsuspecting child that he/she is adopted. A wise parent I know said to his troubled son Timothy, 'We chose you' 'You are special and we love you' Every Christian is a child of God by adoption. « for you did not receive a spirit that makes you a slave again to fear, but you received the Spirit of adoption. And by him we cry, 'Abba, Father.' The Spirit himself testifies with our spirit that we are God's children. » (Romans 815) The presence of the Holy Spirit in our lives is proof that we are God's children. « Because you are sons, God sent the Spirit of His son into our hearts, the Spirit who calls out 'Abba, Father' so you are no longer a slave but a son; and since you are a

son, God has made you also an heir. » (Galatians 4:6); The word Abba means daddy, papa a very intimate form of address indicating that the believer has a deep personal relationship with God established by the Holy Spirit.

5) Spirit of grace
The Holy Spirit, « the Spirit of grace » (Hebrews 10:29) makes available to us all that the Son of God has done to bring about our salvation and new life. Our salvation does not depend on our own efforts but on the Spirit. It is wholly a matter of grace.

6) Spirit of Glory
The Spirit of glory is the Spirit of God and rests particularly on those who suffer for Christ's sake. Peter writes in his letter about suffering for being a Christian. (Christians are persecuted today just as they were when Peter was writing.) « Dear friends, do not be surprised at the painful trial you are suffering, as though something strange were happening to you. But rejoice that you participate in the sufferings of Christ, so that you may be overjoyed when his glory is revealed. If you are insulted because of the name of Christ, you are blessed, for the Spirit of Glory and of God rests upon you. » (1 Peter 4:12-14) The glory yet to come already rests on those who belong to Christ. The glory of the Lord filled the tabernacle and the temple in Old Testament times. (Exodus 40:35 and 2 Chronicles 7:1) The Christian is a temple of the Holy Spirit and to be filled with the Spirit is to be filled with the glory of God

7) The Eternal Spirit
The author of the book of Hebrews writes about the blood of Christ shed for our redemption «How much more, then, will the blood of Christ, who through the eternal Spirit offered himself unblemished to God, cleanse our consciences from acts that lead to death so that we may serve the living God. » (Hebrews 9:14) The Holy Spirit is without beginning or end. The Spirit is active throughout eternity. When our human spirit is subject to the Holy Spirit it is our guarantee of the life to come. We experience a foretaste of heaven.

SYMBOLS USED TO REPRESENT THE HOLY SPIRIT

The bible uses different symbols or metaphors to illustrate the work of the Holy Spirit. The most common ones, are wind, fire, oil, water, and a dove.

1) Wind

We are already familiar with wind as being a way of describing the Holy Spirit. What can the wind teach us about the work of the Holy Spirit? We noted that we cannot see the wind but only the results it produces. The wind is invisible as is the Holy Spirit. The wind can be gentle or powerful, so also the Holy Spirit. I once witnessed an African Christian demonstrating the action of the Holy Spirit as he used a sheet of paper to make a pencil roll across the floor. He produced a draught which caused the pencil to move. The Holy Spirit can energise and move us to serve the Lord! On the day of Pentecost the disciples experienced the presence of the Holy Spirit as a wind blowing. « When the day of Pentecost came they were all together in one place. Suddenly a sound like the blowing of a violent wind came from heaven and filled the whole house where they were sitting » (Acts 2 :2)

In the Old Testament the Holy Spirit is depicted as the breath of God in the account of the valley of dry bones (Ezekiel 37:5) « This is what the Sovereign Lord says to these bones: 'I will make breath enter you and you will come to life.'» We also note that after his resurrection Jesus breathed on his disciples so that they would receive the Holy Spirit. « And with that he breathed on them and said 'receive the Holy Spirit' » (John 20:22) Wind or breath is a vivid figure of speech that depicts the Spirit of God, the Holy Spirit, as a moving force, a divine energy.

2) Fire

We recall the statement that John the Baptist made about Jesus the one who was to come. « He will baptise you with the Holy Spirit and with fire » (Matthew 3:11) (Luke 3:17) When a forest catches fire it burns up all before it, and cleanses the land. The Holy Spirit works in our lives to cleanse them. Fire figuratively stands for the

consuming of evil. « His winnowing fork is in His hand, and He will clear His threshing floor, gathering the wheat into His barn and burning up the chaff with unquenchable fire » (Matthew 3:12 Luke 3:16). On the day of Pentecost in Jerusalem the disciples experienced what «seemed to be tongues of fire that separated and came to rest on each of them. » (Acts 2:3) The Holy Spirit as fire in the mouth and on the tongue, overcoming evil, made salvation possible as the gospel was proclaimed. In the Old Testament at the time when Isaiah was commissioned to be a prophet he met with God in the Temple. We read « One of the seraphs flew to me with a live coal in his hand, which he had taken with tongs from the altar. With it he touched my mouth and said 'See this has touched your lips; your guilt has been taken away and your sin atoned for' »
(Isaiah 6:1-8) The burning coal cleansed the mouth of Isaiah enabling him to declare the word of the Lord.

3) Oil

David, as was the custom was anointed with oil, as a sign that God had chosen him to be King of Israel. The shepherd boy David was sent for by the prophet Samuel. We read « Samuel said 'Send for him for we will not sit down until he arrives' So he sent and had him brought in. He was ruddy, with a fine appearance and handsome features. Then the Lord said 'Rise and anoint him: he is the one' So Samuel took the horn of oil and anointed him in the presence of his brothers, and from that day on the Spirit of the Lord came upon David in power. » (1 Samuel 16: 12-13). We see here a direct link between anointing with oil and the Spirit of the Lord coming upon David. In the case of King David he was consecrated to the Kingship by the Holy Spirit. The Holy Spirit, the oil of God can be viewed as a « Heavenly Anointing ». John writes to Christians warning them about the coming of the antichrist and about false Christians « But you have an anointing from the Holy One, and all of you know the truth. » (1 John 2:20) Anointing with oil symbolises the anointing of the Holy Spirit. Jesus claimed that he had come to fulfil the prophecy of Isaiah when he read the scroll in the synagogue at his hometown of Nazareth «The Spirit of the Lord is on me because he has anointed me to preach good news to the poor.» (Luke 4:18) Jesus believed that he had been consecrated to the ministry to which he was called. The oil representing the Holy Spirit, is often used to anoint the sick to receive healing « If any one of you is sick ? He should call the elders of the Church to pray over him and anoint him with oil in the name of the Lord. And the prayer offered in faith will make the sick person well; the Lord will raise him up. » (James 5:14-15). One of the gifts of the Holy Spirit is healing, and a little oil on a person's forehead acts as a visual aid- the oil does not heal - healing is the work of the Holy Spirit.

4) Water

Jesus went to Jerusalem for the feast of Tabernacles. At that time all Jews living within twenty miles of Jerusalem were obliged to attend. The feast commemorated God's provision for his people in the wilderness after their escape from Egypt. In celebration of God's providential care for his people during the forty years in the desert the Jews left their homes and slept in booths made of palm branches. The feast commenced around the 15th of October and lasted for seven days. On the last day of the feast the priest went to the pool of Siloam and filled a golden flask with a litre of water. He then carried the flask through the Watergate and into the city. On arrival at the Temple the water was poured out on the altar. It was at this moment that Jesus called out in a loud voice. « 'If a man is thirsty, let him come to me and drink. Whoever believes in me, as the Scripture has said, streams of living water will flow from within him'. By this he meant the Spirit, whom those who believed in him were later to receive; Up to that time the Spirit had not been given, since Jesus had not yet been glorified. » (John 7:37-39) The ceremony gave thanks and glorified God for the water that had quenched their physical thirst. Jesus is saying 'Come to me if you want water which will quench the thirst of your souls!' spiritual thirst. As we read in John chapter 4 the same analogy was used for 'soul thirst' with the woman at the well. Water overflowing and outpouring is a vivid representation of the Holy Spirit. All that lives is dependent on water. Just as water is the bringer of life so is the Holy Spirit. We read in the book of Revelation about « The river of the water of Life » (Revelation 22:1-2) The activity of the Spirit of the living God brings new life.

5) Dove

We have already read about the baptism of Jesus and the descent of the Holy Spirit in the form of a dove. The dove represents gentleness and innocence. The action of the Holy Spirit is not always manifested by mighty powerful happenings. The Holy Spirit can move in a person's life in a gentle way. Sometimes in a Christian gathering a profound silence can denote the presence of the Holy Spirit. In the Old Testament a dove was often offered as a sacrifice to atone for sin. Jesus full of the Holy Spirit sacrificed his life for the sin of the world.

6) Seal

When I was a child I used to be fascinated when my mother used sealing wax! Often parcels containing something precious were made secure with sealing wax applied to the knots in the string. There was no cello tape or parcel tape in those days! Royal and Aristocratic families had their own seal. A document might be sealed with wax and its owner's seal stamped on it. When a person becomes a Christian he\ she is sealed with the Holy Spirit. Paul writes « Having believed, you were marked in him with a seal, the promised Holy Spirit, who is a deposit guaranteeing our inheritance until the redemption of those who are God's possession - to the praise of his glory. » (Ephesians 1:13-14). We are also warned « Do not grieve the Holy Spirit of God with whom you were sealed for the day of redemption » (Ephesians 4:30) A seal is a mark of ownership and proof of identity. The Holy Spirit validates that a believer belongs to God. It is the ratification of his\her status in Christ. The Holy Spirit as a seal assures us that we are followers of Christ and is also the guarantee or pledge of something not yet received. The Holy Spirit guarantees our inheritance, eternal life, until we take possession of it. This sealing of the believer dedicates him/her for ministry in the mission of Jesus Christ.

RECEIVING THE HOLY SPIRIT

1) At the time of conversion

When we become a Christian, we asks Jesus to come and be part of our life. When we repent of our sins and put our trust in Jesus; the Holy Spirit is at work in our lives. When a person asks Jesus to come into his/her life the change that takes place is that they are spiritually united to Christ. This spiritual union is the work of the Spirit. Christ in the believer and the believer in Christ. All Christians have the Holy Spirit. Paul describes Christians as being «temples of the Holy Spirit» The believer's life is now controlled by the Spirit of the living God and not just by his own spirit. To be a Christian is to have the indwelling Holy Spirit. Paul writes plainly « Any one who does not have the Spirit of Christ does not belong to him » (literally *is not of him*) (Romans 8:9) Paul elsewhere urges the believer « examine yourself to see whether you are in the faith, test yourselves. Do you not realise that Christ Jesus is in you -, unless, of course you fail the test.

(2 Corinthians 13:5) The one essential thing that marks the true Christian is that the Holy Spirit, the Spirit of Christ dwells within.

2) Baptism of the Holy Spirit at the time of Conversion

All human beings are different and all of us become Christians in different ways. For some of us it is a gradual awakening. Gently and over a period of time we come to repent of our sins and put our trust in Jesus as our Saviour and Lord. For others it is a dramatic life shattering experience that changes there and then the whole course of their lives. We must be careful not to try and form a methodology for the work of the Holy Spirit. There are many people who receive the baptism of the Holy Spirit as a separate experience sometime after conversion. On the other hand there are people who experience the baptism of the Holy Spirit at the time when they are converted. In the case of the conversion of Saul of Tarsus hands were laid on him by the disciple Ananias and then he was filled with the Holy Spirit. « Brother Saul, the Lord - Jesus, who appeared to you on the road as you were coming here - has sent me so that you may see again and be filled with the Holy Spirit. Immediately something like scales fell from Saul's eyes and he could see again; He got up and was baptised ……. (Acts 9:17-19)

Saul who became Paul was converted and filled with the Holy Spirit as one experience. Immediately afterwards he was baptised in water. Very often people come to faith and are baptised and then receive the baptism of the Holy Spirit. It seems that being filled with the Spirit and being baptised in the Spirit are sometimes interchangeable terms.

3) Baptism of the Holy Spirit as a separate experience after conversion

Many Christians who have been converted, born again, and serving the Lord have felt that there was something lacking in their spiritual life. They have tried their best but it has not been good enough. They have become discontented with their discipleship. They have realised from reading the New Testament and meeting with Christians who seem to be on fire for the Lord, that there is much more to receive from God and so they cry out to God to meet this need. The following three steps will help us to receive the baptism of the Holy Spirit.

a) Ask

We have to ask and keep on asking until we receive. Jesus teaches his disciples to persevere when they are praying. He continues by saying to them « Ask and it will be given you; seek and you will find; knock and the door will be opened to you. For everyone who asks receives; he who seeks finds; and to him who knocks the door will be opened » (Luke 11:9-10) These words directly relate to receiving the Holy Spirit. One of the greatest hindrances to receiving the Holy Spirit is fear. Jesus reassures his disciples that the Holy Spirit is a good gift given by a loving Father. « Which of you fathers if your son asks for a fish, will give him a snake instead? Or if he asks for an egg, will give him a scorpion? If you then though you are evil, know how to give good gifts to your children, how much more will your Father in heaven give the Holy Spirit to those who ask him! » (Luke 11:11-13) This passage makes it clear that it is necessary to ask to receive the Holy Spirit. We are to seek more of God's presence in our lives. We are to knock at heaven's door and it will open and we will receive, and His blessing will be poured out upon us.

b) Yield

To be immersed in the Holy Spirit we have to desire it more than anything else. We must want what God has for us and make Him the most important person in our lives. We have to come to a point of absolute surrender to the will of God. Think about this saying.

Christ on the throne - Self on the cross
Self on the throne - Christ on the cross

We have to allow Christ Jesus to be in charge of our lives. We have to be prepared to let go of control, and allow Him to be in control. This can be a painful process. It will require an attitude that is humble and a willingness to forsake anything that would hinder Christ's activity in our lives for we are called to follow Him with our whole hearts.

c) Receive

Receive and believe go hand in hand. When we believe we receive. It is no good asking God to immerse you in the Holy Spirit if you don't believe that He hears you and that He will answer your prayer! When I received the baptism in the Holy Spirit I had to take a step of faith and keep my eyes on Jesus! The minister who spoke with me used the example of Peter who at our Lord's command got out of the boat on the sea of Galilee and walked towards Him on the water. (see chapter 6) The sea was rough and the boat was buffeted by the waves. « During the fourth watch of the night Jesus went out to them walking on the lake. When the disciples saw Him walking on the lake, they were terrified 'It's a ghost' they said, and cried out in fear. But Jesus immediately said to them: 'Take courage it is I. Don't be afraid.' Lord, if it is you,' Peter replied, 'tell me to come to you on the water' 'Come' he said. Then Peter got down out of the boat and walked on the water to Jesus. But when he saw the wind, he was afraid and beginning to sink cried out 'Lord save me!'

Immediately Jesus reached out his hand and caught him. 'You of little faith' he said 'Why did you doubt?' »(Matthew 14:25-28) To receive the Holy Spirit our faith must overcome our doubts. Our eyes must be fixed on Jesus and not on the problems that we might have. We receive by faith and not by feeling. All of us will have a different experience when the Holy Spirit comes upon us but we will know for certain when He has.

Signs that the Holy Spirit has come on a person
In the Acts of the Apostles, when people received the **Baptism in the Holy Spirit they often spoke in tongues**. This can be seen as positive evidence that the believer had been immersed in the Holy Spirit. We read that in the house of Cornelius. « Whilst Peter was still speaking these words, the Holy Spirit came on all who heard the message. The circumcised believers (Jewish Christians) who had come with Jesus were astonished that the gift of the Holy Spirit had been poured out even on the Gentiles. For they heard them speaking in tongues and praising God. (Acts 10:44-46) This incident is often referred to as the Gentile Pentecost for it was the first time that the Holy Spirit had been poured out on people who were not Jews i.e. Gentiles.

Sometime later Paul visited Ephesus and found some disciples there. He asked them « Did you receive the Holy Spirit when you believed? » They answered « No we have not even heard that there is a Holy Spirit ». So Paul asked «Then what baptism did you receive? » « John's baptism » they replied. Paul said « John's baptism was a baptism of repentance. He told the people to believe in the one who was coming after him, that is, in Jesus » On hearing this they were baptised into the name of the Lord Jesus. When Paul placed his hands on them, the Holy Spirit came on them and they spoke in tongues and prophesied. There were about twelve men in all. » (Acts 19:1-7) Paul realised that these disciples at Ephesus had an incomplete faith and were not full of the Holy Spirit. Maybe this was because they were not speaking in tongues! Speaking in tongues seems to have been a confirmation that a believer was full of the Holy Spirit.

The gifts of the Holy Spirit and speaking in an unknown tongue provides the evidence that a person has received the baptism in the Holy Spirit. Although speaking in tongues is evidence that a person has received the Holy Spirit it does not necessarily follow that if a person does not speak in tongues that he/she has not received the baptism in the Holy Spirit. Paul writes « Not all speak in tongues » (1 Corinthians 12:10) Take time to read Acts for yourselves noting every mention of the Holy Spirit. It will become very clear that the Christians in those first Churches were dependant on the Holy Spirit for their witness and service. They followed His leading and guidance.

When Christians talk about the work of the Holy Spirit in a believer's life it often leads to disagreements. Different terms are used to describe the same or similar experience of His work. The New Testament uses the terms, baptism in the Holy Spirit and being filled with the Holy Spirit. People throughout the ages claim that they have been led by the Spirit, waited for the Spirit, and been strengthened by the Spirit. Hearts have been warmed by the Spirit, lives set on fire, released or set free by the Spirit, filled with love and power. However we experience the presence of God, the Holy Spirit, in our lives we must be prepared to be emptied of self so as to be filled with God. Smith Wigglesworth an early pioneer of the modern Pentecostal movement patterned his life on the principle:

All of self, none of God
Less of self, more of God
None of self, all of God

The purpose of the Baptism in the Holy Spirit
The purpose of the baptism in the Holy Spirit is to enable Jesus to be of Lord of our lives. When he is Lord we will always be ready to be used by Him. When we allow Jesus to take control we can begin to walk in the Spirit. I received the Baptism in the Holy Spirit when I came to the end of myself, buried my pride and my intellectual doubts, and went to visit a fellow Pastor. I said to him « I want to receive the Baptism in Holy Spirit, and I want to receive it right now! ».I discovered four immediate effects on my life as a

result of this experience. I had a new assurance, a greater sense of the nearness of God, a new power to witness and a new vision of the Kingdom of God.

1) Assurance

Before I received the Baptism in the Holy Spirit I admired believers who were so certain of what they believed, they never seemed to doubt. I visited a fifty five year old man in hospital whom I knew quite well and greatly admired as a Christian leader. He had suffered a serious heart attack but he talked to me of his faith and love for Jesus. He asked me to send for his daughter in South Africa to come right away. I think he was aware of his possible imminent death. He wanted me to make arrangements for his funeral and to be sure to include the song « Blessed assurance Jesus is mine O what a foretaste of Glory divine » My friend was so certain of what he believed and of the resurrection to eternal life that his testimony made a lasting impression on me. The Holy Spirit had given him assurance. Through him I became aware of the reality of the things I believed and was able to walk with a new confidence. Often **our** confidence in the Lord leads others to a deeper faith. The Holy Spirit uses us to build up others even though we may not be aware of this at the time. Like my friend I too had that assurance thanks to the Holy Spirit's baptism: so many people have been challenged and encouraged by the faith and assurance of others.

2) Nearness

The second result of receiving the Baptism in the Holy Spirit was a new sense of the nearness of God. He was now present and powerful. No longer did my prayers seem to hit the ceiling, but were answered in wonderful ways. Worship and Praising the Lord became a normal part of my everyday life. Reading the Bible was no longer something to be endured as a duty but a joy as God began to speak personally through His word. The Bible came alive as each day God impressed upon my mind new truths It was as if the Holy Spirit himself was underlining certain passages of scripture that were particularly relevant at that moment in my life. God was guiding me through his word and my walk with Him became an exciting discovery. All the time the Holy Spirit was revitalising my relationship with Him and directing my life according to His purpose and plan. The Holy Spirit made me thirsty for more of Jesus. The more I received the more I desired to receive! The Lord opened new doors for me and I met and learnt a great deal from Christians who had, had a wide experience of the things of God.

3) Witness
The third result of receiving the Baptism in the Holy Spirit was a new desire and ability to lead other people to the Lord. All through the Acts of the Apostles the disciples of Jesus shared their faith and led people to the Lord. The day after I had been ministered to by my friend and had received the Baptism in the Holy Spirit, I had a visit from « a man of the road » whom I knew. He was called Johnny Thompson. He had been sleeping rough. He had come to ask me for money to buy a train ticket to a nearby town. I had heard his hard luck stories many times before and given him money. This time however I invited him into my home, sat him in a chair, gave him something to eat and drink and began to share the Gospel with him. I shared how Jesus loved him and had died for him and how he could receive Jesus into his life. With tears streaming down his cheeks he invited Jesus to be his Saviour and Lord. He left the house rejoicing! I too was rejoicing and excited at this new experience.

4) Vision
On the day of Pentecost in Jerusalem when the Holy Spirit came in power on the disciples of Jesus, not only did they speak in other tongues, prophesy and perform miracles they also received a new vision. Peter commentated on what was happening by telling the people « These men are not drunk, as you suppose. It's only nine in the morning! No, this is what was spoken by the prophet Joel; 'In the last days, God says, I will pour out my Spirit on all people. Your sons and daughters will prophesy, your young men will see visions, your old men will dream dreams. I will pour out my Spirit in those days, and they will prophesy' » (Acts 2 :15-18)
When I received the Baptism in the Holy Spirit the Lord gave me a

new vision of the Kingdom of God. I became much more aware of the supernatural. The will of God and His Kingdom became the most important thing in my ministry. The age of the world to come began to break into my present world. Each one of us has the potential to see visions or dream dreams, through the influence of the Holy Spirit. When we pray we need to visualise the answer. If we can imagine or visualise the accomplishment of the vision or the idea that the Holy Spirit has given us, we will be able to go forward in faith, and begin to put into place the necessary steps to facilitate the plan that God has for his people.

Chapter 10 - The Fruit of the Holy Spirit

The American Evangelist Billy Graham once described the conflict within the believer between the flesh and the Spirit as being like two dogs fighting each other. This conflict is between the flesh, or our lower nature as a result of our fallen condition and the Holy Spirit who renews and regenerates us giving us a new nature. We could say that the flesh stands for what we are by natural birth and the Spirit by what we become by the new birth. This battle between the flesh and the Spirit takes place in the lives of all Christians. This is specifically a battle that all Christians have to **win.** All humanity may engage in moral conflict but it is the Christian who battles spiritually with his fallen nature. Paul writes in his letter to the Galatians « So I say live by the Spirit, and you will not gratify the desires of the, sinful nature. For the sinful nature desires what is contrary to the Spirit, and the Spirit what is contrary to the sinful nature. They are in conflict with each other, so that you do not do what you want. But if you are led by the Spirit you are not under law.» (Galatians 5:16-18) I am sure that I am not alone when I find myself wanting to do those things that I should not be doing, and not wanting to do those things I should be doing! It is not unusual for the Christian to feel that a sort of 'tug of war' is taking place between his/her will and God's perfect will. How does the Christian win this battle? By himself, in his own strength he cannot be victorious. As Paul wrote « I can will what is right but I cannot do it » (Romans 7:18)

The Holy Spirit works powerfully in the believer's life so that he/she becomes a new creation. We are born with a sinful nature but God wants to change that nature. The process of change can be painful and long. The Holy Spirit within us changes us and cultivates new fruit in our lives. Paul wrote « The acts of the sinful nature are obvious : sexual immorality, impurity and debauchery;

idolatry and witchcraft: hatred, discord, jealousy, fits of rage, selfish ambition, dissensions, factions and envy: drunkenness and orgies, and the like. » (Galatians 5 : 19-21) He contrasts the old life without Christ with the new life in the Spirit; « But the fruit of the Spirit is love, joy, peace, patience, kindness, goodness, faithfulness, gentleness and self - control. Those who belong to Jesus Christ have crucified the sinful nature with its passions and desires. » (Galatians 5:22) If we crucify our sinful nature and walk in the Spirit, the fruit of the Spirit will grow and become evident in our lives. We notice that fruit is in the singular, meaning that each of the qualities listed will grow together in a Christian's life. It is not a matter of one believer having peace and joy and another having patience and self -control but of all believers having in varying degrees all the fruit listed. Fruit takes time to grow and has to be cultivated. There are many things that can hinder the growth of fruit in the natural realm, it is the same in the spiritual realm. The person who lacks patience can only develop that quality in a trying situation! It is easy to have inner peace when there is no outside pressure! Often the fruit shows itself and grows in adverse conditions. A poster in a classroom where my wife was teaching difficult children said « It's easy to be an angel when no-one ruffles your feathers ». That is indeed true.

LET US EXAMINE THE INDIVIDUAL FRUIT AND THEIR CULTIVATION

1) Fruit of Love

Paul puts love first in his list. The word for love here is the Greek word *agape*. This is the unconditional sacrificial love that Jesus demonstrated by his death on the cross. This love is characteristic of Christianity and expresses an idea previously unknown before Jesus came. First and foremost it is love toward God. When challenged by a teacher of the law to state which of all the commandments was most important Jesus answered « The most important one is this 'Hear, O Israel, the Lord our God, the Lord is one. Love the Lord your God with all your heart and with all your soul and with all your mind and with all your strength. The second is this 'Love your neighbour as yourself;' There is no commandment greater than these » (Mark 12:30) A Christian's first love is love for God. That love will be unconditional and obedient. We will remain faithful to our God whatever the circumstances. The Holy Spirit helps us to love and serve God. The second commandment is to love your neighbour as yourself. If we are to love our neighbours we must be able to love ourselves. Many people hurt by the adversities of life do not love themselves and feel inferior, unlovely, rejected, and worthless. The Holy Spirit assures us that God loves and values us and helps us to love and value ourselves and love our neighbour. This love is not based on feelings, and it does not always follow **natural inclinations**. This love is not just towards those who might return that love but it seeks the welfare of all. It is a love that seeks the opportunity to serve and to do good to « all men, especially towards them that are of the household of the faith » (Galatians 6 :10) In the last century many admired the work of the Hungarian nun Mother Theresa. She worked tirelessly to comfort and help the elderly, sick and dying on the streets of Calcutta. Her love was Christian love, a tough love not based on sentimentality but to meet human need. We are not all called to make the sacrifices that she made but we are all called to love each other as Christ has loved us. **Love is the distinguishing mark of the disciple of Jesus.** We cultivate that love in our lives as we allow the Holy Spirit to live in us more and more.

2) Fruit of Joy

This joy is very different from human happiness. It is a joy that does not come from earthly possessions or situations, its foundation is God. The Christian is joyful because of his faith and salvation. The Christian delights and shares in the joy of others. Even in times of persecution the Christian is able to rejoice; (Matthew 5:11-12 Acts 5:41) The letters JOY have often been used as an acrostic J=Jesus, O = Others, Y= Yourself. True Joy comes when Jesus is first in your life, other people second and yourself last. In the book of Nehemiah we read that the exiles had returned from Babylon and despite great opposition they have rebuilt the walls of Jerusalem and the Holy Temple. It had been a very great work and had demanded great sacrifice and perseverance. When the work was completed Ezra the scribe read from the book of the law of Moses in the square by the Water Gate. He read it from daybreak until noon and all the people listened and some began to cry. « Nehemiah said 'go and enjoy choice food and sweet drinks and send some to those who have nothing prepared. This day is sacred to our Lord. Do not grieve for the joy of the Lord is your strength' » (Nehemiah 8:10). Even when God calls us to do difficult things we should not grumble or complain but work with joyful hearts! Jesus spread joy. He was not just a man of sorrows but also a man of joy! He gave to his disciples that same joy that he had « I have told you this so that my joy may be in you and that your joy may be complete. » (John 15:11) A glum unsmiling Christian is no help to the witness and growth of the Church of Jesus Christ, but a joyful Christian, attracts others to the faith. Real authentic joy comes from the work of the Holy Spirit in a believer's life and does not vary with circumstances.

3) Fruit of Peace

Inner unrest and lack of peace and tranquillity are characteristic of the 21st Century. The search for peace and happiness is relentless. Many years ago when my mind was in turmoil and I was trying to make sense of this life I stumbled on a book by Billy Graham entitled « Peace with God » .While I waited for a train at Uxbridge station I began to read it. I was not a believer at the time but the more I read, the truth, that only faith in God could bring inner peace began to make sense and my pilgrimage of faith began. I also realised that peace with God was the only way that human beings could build harmonious relationships. I had been a member of the secular « Peace Movements » of the fifties and sixties, CND the Committee of 100 etc. As I continued to read this book I began to understand that the only way peace could come was through the Kingdom of God. The fruit of the Spirit peace, is not a passive peace or just the absence of trouble, it is a desire that all the goodness and blessings of God might be experienced in one's own life and in the lives of others. This peace cannot be obtained by human knowledge, demonstrations or marches, because it is a gift of God. The world is unable to give us this peace because it has rejected Jesus. Peace with God means to be reconciled with God through the Cross of our Lord Jesus Christ. The « God of Peace » and the « Prince of Peace » are titles used by the writers of the New Testament to describe Jesus. When peace as a fruit of the Spirit radiates from the heart and mind of the believer, others will see this quality of Jesus. This means that we will live at peace with others and be prepared to « turn the other cheek » when we are injured or insulted. We will be ready to forgive our brothers or sisters time and time again whatever they may do to us. The person of peace leaves all revenge to the Lord. Allow the « Peace of Jesus » to guide you as you seek to do God's will in this troubled and restless world..

4) Fruit of Patience

People often use the term « He has the patience of a saint! » There is also the saying « Patience is a virtue posses it if you can, seldom found in woman, but never in a man! » The fruit of the Spirit **patience** perfects Christian character. It enables us to overcome every obstacle. Generally speaking the word is used in regard to people and relationship's rather than circumstances. The word for patience in Greek can also be translated as longsuffering. Longsuffering is that quality of self-restraint in the face of provocation. Again the teaching that Jesus gave concerning « turning the other cheek » (Matthew 5:39) is relevant. Long suffering is the opposite of anger. The fruit of the Spirit, patience or long suffering in a believer ensures that he will not become bitter:- bitterness destroys. We are told to « get rid of all bitterness, rage and anger » (Ephesians 4:31) The person who is longsuffering is not resentful against God, or circumstances, or fellow human beings. It has been said that the secret of patience is « doing something else in the meantime », that « something else » for the disciple of Jesus is to trace the hand of God in the circumstances that he faces, commit his situation and way forward to God, and trust Him in all things.

5) Fruit of Kindness

Can you think of someone you know who is always ready to help

139

by acts of kindness. The person who sees a need and does something about it. Christians who have the fruit of the Spirit, kindness, are the ones on whom you can rely. There are people in the Church who manage to hurt others by unkindness, sometimes unwittingly by the words they speak, that should not be so. The Holy Spirit should be at work in a believer's life so that he/she seeks to help no matter the cost to himself. Kindness is not exclusive to Christians. In nearly every secular community there are people who have a reputation for being kind. Not everybody is of a kindly nature, but when a new kindness becomes evident in someone's life this is a testimony to the work of the Holy Spirit, an outward sign of God at work. Evidence of this change is often more powerful that a thousand words. Kindness is also the ability to identify with other human beings whose path through life is difficult. Acts of kindness means putting the interests of others above one's own. It is the opposite of selfishness and implies a generous heart where Christ dwells. We are « saved to serve » and to follow the leading of Jesus. We need to cultivate the fruit kindness. Ask The Holy Spirit to open your eyes and enable you to change your attitude and look at people in a different way with kindness and love.

6) Fruit of Goodness

The word goodness has the sense of being morally pleasing to God. The good person is utterly without guile! The standards of the world are very different from the standards Christ taught. In the world there are cunning and crafty people, much treachery and deceit. Many motives are mixed but the believer's motivation should be transparently honest. The world seems to have grown more and more complex but for the Christian with the fruit of goodness it becomes more simple. The centre of his/her life has changed from self to Christ. In fact he/she can have the mind of Christ! That mind is good as only God is good. Goodness then can be equated with Godliness. Paul writes to the Church at Rome « Do not be overcome by evil but overcome evil with good » (Romans 12:21) The fruit of the Holy Spirit goodness enables the believer to see the best in other people, to overlook their faults and to search for their point of view, to better understand their behaviour. Goodness is a powerful weapon in combating all evil. Cultivate the fruit of goodness by allowing the Holy Spirit to draw your thinking closer to that of Jesus.

7) Fruit of Faithfulness

Paul understood faithfulness as fidelity to God and His son Jesus Christ. The word means trustworthiness, the person who is reliable. It can also mean submission to the will of God. Jesus said « Take my yoke upon you and learn from me, for I am gentle and humble in heart, and you will find rest for your souls. For my yoke is easy and my burden is light » (Matthew 11:29-30) Proud men find it difficult to submit. Many problems in today's Church stem from the inability of people to submit to the will of Christ and the leadership of those in authority. The need for this fruit in the life of the believer is paramount. When this fruit is seen in Christian lives there is unity. Who would you have alongside you in a conflict? Who is the one you can depend upon in all circumstances? It is the person who has cultivated the fruit of faithfulness. This was evident in the life of Caleb in the Old Testament. God said « Because my servant Caleb has a different spirit and follows me wholeheartedly I will bring him into the land » (Numbers 14:24) The spirit of Caleb is one of loyalty, faithfulness and wholeheartedness. The word can also have the sense of being teachable. There are Christians who are too proud to learn! They think they know it all and have all the answers. The word disciple means being a learner and a pupil of the master. The cultivation of the fruit of faithfulness is essential for all who want to follow Jesus and mature in the faith.

8) Fruit of Gentleness or Humility

This fruit can be translated by gentleness, forbearance, and kindness. The word humble or lowly is often used. Humility in Greek and Roman times implied having a servile and grovelling spirit, suggesting weakness and a cringing spirit. Today we too often associate humility with weakness. There are so many misconceptions about the real meaning of the word. It has sometimes been confused with an inferiority complex or lack of ambition but again these are false conceptions. Paul wrote «Do not think of yourself more highly that you ought, but rather think of yourself with sober judgement, in accordance with the measure of faith God has given you» (Romans 12:3) Progress for Paul was progress in humility. «Each of you» writes Paul « should look not only to your own interests, but also to the interests of others. Your attitude should be the same as that of Christ Jesus: who being in the nature of God, did not consider equality with God something to be grasped, but made Himself nothing, taking the very nature of a servant, being made in human likeness. » (Philippians 2:4-7) The humble person is gentle and forbearing thinking of others rather than himself. This fruit of the Holy Spirit is one that is marvelled at by our self seeking world and is a wonderfully helpful quality.

9) Fruit of Self-Control

The final fruit in Paul's list is self-control. The Greek word for this fruit is often translated temperance but this limits its meaning and application. Modern translations use the term self-control. This means the mastery of self. It means to have control over our desires and our love of pleasure, to have control over our attitudes, our tongues, in fact our very behaviour. The fruit of self control affects our thinking and our reactions. We desire to align our will with God's will. In other words we have offered our very selves on the altar of self sacrifice. We are no longer controlled by our selfish nature but by the Holy Spirit and the fruit self- control is evident in our lives. Paul compares the Christian to an athlete who disciplines his body so as to win the prize! (I Corinthians 9:25) In a similar way a Christian gains mastery over the his bodily desires by living a disciplined life. We reject those un Christ-like things that try to take us over. The mastery of self means mastery over our basic desires such as sexual immorality, self indulgence, and self preservation. Mastery of self produces a personality that is controlled by the Spirit as Christ takes the central place in the believer's life. Cultivate the fruit self-control so as not to fall back into the old life controlled by selfishness and sin. Remember it takes time to cultivate fruit!

CULTIVATING THE FRUIT OF THE SPIRIT

As all keen gardeners know, it is necessary that the conditions are right for the cultivation of good fruit, the soil, the sun, the rain, all affect its quality. There are two conditions that are vitally important for the cultivation of spiritual fruit.

1) We must crucify the flesh

The first Christian confession of belief in Jesus as the Christ was Peter's. Jesus was with his disciples near Caesarea Philippi when he put a question to them . « 'Who do people say I am' They replied 'Some say John the Baptist; others say Elijah; and still others one of the prophets' 'But what about you?' he asked 'Who do you say I am?' Peter answered 'You are the Christ' Jesus warned them not to tell anyone about him. » (Mark 8:27-30) Immediately after this Jesus began to teach his disciples that he would be suffer many things and be crucified. His ministry would terminate in his death and resurrection in Jerusalem. Peter was horrified. Jesus took him aside and rebuked him. « He then called the crowd to him along with his disciples and said. 'If anyone would come after me, he must deny himself and take up his cross and follow me. For whoever wants to save his life will lose it, but whoever loses his life for me and for the gospel will save it. What good is it for a man to gain the whole world, yet forfeit his soul? Or what can a man give in exchange for his soul? » (Mark 8:34-37) In Luke's version of this event the word daily is added. « If anyone would come after me, he must deny himself and take up his cross daily and follow me » (Luke 9:23) To 'take up the cross' was our Lord's vivid figure of speech for self-denial. The Christian is to totally reject his old nature and crucify it. Being crucified is to suffer agony and this will be a painful process. All Christians suffer the pain of inner conflict in their fight against the lusts of the flesh. Crucifixion is a slow lingering death but a certain one. True Christians do not succeed in destroying the flesh completely whilst on this earth but they have nailed their old selfish nature to the cross and crucifixion has begun.

When we came to Christ we repented. We said no to, that is, we 'crucified' everything we knew to be wrong in our lives. We took our old self-centred nature, with all its sinful passions and desires, and nailed it to the cross. Water baptism symbolised this as we passed through the waters. Paul reminds us that « Those who belong to Christ Jesus have crucified the sinful nature with it's passions and desires » (Galatians 5:24) If we are to cultivate the fruit of the Holy Spirit in our lives it is essential that our sinful nature be crucified. Luke says that every day we should take up the cross, repenting of sin, and dying to the self life. This biblical teaching is widely neglected and the new Christian may find it hard to grasp, but it is one of the conditions and the secret of cultivating the fruit of the Spirit in a believer's life.

2) We must be led and also walk by the Spirit

In conjunction with cultivating the fruit of the Spirit Paul speaks of being « Led by the Spirit » (Galatians 5:18) and 'Walk by the Spirit ' - « Since we live by the Spirit let us keep in step with the Spirit » (Galatians 5:25).

1. The Christian is portrayed as being led by the Spirit

We may speak of a farmer herding his cattle, a shepherd leading his sheep, of soldiers escorting a prisoner and of wind driving a ship. Jesus was led by the Spirit to be tempted in the wilderness (Luke 4:1-2); Christians are 'Sons of God' and are led by the Spirit (Romans 8:14) The Holy Spirit is our leader when he asserts his desires against those of the flesh and puts within us the desire to be holy. He puts this gentle pressure upon us as we yield to his direction and control.

And his gentle voice we hear,
Soft as the breath of even,
That checks each fault, that calms each fear,
And speaks of heaven.

For every virtue we possess,
And every victory won,
And every thought of holiness,
Are His alone.
(Harriet Auber 1773-1862)

2. Keeping in step with the Spirit

There is a clear distinction between being 'Led by Spirit' and 'Walking by the Spirit' (Keeping in step with the Spirit). The former expression is passive the latter active. Many Christians who say that they rely on the Spirit in a passive submissive way, handing over control to the Spirit often find themselves in trouble. The idea of walking or keeping in step with the Spirit means that we have to make an effort ourselves. Walking requires effort by the walker! Keeping in step with the Spirit means to walk in line. To walk in the Spirit is to deliberately walk along the path that the Spirit chooses. We are to set our minds on the things of the Spirit. « Those who live according to the sinful nature have their minds set on what that nature desires; but those who live in accordance with the Spirit have their minds set on what the Spirit desires » (Romans 8:5) Our mindset is of the greatest importance. The things we think about or allow our imagination to focus on will affect receptivity of the Spirit and the fruit manifested in our lives. Scripture tells us that « The peace of God which transcends all understanding, will guard your hearts and your minds in Christ Jesus » The passage concludes « Finally brothers, whatever is true, whatever is noble, whatever is right, whatever is pure, whatever is lovely, whatever is admirable - if anything is excellent or praiseworthy - think about such things. » (Philippians 4:7-8) Just as it is necessary to place a fireguard to protect our children from an open fire, it is necessary to protect and guard the mind. If we are keeping in step with the Spirit our minds will constantly focus on the teaching of Jesus in line with what is revealed by the Holy Spirit through reading the Bible and prayer.

The word of God interpreted by the Holy Spirit will show us what is morally right and what is not. We will be obedient to Christ as revealed in the Scriptures in every area of our lives and in our relationships with other people. Our will must be gradually aligned with God's will so that we obey at all times. We must recall each day that we have died with Christ and have risen to life with Him. We now live a new and clean life with the Holy Spirit living in us, the evil things of the old self are gone having been replaced by the lovely things of the Spirit of Jesus. When we walk or are led by the

Spirit, we allow Him to lead our lives and change us from glory into glory until we go to be with our Lord forever. Life in the Spirit on this earth has an eternal dimension and is a trailer, a sample of the inheritance for every Christian. As many Christians in this life have confessed « The best is yet to come ». We shall all meet again at the feet of Jesus and receive our reward from Him, Hallelujah! Meanwhile we live on earth to please and serve the Lord. This is only possible as we walk in the Spirit asking the Lord to **refill** us every day! (Ephesians 5:18) The word that Paul uses « Be filled with the Spirit » means keep on being filled, over and over again! We need to ask the Lord to fill us each day with more and more of the Holy Spirit. To receive more we have to surrender more of ourselves to the Lord. The Holy Spirit is a faithful friend who will never leave us unless we insult Him, grieve Him or drive Him away. (Hebrews 10:29 Ephesians 4:30 1 Thessalonians 5:19) The Holy Spirit is the helper who will guide us in our decision making and lead us as we serve the Lord. The Holy Spirit will produce fruit in our lives and equip us for service in the Church and in the world. The fruit of this marvellous infilling will grow more and more as we grow closer to Jesus.

Chapter 11 - Gifts and Ministries of the Holy Spirit

One of the most amazing statements that Jesus made to his disciples is recorded in John's gospel. It was at the last supper when He spoke about his imminent death. « Now I am going to Him who sent me, yet none of you asks me 'Where are you going?' Because I have said these things you are filled with grief. But I tell you the truth. It is for your good that I am going away » (John 16:5-7) The disciples were disappointed that he would be leaving them after their three years together. Jesus had lived with them, talked to them, and they had seen the miracles he had performed. They had walked daily with the Son of God on earth! It must have been a wonderful time and now he was saying that it was better for him to leave them. Why? Because the Holy Spirit would come upon them, and upon those who would believe in His name. The Spirit of truth was coming who would teach them all things. Jesus said « I tell you the truth, anyone who has faith in me will do what I have been doing. He will do even greater things than these, because I am going to the Father » (John 14:12) The disciple of Jesus is to continue the ministry of Jesus. The same spirit that was upon Him will be on the believer. It is no wonder that the reformer Martin Luther could write « that on the day of Pentecost there were 120 Jesus' walking the streets of Jerusalem! » We are empowered by the Holy Spirit and so enabled to carry on His ministry. The gifts and ministries of the Holy Spirit have been given to the church to continue the mission of Jesus.

When Christ left this earth to go back to His Father, he gave « Gifts » to his followers. These supernatural gifts are very different from natural abilities. They are given by the Holy Spirit to individuals within the local Church so that they can continue Christ's work. The giving and receiving of these spiritual gifts is clearly taught in the New Testament. Those churches where the « gifts » are seen to be in operation are known as Charismatic Churches from the Greek word for gifts Charismata. The Church as a community of God's people has a supernatural dimension which includes the Gifts and Ministries of the Holy Spirit. The Spirit of God gives those gifts and ministries which are needed to build the Church. God is the giver and He gives to each church as He thinks fit according to His will. Paul believed that in every local church gifts were given to members, not for personal enjoyment, but for the good of all. Paul's teaching about the nature of the Gifts and their correct use may be found in (1 Corinthians 12 -14) (Romans 12) and (Ephesians 4). We see the gifts and ministries of the Holy Spirit operating in the first Christian churches as described in the Acts of the Apostles. Sadly there are many sincere Christians who have never experienced the gifts of the Holy Spirit. Some believe that they were given to the Church at its conception and ceased to exist during the fourth century, when the Church became strong enough to continue without them. This view is unbiblical and is contrary to historical evidence. No wonder the Church went astray!

Paul writes that « To each one of us grace has been given as Christ apportioned it. « ----- It was He who gave some to be apostles, some to be prophets, some to be evangelists, and some to be pastors and teachers, to prepare God's people for works of service, so that the body of Christ may be built up until we all reach unity in the faith and in the knowledge of the Son of God and become mature, attaining to the whole measure of the fullness of Christ » (Ephesians 4 : 7-13) Soon after the risen Christ ascended into heaven the Holy Spirit was poured out upon his disciples on the day of Pentecost. The ministries were given as gifts of grace to the disciples, and spiritual gifts were given to each believer for the building up of the church. It is through these Spirit given ministries that the church advanced after the day of Pentecost. The supernatural gifts of the Holy Spirit were seen to be operating when the Church met together and enabled the gospel to spread like an unstoppable fire throughout the Roman Empire. Tongues, prophecy, miraculous healings, the raising of the dead, great faith, wisdom and discernment were all part of the normal Christian Church in those days! In our own day after the rediscovery of the Baptism of the Holy Spirit at the beginning of the last century, the gospel which is being preached in many parts of the world, is accompanied by miraculous signs. The Churches have rediscovered and are using the gifts of the Holy Spirit in accordance with the teaching of the New Testament and these churches are growing. The gospel is being taken to every corner of the globe. In many places Christians are being persecuted and suffering martyrdom. For the Church to grow in our present hostile culture it is of vital importance that every believer is equipped with God given supernatural gift or gifts.

The clearest teaching about the Gifts of the Spirit is found in Paul's first letter to the church at Corinth. It seems that the church had been richly blessed with spiritually gifted people but unfortunately this had caused deep problems within the fellowship. To their great joy they found that their faith actually worked! Things were happening. There were believers with supernatural gifts of healing, prophecy, teaching, miracle working, speaking in tongues, leadership and so on. So great was the outpouring of the Holy Spirit that His « anointing » came on many in the fellowship but instead of these wonderful experiences leading to greater service for Christ they led to division. Those who had received gifts used them to boost themselves and their own ego. This resulted in jealousy, pride and selfishness which began to split the church. Paul had to remind them strongly that the gifts are given by God - Father Son and Holy Spirit and do not originate from human beings. They are to be used for the glory of God, not for their own glory. Paul writes that the gifts are to be operating in an orderly way especially in public worship. He does not intend to stop the use of any genuine gift, but he says that speaking in tongues, prophecy, words of knowledge and other expressions of the Holy Spirit's activity should be encouraged in an orderly way so that all may benefit. (1 Corinthians 14)

We are all familiar with those who try to sell their products by offering free gifts. All you have to do is claim your gift. There is nearly always some sort of catch in the offer and we need to be on our guard. The gifts of the Holy Spirit are not free gifts because Jesus paid the price for the redemption of mankind by dying on the cross. Often free gifts that are offered are disappointing and of little use. The spiritual gifts that God gives do not disappoint. They are of infinite worth. Paul writes that we should eagerly desire the greater gifts. (1 Corinthians 12:31) We have to ask God for the appropriate gifts to enable the body of Christ of which we are part, to function properly. We have to make the effort to seek our spiritual gift/gifts. If a parcel is undelivered you have to make an effort to go and fetch it from the Post Office and then open it, in fact receive it for yourself. My daughter recently had a package returned to her as having been undelivered. She was perplexed as she knew her friend was still at this address. On further examination she discovered that, as no one had been at home the parcel was put in the local depot to await collection, and a note to this effect had been left at the house. Her friend had been so busy that she had failed to collect it so after a certain length of time it was returned to the sender. How sad when we don't have time or make time to collect what our heavenly Father has ready for us. A pile of unclaimed and unopened parcels benefits no one. God has gifts for us to claim. Through the ministry of the Holy Spirit and by seeking and asking in prayer we receive the supernatural gifts that God has for us. If we are called to minister we are gifted by God and affirmed by our brothers and sisters in the body of Christ, His Church.

THE GIFTS OF THE HOLY SPIRIT

Paul writes of nine spiritual gifts. What are they? How are they to be used?

1) The word of wisdom

This is not human wisdom but the wisdom from on high, **supernatural wisdom.** Paul earlier in his letter to the Corinthians makes it clear that Christ sent him to them « to preach the gospel, not with words of human wisdom, lest the cross of Christ be emptied of it's power » (1 Corinthians 1:17) Paul is saying here that the words he used when he preached to them were not from his human intelligence but rather given to him by the Holy Spirit. Again he says « When I came to you, brethren, I did not come proclaiming to you the testimony of God in lofty words of wisdom. For I decided to know nothing among you except Jesus Christ and Him crucified » (1 Corinthians 2 :1-2) Paul spoke words of Spiritual wisdom not human eloquence! The gift of wisdom is very important for it signifies the speaking of a word of revelation that centres on Jesus Christ. The « Word of Wisdom » is particularly needed in the preaching ministry of the Church, as this gift enables many people to hear God speak into their particular situation. What is of importance with this gift is that both wisdom and utterance come from the Holy Spirit. The « word of wisdom » is not exclusively the domain of the preacher but any believer filled with the Spirit may have a word to share. Sometimes words of wisdom just seem like common sense, but when these are spoken about a situation where the receiver has been struggling to find a solution to a problem, maybe the one who brings the word is unaware of the circumstances, they throw a new light and dimension. My wife was listening to a lady who was greatly troubled about her husband's continual dismissal of her faith in Jesus. « I play worship songs to him every morning while he is having his breakfast but he is not interested and « gets angry » she said. My wife simply suggested that perhaps he was needing her attention and concern and maybe he felt neglected. To which she replied « What a wise head on young shoulders ». The wisdom of the Lord was in evidence there as a gift from the Holy Spirit.

2) The word of knowledge
The second gift of the Holy Spirit that Paul mentions is the **word of knowledge** .He links the word of wisdom with it when he writes to the Colossian Church declaring that in Christ « are hid all the treasures of wisdom and knowledge. »(Colossians 2:3). The word of knowledge makes the things of God more understandable

to his people It maybe spoken in a ministry situation. Perhaps a person has a particular problem and is unsure what to do. A word of knowledge may supernaturally reveal information about their situation and so guide him/her to make the right decision or to take a specific course of action. Sometimes this information is given as a picture or vision. In the Old Testament « the see-er » was one who sees visions, who might see into a common situation, for example where to find lost animals! (1 Samuel 9:3-10:2) We read in (John 4:16-18) that Jesus perceived that the Samaritan woman at the well had had five husbands and was not married to the man with whom she lived! These are two examples of the seer or the prophet who truly perceives and declares hidden things. The word of knowledge is essentially an inspired word of revelation or teaching that brings God's blessing upon the Church. The words, of wisdom and of knowledge, are also closely related to the gift of prophecy. All three are supernatural manifestations of the Holy Spirit. This gift is particularly important when a person comes to you with a problem and asks for prayer. There have been many times when I have not known how to pray for a person and as I have begun to pray I have been given the right words. Quite simply the Holy Spirit has given me discernment.

3) Prophecy
One of the more important Gifts of the Spirit is the **« Gift of Prophecy ».** Paul writes « Follow the way of love and eagerly desire spiritual gifts especially the gift of prophecy » (1 Corinthians 14:1) The chief function of the New Testament prophet was to convey a divine revelation to the Church, in special circumstances and at a specific time. The gift of prophecy is to strengthen, encourage and comfort believers in the body of Christ. (1 Corinthians 14:3) We should speak out a prophetic word in proportion to the faith we have (Romans 12:6) When the Church is assembled together, worshipping the Lord, someone who has the gift of prophecy, and receives a prophetic word from the Lord, should declare it. Sometimes God speaks through pictures that are important for the body of Christ. I was present at a meeting when a person brought a prophetic picture of a « frozen waterfall » which was of special

significance to the Church at that time. Another time in prayer a spiritually mature person declared that Christ was standing at the door of this particular Church building knocking trying to enter! This word from the Lord was of particular help to the leadership of the Church who had become centred on things other than Christ. In the days which followed there was repentance and prayer and the Church began to grow. That particular prophecy was in line with the scriptures conveying the same imagery as the risen Christ's word to the Church at Laodicea (Revelation 3:20) True prophecy is harmonious with God's own word in scripture. The gift of prophecy is instrumental in declaring God's will in particular cases. In the Church at Antioch there were people with the gift of prophecy who confirmed that the Holy Spirit said « Set apart for me Barnabas and Saul for the work to which I have called them » (Acts 13:1-3) Occasionally the gift of prophecy can predict future events. We read how a group of prophets came to Antioch from Jerusalem and one of them Agabus stood up « and through the Spirit predicted that a severe famine would spread over the entire Roman world (This happened during the reign of Claudius.) (Acts 11:27-28). The prophet Agabus again foretold the future when he « took Paul's belt, tied his own hands and feet with it and said The Holy Spirit says « In this way the Jews of Jerusalem will bind the owner of this belt and will hand him over to the Gentiles » (Acts 21:10-13) This prophecy was proclaimed at the home of Philip the Evangelist at Caesarea who had four unmarried daughters who themselves prophesied! (Acts 21:8-9) The gift of prophecy was very evident in the life of the first Christian Churches!

The ministry of a Prophet or Prophetess was primarily exercised in the local Church. (1 Corinthians 14:22) Some prophets were itinerant like Agabus whom we have already mentioned but there were several attached to every Church. (Acts 13:1). The first Christian Churches also encountered the problem of false prophets. Jesus warned his disciples that false prophets would come among them. They would seem to be sheep, genuine disciples, but turn out to be wolves intent on destroying the Church. It is by their fruits that you will recognise them. (Matthew 7:15-20) How can you be

153

sure that a prophecy is genuine? All prophecy should be harmonious with the word of God the Bible. The scriptures are the inspired word of God written by men filled with the Holy Spirit. Any prophecy that breathes a Spirit foreign to Christ cannot be a true prophecy. When a prophecy is given we should always ask ourselves, how much does this reflect the « Mind of Christ » and is it in line with His will? One of the problems with a prophecy can be that the prophet speaks the words that he knows a person wants to hear. Jesus again warns of false prophets « At that time many will turn away from the faith and will betray and hate each other, and many false prophets will appear and deceive many people. Because of the increase of wickedness, the love of most will grow cold, but he who stands firm to the end will be saved. » (Matthew 24:10-13) In (2 Peter 2:1) we read of the problems there were with false prophets. In (1 John 4:1) John says that we should « test the spirits » that are behind the prophetic word. This is as vital today as it was in the Church of John's day

A recent prophecy given to the Church where I was ministering in France has started to be fulfilled. The prophecy was concerning a new set of premises which would be given to them with a car park opposite. Not long ago the leadership learned that the local government in France has a responsibility to make provision for Churches whose buildings were inadequate for the work they were doing. The leaders spent most of that day praying for their situation. The following day there was an evangelistic outreach service many people came, including many children. At the end of the service, the mayor arrived, he was astonished at the numbers there, and saw how cramped they were especially the facilities for the children. The pastor and elders were able to talk to him and ask for his help in finding new premises. He said they should write to his office to put things in motion. This they have done and they prayerfully wait for further news on this project.

True prophecy builds up the community of the Church (1 Corinthians 14:4) Prophecy is for building up not tearing down. This basically means that any utterance that is judgemental or negative in word or manner is false prophecy. There may be an admonition and warning, even an exhortation to desist from evil, but the whole purpose is positive and is for the strengthening of faith, encouragement of believers and the building up of the Church. True prophecy besides being in harmony with the Bible finds consent and agreement in the minds and hearts of others in the Church. There should be a prevailing sense in the community of believers that a prophecy comes from God. The spirit of the one prophesying and his or her words stand under the judgement of others.

I remember a man who asked to give a prophetic word just as a service was drawing to a close. The word given had not been checked, it was negative in content, not in harmony with the word of God and therefore not accepted by those present. It was an example of a false prophet bringing a false prophecy! True prophecy gives glory to God and not to man. Peter writes « As each has received a gift, employ it for one another, as good stewards of God's varied grace; whoever speaks, as one who utters oracles of God…….that in everything God may be glorified through Jesus Christ (1 Peter 4:10-11)

4) Faith
Paul lists **faith** as a gift of the Holy Spirit - (1 Corinthians 12:9). This gift of faith is different from the faith we have for salvation, or faith as a fruit of the Spirit. It is a higher measure of faith by which special, wonderful deeds are accomplished, such as compete healing of a person. In my own ministry I remember being asked by a prominent Evangelist to lay hands on a blind man. I did so with as much faith as I could muster but the man did not receive his sight. On another occasion at a conference a young man came to me asking for prayer. He had a skin disease that stretched up his arm and covered half his body. I prayed in faith for him asking the Lord to heal him completely. I had the gift of faith at the time but almost immediately after I began to doubt. I spent the rest of the conference avoiding that young man! I learnt later that he had been completely healed in an instant! Praise the Lord! The gift of faith

overlaps with the gifts of healing and working of miracles. Jesus taught his disciples that this gift of faith would ensure that their prayers were answered and that they would move mountains! (Matthew 21: 21-22) The gift of faith has its source in God, it is faith that comes from Him. We cannot obtain this gift by our own efforts or by thinking positively. Like all the gifts, faith is apportioned according to God's will. Through this important gift God often brings about healing, as God ministers through us. This gift of special faith uniquely apportioned within the body of Christ can have an extraordinary effect on a Church. Special faith enables the Lord's work to be carried out. It is also in answer to prayers of faith that God provides both resources and personnel, for His work.

When I was a boy I used to watch cricket at the county ground in Bristol. On two sides of the ground were several large Victorian buildings. These impressive buildings were the direct result of the faith of a man called George Muller. He founded orphanages for destitute children. They became known as Muller's orphanages. He opened the doors of one building and soon it was full. He prayed for the food and resources needed to care for the children. God answered his prayers in the most amazing way and the work expanded so that he could build three more houses and fill them with needy children. George Muller had the spiritual gift of faith. Many men of God, in ages past and in the present have had the gift of faith and have been a source of encouragement. We read in the book of Hebrews a list of Old Testament heroes who had this gift (Hebrews 11) « Therefore, since we are surrounded by such a great cloud of witnesses, let us throw off everything that hinders and the sin that so easily entangles, and let us run with perseverance the race marked out for us. Let us fix our eyes on Jesus, the author and finisher of our faith, » (Hebrews 12:1-2) It would be wrong to limit the gift of faith to heroes of the past, to a George Muller, or a Hudson Taylor because ordinary people within our Churches can have the gift of faith. Whether it be balancing the Church budget or engaging in inner city mission the gift of faith is essential to boost the flagging morale of the people of God. The most insignificant member of a local Church may be used to impart faith to the whole body at a crucial moment of decision making.   .

5) Healing

More people today are turning to alternative medicine to find a cure for their ailments and many in the medical profession are taking a holistic approach to curing the sick. In Paul's list of spiritual gifts we read of the gift of healing which is divinely imparted to believers in the body of the Church. This gift is wholly supernatural, the recipient is used as a channel through which God's power flows and so brings healing to the sick. Although the gift is supernatural, the person exercising the gifts may use natural means such as touch, the laying on of hands, or oil. (James 5:14ff) Closely connected with the gifts of healing are the gifts of faith and the working of miracles. These three gifts overlap. On one occasion after I had written an article on Christian healing in a Church magazine I received a very frosty reaction from one particular member of the leadership team. This man would not believe that a person could be physically healed except by the work of the professionals in the secular health service! There are hundreds of people in our present time who can give testimony to their healing by divine means. Evidently he had not heard of them. We need to be clear that Christian healing has nothing in common with what is in secular terms called « Faith Healing » or « Psychosomatic medicine » The local Church's ministry of healing is supernatural in origin as a result of the Holy Spirit present in the body of the Church.

Although God's will is perfect health, this does not mean that human life will be free from all sickness. Paul himself was not free from physical illness, he writes to the Galatians « As you know, it was because of illness that I first preached the gospel to you » (Galatians 4:13) Paul wrote to Timothy about a Christian brother named Trophimus « I left Trophimus sick in Miletus » (2 Timothy 4:20) These were dedicated Spirit filled Christian workers but they were not immune to disease. The Psalmist says « God heals all your diseases » (Psalm 103: 3) but we know from experience that there is no guarantee of freedom from all disease, or that everyone who is prayed for will be healed. Since God's will is health, when disease and sickness come upon us, He will act as our healer. The healing ministry of the Church has continued in one form or another from New Testament times until today. The rediscovery of the gifts of healing during the last century has enabled the Church to be the channel for healing the sick as in apostolic times. God heals today out of compassion for his creation. He requires us to have compassion to carry on his works. God is sovereign and often heals people despite their lack of faith but he also heals in response to faith as he did in New Testament times. (Acts 14:8-10) We must always give thanks to God for healing because all healings are to give glory to Jesus his son. (John 11:4:40 Acts 3:12-13).Death is the end for all humankind but for the believer this is the ultimate healing as we enter God's presence and receive his promised reward.

6) The working of miracles

The working of Miracles is also in Paul's list of the gifts of the spirit. This gift of miraculous power includes all demonstrations of supernatural power. Jesus sent out his disciples saying « 'as you go preach this message.' The Kingdom of Heaven is at hand, heal the sick, raise the dead, cleanse the leper, cast out demons » (Matthew 10:7-8) Healing is included here with the other works of power. We read that the **disciples** of Jesus healed the sick and cast out demons. The gift of miracles is given as a sovereign act of God but is clearly connected to the gift of faith. At the beginning of this chapter I referred to the **greater works** that would be done by believers. These greater works will be a result of the use of this gift. Mark concludes his gospel with the words of our risen Lord « These signs will accompany those who believe: in my name they will cast out demons; they will speak in new tongues; they will pick up serpents; and if they drink any deadly thing it will not hurt them, they will lay hands on the sick and they will recover » (Mark 16:17-18) Those who **believe** says Jesus. **Believing** is an ongoing trust in Christ. It is a continuing faith that the Lord is present with his people, « Christ is the same yesterday, and today, and forever »

(Hebrews 13:8) The living Christ works in the life of the believer; as he did many miracles yesterday, He will do many today! If we truly believe in the promise of « working of miracles » as a gift of the Holy Spirit we become increasingly expectant that He will move mightily, then **we have to act**. Nothing will happen unless we step out in faith. A miracle does not happen by sitting back and waiting. One of the extraordinary miracles recorded in the New Testament was Peter walking on the sea of Galilee. Jesus called to him and Peter got out of the boat and walked across the water. (Matthew 14:28-32.) It would not have happened if Peter had not had the courage to get out of the boat in response to Jesus' call! Trust Christ and then act.

It is important for the Christian to understand what this gift is not. Miracles are not magic. Magic stems from psychic or demonic forces not from God. The gift of working of miracles is not to be associated with exhibitionism. Remember how Satan tempted Jesus to leap spectacularly from the temple to dazzle the crowds! (Matthew 4:4-7) Today when a preacher or evangelist advertises « Come tonight and see miracles happen! » or « Come claim your miracle » he or she is very close to falling into that same temptation. The Pharisees wanted Jesus to perform a miracle but he would not make an exhibition for their satisfaction. (Mark 8:11)   Miracles cannot be programmed. We have a miracle working God but He is sovereign and He acts according to His will. God may not always act by giving the gift of miracles in the way we think because he may have another way of fulfilling His purpose in a given situation. When the chains fell off the imprisoned Peter and the doors opened a miracle had occurred. The believers were praying for Peter's release. Their prayers were answered but they would not believe that Peter was free! (Acts 12:5-17) Many Christians today believe we are entering the end times before King Jesus returns and that will mean an increase in miracles. As the time draws near for the coming of the Kingdom of God on earth, miracles may multiply, as powers of the age to come, break in, on the present age.

7) Discernment

The gift of discernment or the ability to distinguish between spirits is of the utmost importance, and refers to telling the difference between what is of the human spirit, the demonic spirit and the Holy Spirit. Sometimes when someone asks for prayer or laying on of hands for healing, the gift of discernment reveals that there is an undisclosed underlying problem, to the illness. We need to know what is truly the work of the Holy Sprit and what is counterfeit. Discernment is particularly important in relation to the operation of gifts of healing and prophesy. As an example let me tell you about a pale and breathless woman who asked for prayer for a heart problem when an invitation was given for people to come forward for ministry. When I began to pray in tongues the Lord gave me the gift of discernment and I saw that her problem was that she had split up with her husband. When challenged she broke down in tears confessing that she had committed adultery and had left him. She was ministered to, she found forgiveness, and they were eventually reconciled. Her physical condition changed and she was completely healed.

The prophet also needs to be especially gifted with discernment. It is so easy to tell someone what they want to hear. The evil one is good at posing as an angel of light. The prophet must always be on his or her guard. The gift of discernment of spirits is vitally important in this ministry. We must be sure that in the realm of the angelic we are not deceived. The gift of discernment helps us to judge the source of the spirit, angelic, merely human or demonic, and enables us to judge whether a prophecy is truly from God.

8)and 9) Speaking in tongues and interpretation

The final two gifts in Paul's list are **«speaking in tongues and interpretation»**. They are twin gifts that operate together in the assembly of believers. **In public worship one should not function without the other.** The gift of speaking in tongues is the most controversial one in the whole list. Many sincere people have been perplexed by Christians claiming to speak in tongues. The issue is made more difficult as this gift is not mentioned in the Old

Testament or the Gospel accounts of the ministry of Jesus. However it was a gift that was important in the Churches in the Acts of the Apostles. Today there are sincere believers who cannot see the point of speaking in tongues and will argue that they are not relevant for today's church. They are mentioned in the New Testament as being important and tongues and interpretation of tongues operate on a level above and beyond the mind. These gifts enable the believer to relate with God in a more direct and intense way. In the Acts of the Apostles and Paul's letters different kinds of speaking in tongues are described. (1 Corinthians 12:10)

The individual **believer is given an unknown language to pray and to praise** God the Father. Many times we do not know how to pray or what to pray for but the Holy Spirit comes to our aid. **We speak in tongues as our own devotional language**. In worship a whole assembly of believers under the influence of the Holy Spirit may begin to glorify God by **singing in the Spirit**. i.e. in tongues. The gift of devotional tongues helps us to relate more directly to God and be more conscious of what he is trying to say to us. Praying in tongues over the word of God, the Bible, reveals to us more clearly what God is saying through His written Word. In ministry situations praying in tongues helps to enable the other spiritual gifts to operate. There is no limit to the use of tongues in our devotional life. It is a gift that all believers may receive. Paul writes « I want you all to speak in tongues » (1 Corinthians 14:5) and « Eagerly desire the greater gifts » (1 Corinthians12:31). Remember that all gifts must operate in love.

In his letter to the Church at Corinth Paul gives us a glimpse of the Church coming together to worship and praise the Lord. He gives instruction on the nature of spiritual gifts and how they should be used in the assembly of the Church. Speaking in tongues seems to have been an ongoing ministry of the Church. **Paul makes it clear that tongues in public must always be accompanied by the gift of interpretation**. It appears that the problem at Corinth, was not speaking in tongues but failure to give an interpretation. Tongues with interpretation encourage and strengthen the church.

The result is that God speaks to His people directly both to the individual Christian and to the gathered Church. The gift of tongues with interpretation is to be used in an orderly way not with everyone speaking at once! « All this must be done for the strengthening of the Church. If anyone speaks in a tongue, two - or at the most three - should speak one at a time, and someone must interpret. If there is no interpreter the speaker should keep quiet in the Church and speak to himself and to God » (1 Corinthians 14:26-30) It is interesting that Paul now speaks about the gift of Prophesy and how the people should « weigh carefully what is said » Again things are to be done in an orderly way with two or three people with the gift of prophecy speaking out and others carefully weighing up what has been said. He also writes « And if a revelation comes to someone who is sitting down, the first speaker should stop » It seems that when the church assembled for worship, speaking in tongues and prophecy were linked together and were a normal part of the meeting. Speaking in tongues, while a blessing to believers is a sign to unbelievers. (1 Corinthians 14:22) It should be evident to the unbeliever of a supernatural utterance. Hearing the gift of speaking in tongues can convince a seeking person to look more deeply at the Christian faith and can lead to conversion.

We have considered in detail the gifts of the Holy Spirit in Chapters 12-14 of 1 Corinthians. These gifts seem mostly to be used in the context of the Church gathered together for worship. They are to be exercised in an orderly way. The list of gifts or God given abilities in Romans 12 vs. 4-8 seem to be for use in the context of the general life of the Church and it's ministry. Paul again uses the illustration of the Church being like a body composed of many members. Just as the different parts of the body have different uses and function differently so also in the Church each member has a different gift or gifts given by God. All are called to serve Christ in different ways with different gifts. Just as in the body each part is vital for the body to be healthy so also in the Church each member is important for its proper function. (Romans 12:4-5)

THE LIST OF GIFTS IN PAUL'S LETTER TO THE ROMANS

1) The gift of prophesying

The gift of prophecy overlaps with the list of gifts we have already considered. This gift used in public worship for the building up of the Church can also be used in counselling an individual for the building up of their faith. In general the word means « Speaking forth the mind and counsel of God » This can mean inspired utterances in preaching or on a one to one basis. The person with the gift is to exercise it in proportion to his/her God given faith.

2) The gift of serving or administration.

« If it is serving let him serve » vs7 In every church there are opportunities to serve. This service can take many forms but the word here seems to suggest administration. Every church fellowship needs a degree of organisation. It is true that some people are more gifted than others! Some people are very capable of organisation and administration and others not so. It is a practical gift given by the grace of God. It can also be understood as a ministry. Paul also lists the gift of administration in (1 Corinthians 12:28)

3) The gift of teaching

« if it is teaching, let him teach » vs7 Paul is concerned if someone is gifted by God as a teacher or communicator that he/she should have the opportunity to use it for the building up of the church. In all these gifts there is an overlapping of the supernatural with the natural! The most important thing is that more is learnt about God in the church. How much this gift is needed today in the local church.

4) The gift of encouraging or exhorting

« If it is encouraging, let him encourage » vs8 Encouraging has the sense of inspiring others in the church by stimulating their faith. It is the perfect antidote to discouragement and in our churches today there are a lot of discouraged people especially when no progress in spreading the gospel seems to be happening. Some translation of this passage use the word exhortation instead of encourage. The word has the sense of « earnestly admonishing ». In other words to urge, advise or correct!

5) The gift of contributing to the needs of others
« If it is contributing to the needs of others, let him give generously » vs8 We are called to give generously with all our hearts. The gift of being a generous giver to those in need is important if a church is to remain faithful to it's master. When Paul was saying farewell to the elders of the church at Ephesus, Luke writes « You yourselves know that these hands of mine have supplied my own needs and the needs of my companions. In everything I did, I showed you that by this kind of hard work we must help the weak, remembering the words the Lord Jesus himself said 'It is more blessed to give than to receive' » (Acts 20:34-35)

6) The gift of leadership
« If it is leadership, let him govern diligently » vs.8 If a person is called and gifted by God as a leader that person must lead! We must accept that if a person is a leader in the church he/she has been given authority by God. Many in our churches today complain about the lack of leadership and look for a strong leader. When such a person begins to lead the church the others must follow. You cannot lead people if they are not prepared to follow or accept authority.

7) The gift of showing mercy
« If it is showing mercy, let him do it cheerfully » vs.8 Other versions of the New Testament translate 'showing mercy' as 'having sympathy for other brothers and sisters in the church' or 'helping others in distress' All help must be given in a cheerful manner. The gift of 'helps' is also listed in the first letter to the Corinthians.
Paul writes of the gift « of being able to help others » which is probably the same gift (1 Corinthians 12:28)

Peter also writes about the believer using the gift he/has received to serve others.

« each one should use whatever gift he has received to serve others, faithfully administering God's grace in its various forms. If anyone speaks, he should do it as one speaking the very words of God. If anyone serves, he should do it with the strength God provides so that in al things God may be praised through Jesus Christ. To him be the glory and the power for ever and ever. Amen » (1 Peter 4:10-11) None of us should exercise the spiritual gift God has given us for our own benefit but to serve others. He distinguishes between speaking gifts and serving gifts. When exercising a 'speaking gift' it is to be God that is speaking through a person. When it is a serving gift it is to be administered in God's strength, not our own ability. Finally we use our God given gift or gifts so that God may be praised through Jesus Christ. He is to have all the glory.

THE MINISTRIES OF THE HOLY SPIRIT

Finally a word about the ministries of the Holy Spirit that Paul writes about in Ephesians. These ministries are given to prepare God's people for works of service. Imagine a professional football team without its coaching staff. The team would not function as a unit and each individual would do his own thing! There would be no strategy or tactics and that team would soon suffer defeat. Those with the ministries of the Holy Spirit are the coaching staff of the Church! They bring, guidance, discipline, encouragement, direction and unity to the Church. The ministries of the Holy Spirit are leadership gifts for the people of God. Paul writes about the ascended Christ saying « It was he who gave some to be **apostles, some to be prophets, some to be evangelists, and some to be pastors and teachers** to prepare God's people for works of service (Ephesians 4:11-12)

1) The Apostle

The Apostle is head of the list and we immediately recall the twelve disciples of Jesus who were called Apostles. The word means men (or women) who are sent by God. They are people with a mission. They are messengers and ambassadors for the Kingdom of God. The New Testament does not restrict apostleship to the twelve. Paul and others like Barnabas (Acts 14:14) Andronicus and Junias (Romans 16:17) were called apostles. **The role of the Apostle in today's church is to give leadership, establish the Church's vision, and to offer direction and encouragement.**

2) The Prophet
The role of the prophet is to proclaim the message of God and to foretell the purposes of God. The Church is dependant on the prophetic ministry to develop kingdom strategy and keep it faithful to God's purpose. **The prophet like the Apostle exercises leadership in the local Church. Some prophets have a wider ministry bringing words of prophecy to many congregations**

3) The Evangelist
The evangelist is the « **fisher of men** » and casts his net widely for the Kingdom of God. Both prophet and evangelist may be part of the ministry team of the local Church. The evangelist like Phillip in the Acts of the Apostles is able with the aid of the Holy Spirit **to lead individuals to faith in Jesus Christ.** (Acts 8:26-40) This simple one to one is the way that evangelists operated in the first Christian Churches. There was no TV or TV Evangelists in those days! The large arenas were more likely filled with lions and Christian martyrs!

4) The Pastor
The pastor is identified in the New Testament as being the **Shepherd of the flock**. The shepherd cares for and feeds the sheep. Peter the disciple of Jesus and leader of the early Church besides being called to be a « fisher of men » was also commissioned to take care of the sheep in God's flock and to feed the lambs.

The pastor gives help, care and support to the Church where he belongs. He is responsible for 'feeding the lambs,' those who have just come to know the Lord and 'feeding the sheep,' those who are maturing in faith. (John 21:15-19).
5) The Teacher

Linked with the pastor is the teaching ministry. **Jesus was known as 'Rabbi' teacher.** He taught the people and they hung on his every word! All men marvelled at the authority that he had. **The ministry of teacher in the church is one of instructing the believer in the teachings of the Old and New Testaments. He or she is called to teach sound doctrine so that the church remains faithful to the word of God, is united and matures in the faith and has Christ at its centre.**

All these ministries given by the Holy Spirit are for preparing God's people for works of service, whilst the gifts of the Holy Spirit given to individual believers are for the building up of the body of Christ

Chapter 12 - Belonging to the Church

What does the word « Church » mean for you? Do you think of a building with a spire or a square tower? Perhaps you see the Church as an organisation which makes rules and gives an opinion on moral issues. In fact the Church is a group of believers meeting together for a certain purpose. The word Church comes from the Greek word *ekklesia* which was a common word for a group of citizens meeting together to discuss the affairs of state. This word was adopted by the early Christians to mean the whole company of the redeemed, assembled together; that is to say all people who believe in Jesus and are saved. In the New Testament we find that the word Church is used to refer to different groups of Christians. It may be a local congregation, all the groups of believers in a wide area or a particular district or the leaders of the Church assembled together, as in the council of Jerusalem. (Acts 15:12) What is the nature of the Church? The New Testament uses several different metaphors to describe the Church of Jesus Christ, the **building,** the **body**, and the **bride** are the three most important ones.

1) The Church like a building The disciple Peter who was the acknowledged leader of the first Christian Church wrote about the Church being a building, a spiritual temple made up of living stones whose foundation stone is Christ. « As you come to him, the living Stone - rejected by men but chosen by God and precious to Him - you also like living stones, are being built into a spiritual house to be a holy priesthood, offering spiritual sacrifices, acceptable to God through Jesus Christ » (1 Peter 2:4-5). When a house is built it is important that it has a secure foundation. The Church's one foundation is Jesus Christ her Lord. Paul writes to the Church at Corinth reminding them that Christ is the foundation on which the Church is built, and that the believers are responsible for building it.

He says «no one can lay any foundation other than the one already laid, which is Jesus Christ (1 Corinthians 3:11). It is good for us to recall the commission that Jesus gave to Peter at Caesarea Philippi. Simon Peter had confessed that he believed that Jesus was the Christ the Son of the living God. This was the first Christian confession of faith and it can be argued that this was the moment the Church was born. Jesus replied « Blessed are you Simon son of Jonah, for this was not revealed to you by man, but by my Father in heaven. And I tell you that you are Peter, and on this rock I will build my Church and the gates of Hades will not overcome it. » (Matthew 16:17-18).We note that Peter's faith did not depend on his understanding but on God revealing the truth to him. We also need to recognise that our faith is not just based on head knowledge of Jesus but on the truth that God has revealed to us. There are different interpretations of this text that have led to confusion of Peter's authority in the Church. My understanding is that the rock on which the Church is to be built is not the person of Peter but his faith in Jesus. He was a great leader but there is no hint that he or any other of the disciples had any conception that an absolute primacy had been conferred on him!

Christ must be at the centre, holding the Church together, in everything it is, and does. Each living person is different as is each living stone. The use of the word « living » implies that a person is alive in Christ. Imagine stones being quarried and shaped to become part of a building. Each stone has to be worked upon by a mason with the right tools so that it is shaped to take its particular place. So within the Church the believer is shaped by the Lord, made holy, sanctified so that it he/ she is built into a spiritual house! Peter understands that God is at work building His Church, erecting His building stone by stone! Just as each stone is placed in the building so the Lord places us alongside others. We are to be like priests in the Temple offering sacrifices to God on behalf of an unbelieving world. The picture of a Holy people worshipping God and of a praying people making intercession for others, and declaring the wonderful deeds of God, is the church manifesting divine power. The Church is not primarily a human organisation, but a supernatural society of moral excellence continuing the ministry of Jesus in every age.

2) The Church as a body

The apostle Paul in his understanding of the nature of the Church uses a more functional approach. He describes the Church as the body of Christ. When we think of a human body we think of a living organism where each organ has a part to play so that the body functions correctly. « The body is a unit, though it is made up of many parts: though all its parts are many, they form one body. So it is with the Church of Christ. For we were all baptised by one Spirit into one body -whether Jews or Greeks, slave or free - and we were all given the one Spirit to drink.» (1 Corinthians 12:12-13) He makes the point that each part of the body is important and necessary. Each person is important in the Church. In a body all the organs have a different function so that the body is healthy, so also in the church all of us are different and have different gifts and ministries. There are many different ways of serving the Lord and in a healthy Church every person will play their part using the gifts and abilities that God has given them. God has created the human body according to his blue print, every part is where he wants it to be so that the body lives and functions correctly. « Now the body is not made up of one part but of many. If the foot should say 'Because I am not a hand, I do not belong to the body ' it would not for that reason cease to be part of the body. And if the ear should say 'Because I am not an eye I do not belong to the body' it would not for that reason cease to be part of the body. If the whole body were an eye where would the sense of hearing be? If the whole body were an ear where would the sense of smell be? But in fact God has arranged the parts in the body, every one of them just as he wanted them to be. » (1 Corinthians 12: 14-18)

THERE ARE LESSONS WE CAN LEARN FROM THIS ANALOGY

a) God in Christ is head of his Church. He is responsible for its existence and the way each person works in the Church, just as the head controls all parts of a human body which together make up the whole.

b) There is to be no jealousy or rivalry in the Church. Each person is valued for the contribution he/she makes. We must respect, accept and encourage each other's contribution to the mission of the Church.

c) God has given to us different gifts and abilities as he wills. We cannot all be preachers in the one congregation. If everyone got up to preach at the same time no one would be able to hear what was being said! All of us are different and can serve the Lord by making our own unique contribution to the life of the Church.

d) We all need each other. When the Church meets « The eye cannot say to the hand I don't need you. And the head cannot say to the feet I don't need you! On the contrary, those parts of the body that seem to be weaker are indispensable. » (I Corinthians 12:22) All contributions to the life of the Church are of equal value. Humble service such as cleaning the floor is just as important in God's eyes as leading the worship.

e) There should be no hint of division in the church Members should have equal concern for one another. In the Church writes Paul « If one part suffers every part suffers with it ; if one part is honoured, every part rejoices with it » (1 Corinthians 12:26) Divisions and splits, caused by human sinfulness and Satan's activities have been the biggest hindrance to the Church's mission in every age.

f) All members of the Church have God given gifts. In some cases these will be supernatural in other cases natural abilities. Every new believer within the Church must find his/her place in the congregation. The mature Christians should encourage newcomers to serve the Lord.

g) 'Square pegs in round holes.'
It is important that we aim to have every person serving the Lord but at the right time, in the right way, and for the right reasons.

3) The Church as a bride
The New Testament describes the Church as being like a bride adorned in all her finery awaiting the coming of the bridegroom. Christ is identified with the bridegroom and the term is used fourteen times in the gospels and the book of Revelation. Paul writes to the Church at Corinth « I promised you to one husband, to Christ, so that I might present you as a pure virgin to Him. » The Church is to be as pure and beautiful as a virgin bride. When two people get married it is always a special occasion. Two become one and together they start a new life. It is a time for celebration and everybody dresses up for the occasion. The bride in particular is dressed to look her best. Marriage customs differ in different parts of the world. In the west the bridegroom usually waits for his bride to walk towards him down the aisle. Marriage traditions in Eastern countries are completely different At the time when Jesus lived, marriages among Jews were arranged by the young people's relatives, often at the very early age, of eleven or twelve. The bride was paid for by the bridegroom, after which the betrothal took place before two witnesses and rings were exchanged followed by a benediction. From this moment the young couple were regarded as being as much bound to one another as if they were already married. The marriage proper took place at a later date. Joseph and Mary were betrothed before Jesus was born. (Luke 1:26-27 & Matthew 1:18) A wedding was a great occasion involving the whole community. It consisted of two parts, the wedding procession and the marriage supper. In the parable that Jesus told, the ten young girls were going to keep the bride company until the bridegroom arrived to fetch her. This could have been at any time, that night, the next night or even after two weeks! No one knew for certain

when he would arrive! The wedding procession followed the bridegroom when he arrived to fetch his bride and take her to her future home. The procession was accompanied by shouting, singing and dancing and the bridegroom would be splendidly attired. Meanwhile the bride wearing a veil and adorned with embroidered clothes and jewels waited for the bridegroom to arrive. The bride and groom would set off together with the wedding guests to their new home. They would share a banquet with their guests which often included all the people of that town. The marriage feast lasted for a week or more. The bride waiting for the bridegroom to come is a picture of the church waiting for the return of Jesus.(Revelation 21:2)

Paul elaborates on the relationship between the bride, and bridegroom in terms of husband and wife in his letter to the Ephesians. (Ephesians 5:22-32) Christ loves the church and cares for it. The church on the other hand must submit to the authority of Christ, as a wife, out of love, submits to her husband. The church as the bride of Christ emphasises the eternal dimension. Just as we are saved for eternity so the people of God, the Church, is for eternity. The church will be part of the wedding feast of the lamb at the end time. John writes « Then I heard what sounded like a great multitude, like the roar of rushing waters and like ,loud peals of thunder, shouting:
'Hallelujah!
For our Lord God Almighty reigns.
Let us rejoice and be glad and give him glory!
For the wedding of the Lamb has come, and his bride has made herself ready.
Fine linen bright and clean was given her to wear'
(Fine linen stands for the righteous acts of the saints)
(Revelation 19:6-8)

The local Church
The activities of a local church vary greatly. In some the spiritual activities are dominant and take precedence, in others a lot of effort is put into social events. Some support overseas missions, others help the poor and needy in their own town. There is great diversity.

What were the activities of the New Testament church in Jerusalem?
We notice at least nine characteristics of that church as described in (Acts 2:42-47)

1. They were a learning Church vs. 42
« They devoted themselves to the Apostles' teaching. » There is a half truth that says « Christianity is caught not taught. » This may be true when receiving Christ as Saviour and Lord, but if Christians are going to reach maturity the faith must be taught through the preaching of sermons or studying the Bible in small groups, and as the early Christians did, believers must devote themselves to learning.

2. Fellowship was an important characteristic. vs. 42
Christians spent time together, shared meals, encouraged and supported each other. It is important that fellowship should centre on Christ and the Holy Spirit. (There might be for example close fellowship between members of a golf club but it is because they all share the same interest, and at the centre is the game of golf!) All our fellowship with one another should have Christ at the centre. When we meet together as the Church, wouldn't it be great if Christ was at the centre of our conversations, what he is doing in our lives and how we would like to serve Him better! The Holy Spirit would be honoured and experiences shared and faith would grow.

3 They Broke Bread together vs. 42
They focused their thoughts on the last supper where Jesus had explained what his death would mean. When we share together the bread and wine we remember the death of Jesus and what it means for us. We enter into deeper fellowship with Him and one another, and in quietness commit our thoughts and lives again to his service searching our hearts and asking for forgiveness.

4. They prayed together vs. 42
We note here that the church took part in formal times of prayer in the Temple (Acts 3: 1) and in smaller groups praying together in

their homes. (Acts 12:12-17) The evangelist R.A.Torrey said « Prayer is the key that unlocks all the storehouses of God's infinite grace and power. All that God is, and all that God has, is at the disposal of prayer» How often do you pray together with a group of believers or even with your family? What about saying 'grace' before a meal or committing the day to God with the whole family's day's activities laid before the Lord. It would make such a difference.

5.Miracles were happening «Miraculous signs were done by the Apostles» vs.43

In the very next chapter we read of a beggar crippled from birth being healed
(Acts 3:1-10) The apostles and new converts in the first Christian churches carried on the ministry of Jesus. Miracles of healing accelerated the spread of the good news that the Kingdom of God had come!

6. The believers were « Together » Sharing and Caring for one another vs.45

«All the believers were of one heart and mind. No one claimed that any of his possessions was his own, but they shared everything they had » (Acts 4:32) They had generous hearts so that they willingly shared what they had! The love of Christ in their hearts was expressed in practical caring for one another. We read also that «There was no needy persons among them. » (Acts 4:34) The early church displayed a singleness of purpose and concern for the disadvantaged. They cared for the widows among them no matter their nationality. (Acts 6:1-7). Widows often did not have the means to feed and look after their family, and were on many occasions victims of exploitation.

7 They met together regularly vs. 46

The Church met together in the Temple Courts in large numbers and as small groups in their homes. In their homes they broke bread together and prayed. Meeting together always demands commitment and prioritising the use of time. How sad when Christians, both new converts and those of long standing, are negligent in meeting on Sunday or in midweek house groups. Should we not say with the Psalmist « I was glad when they said to me let us go into the house of the Lord. » (Psalm 122)

8 They were a Praising Church vs. 47

They praised God together in the Temple Courts and in their homes. They were a praising people giving glory to God no matter the circumstances. They even praised God in prison! (Acts 16:25) They continued the Jewish tradition of singing Psalms but added their own « spiritual songs » (Ephesians 5:19-20 Colossians 3:16 Hebrews 13:15 1 Peter 2:9)

9 They were a Growing Church vs. 47

What was it that produced the growth? What was their strategy? Today much has been written on church growth and a whole movement has emerged concerning this subject. The Church in Jerusalem was born of the Spirit, led by the Spirit and it grew by the Spirit. The people witnessed to their faith, they were excited by Jesus and filled with a contagious joy!

There are many different sorts of local churches, each one having its strengths and weaknesses. In the New Testament we read about the risen Christ's message to the seven churches of Asia. The Lord commended and condemned each of those churches, who were facing different circumstances. (Revelation 2-3) There is no uniformity in the local church and you will never find a perfect one. There are a bewildering number of churches and denominations. These different denominations or groups of churches are for the most part accidents of history, often coming into being as a result of schism. Even those churches that claim to be non-denominational have to have structures and government which are often similar to denominational churches. What then should the new convert look for in a local church? A mature Christian moving to another part of the country or going abroad is faced with the same question.

1) The church should be a place where the gospel is preached and the ministry is Bible centred.

2) Christ at the centre of the church's life. It is so easy for a church to become inward looking and little more than a social club.

3) The leadership of the local church is very important. If the leadership is not esteemed and affirmed by the congregation its authority will be diminished and the members will not be submitted or obedient.

4) The prayer life of the local church is very important. Without prayer very little will be accomplished for the Kingdom of God. Always look to see if the church is a praying people.

5) « The church exists by mission as fire exists by burning » wrote Emile Brunner.
Evangelism, and missionary endeavour should be an important part of church life. If a church has no concern for the lost, and is not continuing the work of Jesus it is built on the wrong foundation!

6) Unlike human institutions the church accepts all kinds of people. There is usually something wrong if a church consists of people who are all of the same class and background, age or sex! The church has a place for both the rich and the poor, for the young and the old, for people of different nationalities for « we are all one in Christ Jesus » (Galatians 3:28) James the brother of our Lord give some very practical teaching about favouritism in the churches in his letter. He writes « My brothers, as believers in our glorious Lord Jesus Christ, don't show favouritism. Suppose a man comes into your meeting wearing a gold ring and fine clothes, and a poor man in shabby clothes also comes in. If you show special attention to the men wearing fine clothes and say 'Here's a good seat for you' but say to the poor man 'sit on the floor by my feet' have you not discriminated among yourselves and become judges with evil thoughts.»(James 2:1-4)

7) When looking for a local church check out if the church has a vision and what it is. « Where there is no vision the people perish » (Proverbs 29:18 A.V)
These are just seven things to look for in a local church. This list is by no means fully inclusive and there are other characteristics one could look for but the seven above are all very important for a healthy church. The Church « Webb site » can reveal a lot!

I remember attending a meeting in Liverpool that was addressed by Arthur Blessit. Arthur was well known at that time as a leader of the 'Jesus people' and for carrying a large wooden cross on his shoulders throughout the countries and continents of the world. He said to me after the meeting words that I have never forgotten « If you are called to lead - you must lead - leadership is very important » There are many different styles of leadership. In the New Testament Church the « council of Jerusalem » was the governing body. They made decisions that affected all the other local churches. They gave authoritative ruling on whether Gentile Christian had to undergo the Jewish rite of circumcision and obey the Jewish law of Moses.(Acts15:1-35). In the fourth century the Roman catholic church set up a rigid hierarchical form of government. The protestant churches on the whole developed government by consensus. In some churches the authority rests in a Bishop or Patriarch, in others a council made up of delegates from local churches. Some Pentecostal groups are governed by a group of leaders delegated as Apostles. The outward shape of a church's governing body is not as important as the qualities the leaders possess. It is good to aspire to be a leader in the church if God has called you for this. The apostle Paul lists the qualities church leaders should possess in his letters to Timothy and Titus. (1 Timothy 3:1-16 & Titus 1:5-16) Leadership in the Christian church is not appointed but anointed. Any leader must be called by God, anointed by the Holy Spirit, and affirmed by the church. Maybe you who are reading this book feel that God is calling you to leadership. Your first step in answering that call is to talk, pray, and discuss it with your minister.

No person can remain a Christian in isolation. You need to become a member of a local Church. Imagine a blazing fire giving out lots of heat. As it begins to die down someone throws on another log or an armful of sticks. One stick set alight soon dies out, two sticks will do a little better, but an armful will make a fire. If one of these sticks goes out the others soon light it again. If another stick is green or damp the others soon set it ablaze. A fire reminds us of a church where people help and encourage each other in the faith. Our fellowship with other believers helps us to keep our spiritual fervour. I repeat no church is perfect but is better to belong to the most imperfect church than to no church at all! The author of the book of Hebrews writes « Encourage one another daily » (Hebrews 13:3). In the New Testament, Barnabas was known as the great encourager. We need more like him in today's churches! Words of encouragement spoken sincerely build up people and strengthen the church. On the other hand criticism destroys faith and fellowship and gossip leads to unrest and hurt!

The Christian Church is a fellowship of believers throughout the world, wherever we travel we can find brothers and sisters in Christ. As members of a church we are sustained by the prayers of others, especially in difficult times, and in turn our prayers and encouragement enable others to walk in faith and victory. We are called by Jesus to « go and make disciples of all nations » and it is as part of the Church that we can fulfil His purpose. The Church is there for those who are outside it as well as for those within it. Think of a bicycle wheel, each spoke is joined to the hub in the middle, in the same way every believer is joined to God by faith in Jesus Christ. Each spoke is also joined to the circumference of the wheel, and so each believer is related by love to one another. This relationship is described in terms of the family. There are brothers and sisters, fathers and mothers, sons and daughters, within the family of God, the fellowship of the Church. The wheel is useless if the spokes become detached from the hub or from the rim. The Church becomes useless if the relationship of its members with God breaks down, or if the relationship between its members is fractured.

Chapter 13 - Worship and the Lord's Supper

There was a vast crowd of people filling the cathedral. Christians of all denominations had gathered together for a special celebration. Every seat was taken and late comers were standing at the back. As one, the whole congregation stood and worshipped God with heart and voice. The atmosphere was electric and all glory was given to God. The Bishop said later that the worship of the people had been like a « Great explosion of love and praise! » One could say it was worship at it's best! There are many ways of worshipping God but Christians worship the same God. When a Church gathers together on a Sunday its principal purpose is to worship God. The Bible, the preaching of word of God, and the celebration of the Lord's supper are the focal points. The design of the building used for worship reveals the emphasis the church places on « The Word » and « The Sacrament of the Lord's supper » In most Catholic Churches there is a « High Altar » for the celebration of the mass. This is usually the first thing that you see as you enter the building. It says to the observer that the celebration of the « Mass, Eucharist, Holy Communion or Lord's supper » is the focal point of that congregation's worship. (All four terms are used to signify the commemoration of the supper Jesus shared with his disciples just before his arrest, trial, and crucifixion.) In many reformed Churches the pulpit is large, and centrally placed, with a small communion table in front of it indicating that here the emphasis is on the reading and preaching of the word.

There are many ways that people engage in worship. The use of musical instruments was an essential part of Jewish worship. The Psalmist says « Praise him with the sounding of the trumpet, praise him with the harp and lyre, praise him with tambourine and dancing, praise him with strings and flute, praise him with the clash of cymbals, praise him with resounding cymbals. Let everything that has breath praise the Lord! » (Psalm 150) Worship was a time when everyone participated, playing musical instruments, singing and dancing before the Lord! Unfortunately with the invention of the organ played by one person, and the development of trained choirs, many people may feel more like spectators than participants. Fortunately many churches today are encouraging a wider participation with orchestras, and instrumental music groups. The use of colourful images and icons can stimulate our senses in worship and from earliest times Christians have used symbols, such as a cross, an anchor, or a fish. These symbols have been discovered etched into the walls of the catacombs in Rome and on the walls beside a primitive baptistery under the church of the Holy Sepulchre in Jerusalem. Soon after the church came into being heresies arose. People added or emphasised some particular doctrine to the exclusion of other important truths of the faith. To combat these errors the church fathers formulated « creeds » (Those things that all Christians believed). Today many Christians regularly affirm their faith by saying the Apostle's or Nicene creeds, as part of worship

 From the Byzantine period many church buildings displayed beautiful works of art, these include stained glass windows and murals to help the worshipper understand Bible stories and appreciate the beauty of all that God has created. Portable images such as icons have in some traditions become worship aids. The reformers in the 16th century changed this in part by destroying all that they saw as idols, substituting for them a simple more severe, cerebral style of worship. Today there is more appreciation of colour and beauty as aids to worship, with the use of flowers and coloured banners! From earliest times candles and lamps have been used in Christian worship, expressing « Jesus the Light of the World », the light that has overcome darkness. (John 1:6-14) Movement has been part of worship from the very beginning with processions and dancing; the use of banners, clapping and lifting up hands to the glory of God. Some Christians are helped in worship by the burning of incense or the beads of the rosary. Our whole body, and all our senses, can be used in our worship, if they are used in Spirit and in truth. When our worship just becomes a form of words or going through the motions of dead tradition, it is not the sort of worship that God wants. Jesus said «God is Spirit, and his worshippers must worship in spirit and in truth » (John 4:24)

The Sabbath day for the Jewish people is Saturday, that is the day when they meet together in the Synagogue to worship God. We have a picture of Jewish worship during the lifetime of Jesus in Luke's gospel. The Rabbi stood up to read the scripture and then sat down to give his sermon. (Luke 4:16-30). The Christian church at the beginning was predominantly Jewish and consequently the patterns of early Christian worship were very similar to that of the Jews. The centres of Jewish worship were the Temple in Jerusalem and the local synagogues. In the early chapters of the Acts of the Apostles the Christians worshipped God in the Temple and in their own houses. (Acts 2:46-47). Very soon they changed their day of worship from « The Sabbath, » Saturday to « The Lord's Day » Sunday. They did this to commemorate the resurrection of Jesus. Every Sunday Christians meet together all over the world to celebrate Jesus their Risen Saviour and Lord. When we meet in His Name he is present with us. « For where two or three come together in my name, there I am with them.» (Matthew 18:20). The form the worship takes, whether it be formal or free, or the number of people present does not matter as long as it is led by the Holy Spirit. We meet together to worship, to learn, to pray, to encourage one another and so grow in the faith. Meeting together to worship God on Sunday must take priority over other things. The author of the book of Hebrews makes this very clear. He says « Let us not give up meeting together, as some are in the habit of doing, but let us encourage one another - and all the more as you see the Day approaching. » (Hebrews 10:25)

The Hebrew word for worship most often used in the Bible is *proskuneo* which means to make obeisance or do reverence to. The word is derived from the word to kiss! It means that in worshipping God we come to greet him with a kiss! Adoration as well as homage and respect for God is central in our worship. David and the other

writers of the Psalms expressed their worship in terms of adoration « I love you, O Lord my strength. The Lord is my rock; my fortress and my deliverer: my God is my rock, in whom I take refuge » (Psalm18:1-2). The Jews sang Psalms during their worship. At the great Jewish festivals, for example, Passover, Harvest and the Feast of Tabernacles, they sang Psalms as they went up to the Temple. Each of (Psalms 120-134) is called a song of Ascent. For many centuries the chanting of Psalms was normal in Christian Worship. Today many Hymns and worship songs echo the Psalms! The early church also used « Spiritual Songs » in their worship. « Let the word of God dwell in you richly as you teach and admonish one another with all wisdom, and as you sing psalms, hymns, and spiritual songs with gratitude in your hearts to God. » (Colossians 3:16) The word is always at the centre of worship whether it be sung, read, or taught. This word is inspired by the Holy Spirit. Paul writes « be filled with the Spirit . Speak to one another with psalms, hymns, and spiritual songs; Sing and make music in your heart to the Lord, always giving thanks to God the Father for everything in the name of our Lord Jesus Christ. »
(Ephesians 5:19)

There are several quotations used in the New Testament that may have had their origin as a spiritual song or hymn. For example
    « Who being in very nature God,
    did not consider equality with God something to be grasped,
    but made himself nothing, taking the very nature of a servant,
    being made in human likeness;
    And being found in appearance as a man, he humbled himself
    and became obedient to death - even death on the cross!
    Therefore God exalted him to the highest place
    and gave him the name that is above every name,
    that at the name of Jesus every knee should bow,
    in heaven and on earth and under the earth,
    and every tongue confess that Jesus Christ is Lord,
    to the glory of God the Father » (Philippians 2:6-11)

These words have been adapted for the more modern hymn « At the

name of Jesus every knee shall bow » (author Caroline Marie Noel)
Another possible example is found in Ephesians
    « Wake up, O sleeper, rise from the dead,
    and Christ will shine on you. » (Ephesians 5:14)

The modern song « Shine Jesus shine » by Graham Kendrick echoes these words.

The early church may have used these words in Paul's letter to Timothy as an inspirational missionary hymn.
    « He appeared in a body, was vindicated by the Spirit,
    was seen by angels was preached among the nations,
    was believed on in the world, was taken up in glory »
    (1 Timothy 3:16)

Each of these quotations of possible hymns or spiritual songs emphasizes the reality of the incarnation, the humanity of Jesus. He really did come among us. They emphasize his divinity, his resurrection and ascension and his reign in glory. Worship should reflect both the humanity and the divinity of Christ.

In the book of Revelation we find that John shows us a series of pictures that do not always seem to follow in logical order. John had been put in prison on the Isle of Patmos by the Romans, because of his faith in Christ, consequently he was writing in a way that Christians could understand but not his Roman captors, so much of his language is metaphorical. His vision was the result of looking beyond this life to the life of the world to come. It was as though a curtain or veil had been removed so that he glimpsed what was happening in heaven. We see pictures of the failure of the Churches on earth, the battle between good and evil, the final destiny of the saints and finally all creation worshipping God. We have a picture of the Lord God Almighty and His holiness. « Whenever the living creatures give glory, honour and thanks to him who sits on the throne and who lives for ever and ever, the twenty four elders fall down before him who sits on the throne, and worship him who lives for ever and ever. They lay their crowns before the throne and say:

    You are worthy, our Lord and God
    To receive glory and honour and power,
    for you created all things,
    and by you they were created and have their being. »
    (Revelation 4:9-11)

This glimpse of worship in heaven helps us to understand the greatness of the God we are worshipping. In our mundane earthly setting we often forget that He is Holy and lives for ever and ever and is worthy of receiving our worship! He has created all things and beside him our little crowns of achievement are insignificant. We are lost in wonder, love and praise when we consider His greatness. Whatever form our worship may take, whatever aids we use, may God and Jesus be at the very centre and may we penetrate the veil that separates heaven and earth.

The clearest picture we have of the Church at worship in new Testament times is in Paul's letter to the Corinthians where he writes to correct the faults in their worship and deals with their problems. We must take into account that this Christian church was composed mainly of Gentiles who were probably sailors, dock workers, and people with moral standards that were unacceptable to the Jews! The Holy Spirit was much in evidence but so also were the works of the flesh! Reading between the lines it seems as though their worship services had become chaotic!
Paul reminds them of :

1. The need for order
Paul has already rebuked the Church for the way it was behaving during the celebration of the Lord's Supper (1 Corinthians 11) Now in their meeting for worship there is a similar disorder. Individuals are going ahead with their own personal preferences instead of being sensitive to the needs of others. They had a spiritual gift and they were going to exercise it whether the Spirit was leading them or not!

2. The need for participation

Paul envisages all members of the church bringing a distinctive contribution to the worship. A hymn, a lesson, a tongue or an interpretation. (1 Corinthians14:26) This contribution should be for the good of all, for the edification of the Church, not for one's own personal gain and glory.

3. The need for control.

Having made it clear that the public speaking in tongues should be accompanied by interpretation Paul limits the number of times tongues/interpretation should be used in the meeting. Speaking in tongues and prophecy are not uncontrollable phenomenon!
(1 Corinthians14:27)

4. The need for Leadership and consistency

Always there should be a person presiding over the Church's worship, things are to be done in an orderly manner, someone has to take charge and prophecy has to be tested. He reiterates that everyone can be used in worship « you can all prophesy in turn so that everyone may be instructed and encouraged » (1 Corinthians 14: 31) We limit the Holy Spirit when we always expect certain gifts only from certain people!

5. The need for prophecy to be tested.

Weighing up the authenticity of the prophesy is the responsibility of the whole Church (1 Thessalonians 5:21) (1 John 4:1-6). There have always been false prophets. Many instances are quoted in the Old Testament especially in the book of Jeremiah. There are people of our generation whose prophecies appear not to be genuine. Prophecies must be tested, it is easy to get carried away on the spur of the moment and play into Satan's hands!

The time of ministry in the context of worship is important for the spiritual growth of the individual believer and the edification of the Church.
It is a time when burdens can be laid at the foot of the cross and sins confessed and forgiven. This ministry in the Spirit is often

accompanied by tears or laughter. Occasionally a person may sink to their knees or rest in the spirit stretched out on the floor. Sometimes onlookers are concerned about the person who has been « Slain in the Spirit ». In most cases their fears are ungrounded. Throughout the history of the Christian church such phenomena has been observed when the Holy Spirit is at work in a gathering of believers! During times of ministry many people have received deliverance from demonic oppression or possession. This again might result in people crying out, shaking or falling prostrate to the floor. When physical phenomena accompany the working of the Holy Spirit, the new believer observing this should not be afraid or surprised but continue praying and praising God. The time of ministry is an opportunity for people to respond to the preaching of the gospel and give their hearts to the Lord. It important that those who are part of the ministry team are able to lead those who have responded to the Lord. Many who come for prayer have specific problems or lack assurance. It is important that at all times confidentiality is maintained, much harm has been done by gossip in the Church! This time of responding to the preaching of the word is often a time when a person rededicates his/her life to the Lord, offering to serve Christ both in the Church and the world. In a living Church, times of ministry are an essential part of the worship, this often includes the laying on of hands and anointing with oil.

In the New Testament we find the ministry of the Laying on of hands for five reasons.

1. Healing the sick
Jesus imparted healing by the Laying on of Hands. (Luke 4 vs. 40, 13 : 13) and so believers are encouraged to impart healing by the Laying on of Hands.(Mark 16: 17) (Acts 9 :17) (Acts 28 :8-9)
Elders are to anoint with oil (by their hands) and pray for healing. (James 5 : 14 -16)

2. To impart Blessing
Jesus imparted the blessing of God to children (Matthew 19 :13-

15)(Mark 10 :13-16) Jesus put his hands on John and said « Do not be afraid. » (Revelation 1 :17)

3. To impart the Baptism of the Holy Spirit
Believers in general, as well as leaders, were involved in imparting the baptism of the Holy Spirit by the laying on of hands.(Acts 8 : 14-24) (Acts 9 :10-17) (Acts 19 : 6)

4.To impart Spiritual Gifts (1 Timothy 4 : 14) (2 Timothy 1 : 6) (Romans 1 : 11) To those who have the «Call of God » on their lives to enable them to fulfill that call. (Acts 13 : 1-3)

5. To set people apart for a specific work
Established workers for the Lord are set apart for specific work by the laying on of hands. (Acts 13 : 2-3) The commissioning of Deacons also involved the laying on of hands by the leadership (Acts 6:1-6) Worship is the natural context in which to receive this ministry.

6 Anointing with oil
In some traditions (Roman Catholic) believers are anointed with oil during the hours preceding their death. James instructs the elders or leaders of the Church to anoint the sick with oil for healing in the name of the Lord. (James 5:14-15)

Christians worship their risen Lord in the power of the Spirit each week on the Lord's day. In the worship service there will normally be times of praise and thanksgiving, of reading the word and preaching. There will be praying together including adoration and thanksgiving, as well as intercession for our own needs and the needs of others We will also find the exercising of the gifts of the Holy Spirit and times for response and for ministry.

 « Celebration of the Lord's supper » Jesus celebrated the Jewish Passover with his twelve disciples during the evening before he was arrested. This has been called « The Last Supper » The Passover meal was a feast instituted by God to commemorate the deliverance of Israel from Egypt. (Exodus 12). Jesus desired to eat this meal with his disciples before he was crucified. We read in Mark's gospel that « while they were eating, Jesus took bread, gave thanks and broke it, and gave it to his disciples saying, **« Take it; this is my body »** Then he took the cup, gave thanks and offered it to them, and they all drank from it. **« This is my blood of the covenant, which is poured out for many »** (Mark 14 :22-24) Jesus by using bread as a symbol of his body, which would be crucified, and wine as a symbol of his blood, which would be shed at the crucifixion, gave new meaning to the Passover meal. Just as the Israelites were delivered from slavery in Egypt, so those who believe in Jesus will be delivered from the slavery of sin. Three of the gospels give accounts of the « Lord's Supper » (Matthew 26:26-28 Mark 14:22-24 Luke 22:17-20) John's gospel seems to imply that the « Farewell Discourses and foot washing » were a part of that same evening. (John 13-17) The celebration of the Lord's Supper was a regular part of Christian worship in the early Church. (Acts 2:42,46 Acts 20:7) Paul used the framework of the Jewish Passover to interpret the Lord's supper in his letter to the Corinthian Church and to correct some of its failings. He warns them about compromise. (1 Corinthians 10:14-22) He writes « The sacrifices of pagans are offered to demons not to God, and I do not want you to be participants with demons. You cannot drink the cup of the Lord and the cup of demons too; you cannot have a part in both the Lord's table and the table of demons » (1 Corinthians 10:20-21) We are to take the celebration of the Lord's Supper very seriously indeed! « A man ought to examine himself before he eats of the bread or drinks of the cup. For anyone who eats and drinks without recognizing the body of the Lord eats and drinks judgement on himself » (1 Corinthians 11:28-29)

THREE THINGS ARE EVIDENT FROM PAUL'S TEACHING

1. The Lord's supper is exclusively for those who believe that Jesus is Lord. In the early church the preaching of the word was to all and sundry. At the commencement of sharing the bread and the

wine all unbelievers were asked to leave! Today different churches have different rules. Some offer the bread and the wine, only to those who have been baptised and confirmed, others to those who have been baptised as adults. Some churches insist on church membership while others offer the bread and wine to all who love the Lord Jesus as Lord and Saviour.

2. Those who participate in the Lord's Supper must prepare themselves by spiritual examination, confessing their sins and asking for forgiveness. Those who do not do this Paul warns will be weak or even dead spiritually. (1 Corinthians 11:30) Some Churches meet for this very purpose on Saturday evening before they participate in the Lord's supper on the following day.

3. The Christian should not neglect the Lord's Supper
We receive a special blessing when we remember our Lord, his sacrifice on the cross, and the means of our salvation.

There has been more debate and differing views over this subject than any other Christian doctrine. Today it divides the Christian Churches so that unity becomes impossible. Those of the Catholic tradition use the term mass, others use Holy Communion or the Eucharist. The reformed tradition speak of the Lord's Supper and Breaking of Bread. All these different titles originate from the same event. In the medieval church, there was a great emphasis on mystery. There was much controversy as to what was taking place when believers took the bread and wine together. Some believed that the bread and wine changed in substance after the prayer of consecration offered by the priest. We call this transubstantiation. The bread became the body of Christ and the wine his blood. This was known as the real presence, or Eucharistic presence. It was named the feast of Corpus Christie. The sacrifice of Christ's body was emphasised. At the time of the reformation these beliefs were challenged. One of the reformers, Zwingli, maintained that the Lord's Supper was a memorial rite and no change took place in the elements whatsoever! For the most part the Protestant churches have taken this view that the Lord's Supper is a time of remembering the sacrifice on the cross and of giving thanks for our salvation. We do this in remembrance of Jesus. It is a means of receiving grace and blessing.

The power of remembering is very great. When we recall special events we recreate them in our imagination. Our memory brings them alive, making them seem that the event occurred a very short time ago! The Passover meal is a meal of deliverance commemorating the exodus from Egypt. When it is celebrated in a Jewish family they enter into it as if taking part in the event itself. At that last meal Jesus was urging his twelve disciples not just to remember Him but to enter into his crucifixion and receive the benefits of it. The believer today when he/she participates in the Lord's Supper shares in what God has done and brings the event into the present.

The Lord's Supper is a meal of thanksgiving. It is a time of giving thanks to God for what he has done by sending Jesus so that we might be reconciled to Him and receive the gift of everlasting life. The word Eucharist means thanksgiving. The Lord' Supper as we have seen is a time of remembering. We remember the sacrifice of our Lord on the cross and His suffering. The Lord's Supper as a reinterpretation of the Jewish Passover is a memory aid that helps us to be delivered from the slavery of sin. The Lord's Supper is a time when we meet with the Lord. You might find the words of the Hymn by Horatius Bonar helpful -

> « Here O my Lord, I see Thee face to face:
> Here would I touch and handle things unseen;
> Here grasp with firmer hand the eternal grace,
> And all my weariness upon Thee lean.
>
> Here would I feed upon the bread of God;
> Here drink with Thee the royal wine of heaven;
> Here would I lay aside each earthly load,
> Here taste afresh the calm of sin forgiven.

This is the hour of banquet and of song;
This is the heavenly table spread for me;
Here let me feast, and, feasting, still prolong
The hallowed hour of fellowship with Thee.

When Christians celebrate the Lord's Supper they look backwards to a past event, they experience a present reality, and look forward with expectation to the coming of the fullness of God's Kingdom symbolised by the wedding supper of the Lamb! (Revelation 19:9)

When we take the bread and eat it we feed on Jesus the living bread. We recognise afresh that **He is living in us by the power of the Holy Spirit**. When we drink the wine, symbolising his blood, **we are assured that all our sins have been forgiven**. We know that it is by the shedding of the blood of Jesus that Satan is defeated and we have the victory. There is power in this blood, and many have received healing as they have taken the cup and drunk from it.

Sunday worship for all believers is the climax of their week. The Lord's day is a special time of celebration of our faith. It is an opportunity to engage in worship with fellow believers. It is true that we can worship the Lord in private and should do, but the fellowship around the risen Lord with our brothers and sisters in Christ is unique.

Worship is an essential part of a Christian's daily quiet time. It is good to praise the Lord with our voices. There are many Christian worship CD's that can help us with praise and adoration as we worship the Lord with the help of the Holy Spirit in our daily lives.

Chapter 14 - Knowing and Reading Your Bible

At the time of writing this chapter it is St Valentine's day! Young people in particular wait with expectant hearts for the arrival of the postman, will an envelope drop through the letter box? Perhaps the card will be from an anonymous secret love, or a token of a longstanding love. All of us joyfully receive a love letter from someone we love. It reassures us that we are loved, giving us strength for the present and hope for the future. There is joy when we think about a long term life changing relationship with someone we love and who loves us. The Bible itself is like a love letter, to the believer, from God! It enables him/her to enter into a living relationship with Him. This relationship is based not on fear but love. « God so loved the world that He gave His one and only Son that whoever believes in him shall not perish but have eternal life. » (John 3:16) The Bible reveals what is on God's heart and his love for every person he has created. Jesus showed us what God the Father is really like. There is a story about the great Biblical scholar and theologian Karl Barth. One day he was asked, by one of his students « With all your study of Theology, what is the greatest discovery you have made? » The great man answered with the first line of a children's Hymn « Jesus loves me, this I know because the Bible tells me so ».

God communicates with us through the Bible. We read that « In the past God spoke to our forefathers through the prophets many times and in various ways, but in these last days he has spoken to us by his Son, whom he appointed heir of all things, and through whom he made the universe. The Son is the radiance of God's glory and the exact representation of his being, sustaining all things by his powerful word. » (Hebrews 1:1-3) The Bible contains the history of his people Israel, the words that the prophets spoke and more importantly a historical record of the life and teaching of Jesus.

God still speaks to us today through the Bible and our part is to listen. When we read a letter from the one who loves us our heart beats with excitement, and expectation, in the same way when we pick up the Bible, the word of God, we wait with expectation for what God wants to say to us. We might use the words of a hymn by Francis Ridley Havergal as a prayer before we open our Bible to read what it has to say.

« Master speak! Thy servant heareth
Waiting for Thy gracious word
Longing for the voice that cheereth
Master let it now be heard.
I am listening, Lord for Thee,
What hast Thou to say to me? »

Year after year the Bible maintains it's place as the best selling book in the world. It is estimated that 50 million copies are sold every year! Some are given as presents at a Christening or dedication of a baby, at weddings, or when people enter the Church through baptism or confirmation. Many are bought by churches for use in the service and others by those who just want to read God's word. All versions sell well whether it be the King James version of 1611 or the The Good News Bible in modern English. Besides being a best seller it is unique. It was written over a period of 1500 years by 40 or more authors and reflects the writer's experience of God and His dealings with humankind. The authors come from many different walks of life, Kings, scholars and philosophers, rulers and thinkers, on the one hand and fishermen, farmers, and tax gatherers on the other. The Bible contains different types of literature. There is history that has been described as His story, showing how God has been with His people from the creation of the world. Personal history and world events are recorded within its pages. The Bible contains songs of praise, poetry, prophecy and apocalyptic literature (describing great and dramatic events to come like the new heavens and the new earth), there are proverbs, (wise sayings) and letters to individuals and to Churches. Above all it is the word of God written by human beings, inspired by the Holy Spirit.

I want you to imagine a scene. You are walking along the promenade of a popular holiday resort. There are about six or seven people near a middle aged man who is dancing around a coat covering an object on the ground. He keeps shouting « It's alive, it's alive, it's alive! » Very soon a small crowd of people gather curious to see what it is that is alive under the coat. He bends down and carefully picks up his coat to reveal a book and then he proclaims in a loud voice "It's the living word of God! , the Bible." He opens the book, and begins to talk about Jesus. That was how my colleague began to proclaim to the visitors on Southport sea-front the truth about Jesus. The Bible is indeed the living word of God inspired by the Holy Spirit. Paul makes this very clear to his young prodigy Timothy, he writes "All Scripture is God-breathed and is useful for teaching, rebuking, correcting and training in righteousness, so that the man of God may be thoroughly equipped for every good work" (2 Timothy 3:16) God has breathed His life into it! As we read it, not only does he speak to us through it but He himself breathes his life into us. How important it is to realise that this book is different from any other.

The Bible has the power to change a person's life. A famous sportsman who was going through a particularly low period in his life was alone in a hotel bedroom with nothing particular to do, seeing a Gideon Bible in his bedside locker he picked it up and began to read. Very soon he became totally absorbed and experienced a strange power at work in his life. Through that incident he accepted Christ as his Saviour and became a Christian. The Gideon society, made up of Christian business men, place Bibles in hotels, schools and colleges. They quietly continue this valuable work and we will not know the full extent of the fruit of their labours until we all get to heaven! I believe that their ministry has been very fruitful indeed. Did you know that the actor David Suchet, known by many for his role of Poirot the Belgian detective in the televised stories by Agatha Christie, underwent a similar experience in a hotel room in America. He was lying in the bath when he had an inexplicable desire to read the Bible. In the hotel room there was a Gideon Bible and he began to read it. He said

" From somewhere I got this desire to read the Bible again. That's the most important part of my conversion. I started with the Acts of the Apostles and then moved on to Paul's letters. It was only after wards that I came to the gospels. In the New Testament I suddenly discovered the way that life should be followed."

Today there are many translations of the Bible. It is good to get advice from your Pastor, church leaders or Elder before buying your own personal copy. There are two reasons for this. The first and more important reason is that you purchase a version of the Bible that has been accurately translated and the text has not been interfered with by those who are members of a sect! (The New world version used by Jehovah's witnesses is one to be avoided!) The second reason is to make sure you buy a version you can understand! The Bible is not to adorn a book shelf, but is to be read daily if possible. The Bible is the Christian's constant handbook and companion..

Can we trust the authenticity of the bible is a question that many people rightly ask? The word canon is used with regard to old and new testament writings. The word means rule or standard. In practice the forming of the « Canon » consisted of collecting together ancient texts that could be accepted as inspired by God. It was the selecting of those writings and texts that were deemed to be reliable and inspired and rejecting those that were thought to be unreliable, spurious or slanted towards some particular sect. The Hebrew Bible - the one used by the Jewish people, consisted of 3 sections or canons. The first part was the five books of the law, Genesis, Exodus, Leviticus, Numbers and Deuteronomy. The second was the prophets which includes the former prophets, Isaiah, Jeremiah, Lamentations, the latter prophets, Ezekiel and Daniel and minor prophets Hosea, Joel, Amos, Obadiah, Jonah, Micah, Nahum, Habakkuk, Zephaniah, Haggai, Zechariah, and Malachi. The third was the writings consisting of the150 Psalms, poetry, Job, Proverbs, Ecclesiastes and Song of Songs. This section also contained the twelve books of history.- Joshua, Judges, Ruth, 1 Samuel, 2 Samuel, 1 Kings, 2 Kings, 1 Chronicles, 2 Chronicles,

Ezra, Nehemiah, and Esther. The Christian Bible contains the Hebrew Bible with the books arranged in a slightly different order, and the canon of the New Testament, a collection of early Christian writings recognized by the Church as the accurate and authoritative expression of the apostolic faith. Writings such as the « Gospel of Thomas » « The Gospel according to Phillip » « The acts of Barnabas » and many more were rejected because they were tainted by early Christian heresies.

One of the marks of conversion is a hunger and avid desire to read and know the Bible. This hunger is a work of the Holy Spirit, new converts have been known to read the whole of the New Testament in two days. Non Christians may have started to read the bible but given up after a few pages. Sadly many new Christians start off with a hunger to read the word of God but after a short time that hunger diminishes! It is the Holy Spirit that makes all the difference. There are those who claim to be Christians in our churches who don't read the Bible from one week's end to the next. I recall a time when I was asked to help a Church, by leading their leader's meeting. I suggested that we started with a Bible Study. One of those present produced some Bibles. I announced that we would look together at John chapter three. To my utter amazement one of the members of the meeting asked another where to find John's gospel. Was it in the old or the New Testament? At first I thought he was joking but as he searched for the passage it soon became apparent that he had very little knowledge of the Bible and he was one of the leaders! Amos prophesied «The days are coming declares the Sovereign Lord when I will send a famine through the land - not a famine of food or a thirst for water but a famine of hearing the words of the Lord » (Amos 8:11)

We can think of the bible as bread. Jesus himself declared that he was « The Bread of Life » and that « He who comes to me will never go hungry » (John 6:35) We discover this bread of life as we read the Bible. All of us depend on food, bread to eat and water to drink. Without them we would soon perish. Similarly we need to feed regularly on the word of God. Smith Wigglesworth, was a well known Pentecostal preacher and evangelist. He came from humble origins and his wife, Polly taught him to read using the Bible. This was in fact the only book he ever read and his habit was to read a portion of it at every meal time! No meal was complete for him without spiritual food. The Bible is also described as « Spiritual milk ». New converts like new born babies need feeding. Peter advises them «Like newborn babies, crave pure spiritual milk, so that by it you may grow up in your salvation, now that you have tasted that the Lord is good » (1 Peter 2:2). The desperate cry of a hungry baby, will not stop until the child is fed! The desire for more and more of the Lord is a hallmark of conversion and that hunger is satisfied by our « feeding » on the word of God..

Jesus compared the preaching of the word of God with scattering seeds. The parable of the sower describes the different responses made by different people to hearing it. (Matthew 13:1-23) Peter reminds new converts, maybe at the time of their baptism that they « have been born again, not of perishable seed, but of imperishable, through the living and enduring word of God » (1 Peter 1:23) A seed is sown in the ground but it is months later that the crop is harvested. Often people hear the word of God, retain it in their memories and respond at a later date. The Bible is described as being like a light to guide us in the dark. «Your word is a lamp to my feet and a light for my path » (Psalm 119: 105) God's word guides us and shows us the next step to take in our life with Jesus. God may not reveal to us the distant future but he will lead us by his word to take the decisions that concern us in the present. There have been many instances of people randomly opening the Bible to receive guidance. Gladys Aylewood opened her Bible at random and received confirmation that God was calling her to go to China as an missionary for Christ! God more often guides as we consistently read the Bible by making certain texts, stories or passages stand out. It is as if the Lord takes a marker pen (His spirit) to show us personally what is His will for us. There are other words used to describe God's word such as a mirror (James 1:23-24) A mirror shows us how we appear to others whereas the Bible reveals to us what we are truly like before God. The word of God is described as being like a fire and hammer. (Jeremiah 23:29) The fire speaks to us of purity and the hammer breaks up hearts which are rock hard.

Paul describes the word of God as being like a sword « Take the helmet of salvation and the sword of the Spirit, which is the word of God » (Ephesians 6:17) The context implies that the sword, the word of God, is essential in combating the devil! We have seen how Jesus used the words of scripture to put Satan to flight. A sword can be used both to defend oneself or to attack another. The book of Hebrews speaks of a two edged sword; « For the word of God is living and active; Sharper than any double-edged sword, it penetrates even to dividing soul and spirit, joints and marrow, it judges the thoughts and attitudes of the heart. Nothing in all creation is hidden from God's sight. Everything is uncovered and laid bare before the eyes of him to whom we must give account » (Hebrews 4:12-13) It cuts through all our defences, excuses and posturing to reveal the truth. It is plain that God has provided a standard for our lives. When we fall short we come under judgement. Nothing in our lives is hidden from God. There is a game we used to play in bible club called 'sword drill' which involves competing to find a text in the bible. Each child holds a New Testament by his/her side.(The sword is in it's sheath.) The leader gives the command « un-sheath your sword! » and then calls out a text for example John 3:16 . The first person to find the text scores a point. The whole game is to help everyone find their way around the New Testament!

Two non biblical descriptions of the Bible are a « manual » and « manifesto ». When we buy a new car or a kitchen appliance it is always accompanied by a manual. This helps us to get the best out of our purchases. It explains where everything can be found and how it should function. The Bible has often been described as a manual for living! Its pages help us to get the best out of our life on earth. Just as we refer to the manual given with a car for information when we have a problem, we can turn to the bible to find the answer when we need help with a life problem. The word manifesto means « a declaration of policy » The Bible reveals to the believer the policy of the Kingdom of God. This is a public declaration of life in the Kingdom of God that is for all people. The Bible is the supreme authority for what we believe and how we act, instructions for living!

Most of us lead busy lives and experience time pressures of one sort or another, but it is important to set aside a specific time every day to pray and read the Bible. This time must become part of the structure of your life whether it be morning, mid-day, or evening. The length of time will vary with the individual but discipline and determination will be needed. Turn off your telephone, unless you are waiting for a very important call. Then ask God to speak to you through His word. It is better to begin by reading Mark or John's gospel than Genesis! Read slowly and prayerfully. It maybe that you start with just a few verses daily and as you become more familiar a chapter each day. To begin with it is better to read one chapter five times than, five chapters one after another. Ask yourself what the passage you are reading means in the context of when it was first written, and then how does it apply to me today? Is there any action I need to take? Is it relevant to my situation and what is the Lord saying to me? Remember always that the Bible is the living word of God. It speaks both to our hearts and minds. D.L. Moody said « The Bible was not given to increase our knowledge. It was given to change our lives!» .

After beginning with a New Testament gospel, read some of the Psalms found in the Old Testament. Many of them were written by David the shepherd boy who became Israel's greatest King. The Psalms reflect strongly how human beings react to their life circumstances, and how God has acted in their situations. The Psalms contain many songs of praise and prayers with which we can identify. Through the ages countless believers have turned to the Psalms to receive understanding and comfort. The 23rd Psalm is a particular favourite of many because it assures us that God is like a shepherd who cares and looks after us. He promises to be with us always. Many have found this Psalm particularly helpful when a loved one has died. Psalm 121 reassures the believer that God is close by and ready to come and help those who call upon His name. The Psalmist writes « The Lord watches over you » vs3 « The Lord will keep you from all harm - He will watch over your life; the Lord will watch over your coming and going both now and for evermore. » vs7-8. Many Psalms for example 136 help us to verbalise our thanks to God for the all the blessings he has given us. It speaks of God's greatness and His love. It tells how God has rescued His people and each verse is accompanied by the refrain « His love endures for ever ». Psalm 150 helps us to praise God with our whole being. « Praise God in his sanctuary » « Praise Him for his acts of power; praise him for his surpassing greatness » Praise God with all kinds of musical instruments, with dancing and singing! « Let everything that has breath praise the Lord » vs6. Some Bibles contain a list of selected passages to use in times of difficulties, many of these are from the Psalms.

There are many Bible reading aids. A good Bible dictionary and a concordance is a wise investment. A Bible concordance helps us to identify where certain texts may be found and a good Bible dictionary help us to understand their meaning. As we mature in the faith we may want to deepen our understanding of passages of scripture a good Bible Commentary will help with this. Consult your Minister, Pastor or a mature believer for advice on which one to buy. Many are helped in their daily reading by using Bible notes. The Scripture Union in the UK produces « Daily Bread ». The crusade for world revival produce « Every day with Jesus » both are particularly helpful. There are notes produced for adolescent Christians by the « Navigators ». There are many Bibles that are simplified for children or adapted for young people. I have fond memories of a book of bible stories I had as a child. It is essential as we become mature Christians to know what is in the Bible. We need to read the New Testament from Matthew's gospel to the book of Revelation. This can be done in a few days or a few months. There are reading plans available that will enable you to read the Bible in a year. Do not forget to pray before you read and to ask the Holy Spirit to help you understand what is written and apply it to your situation.

There are different ways in which the Bible can be studied. When reading a Gospel story for example, our imagination can help us enter into a situation with Jesus. We can identify with the people he helped or with one of the disciples. In our imagination we can be with the disciples when a sudden storm threatened to sink the boat in which Jesus was sleeping! As we apply these situations to our own lives we can call upon Jesus to still our storms and chase away our fears. Another way to read the Bible is to study it thematically using a « Thompson Chain Reference Bible », it is good to trace a certain subject such as the « Love of God » or « Salvation » from Genesis to Revelation. There are many promises that we can claim, when we are familiar with God's word. Promises such as « In all things God works for good of those who love him, who have been called according to his purpose » (Romans 8:28) or « Never will I leave you; never will I forsake you » (Hebrews 13:5) When we have sinned and are overcome by guilt we can claim the promise « If anyone does sin we have one who speaks to the Father in our defence -Jesus Christ, the Righteous One. He is the atoning sacrifice for our sins, and not only for ours but for the sins of the whole world » (1 John 2:1-2) When we are afraid we can stand on the promise « perfect love drives out fear » (1 John 4:18) or when we feel the pull of the world trying to destroy our faith « Everyone born of God overcomes the world » (1 John 5:4). As we make these promises our own we will begin to realise their truth. In the Bible we will discover words of wisdom and guidance, poems and prophecies that will enrich the soul.

When a Christian becomes more familiar with the Bible he will remember certain texts, stories or teaching that are particularly relevant. It is good to commit to memory texts and whole passages of the Bible. When I was a child I was made to learn by heart the ten commandments, the 23rd Psalm, Paul's passage on love 1 Corinthians 13 and the way to the Father in John 14. These have never left me, they are part of my life. Proclaiming texts out loud in certain situations helps combat the devil. Just as Jesus dealt with the devil using words of scripture so can we. Jesus gave to his disciples the authority to deal with Satan. « I saw Satan fall like lightening from heaven. I have given you authority to trample on snakes and scorpions and to overcome all the power of the enemy: nothing will harm you » (Luke 10:18-19) We proclaim the victory over Satan « We overcome all the power of the enemy » by quoting the Bible at him. Jesus also gave his disciples authority by proclaiming the word of God to « bind and to loose ». « Whatever you bind on earth will be bound in heaven, and whatever you loose on earth will be loosed in heaven » (Matthew 16 :19) Memorised scripture is particularly important in spiritual warfare. The word of God is the Christian's sword without it he/she is defenceless!

I was sent an e-mail last week from a friend it said
« Ever wonder what would happen if we treated our Bible like we treat our mobile phone?

What if we treated it like we could not live without it?
What if we gave it to Kids as gifts?
What if we used it when we travelled?
What if we used it in case of emergency?
This is something to make you go ...hmm...where is my Bible?
Oh and one more thing.
Unlike our cell phone, (mobile) we don't have to worry about our Bible being disconnected because Jesus has already paid the bill.
Makes you think « where are my priorities?»

Chapter 15 - How Do Christians Pray?

The first instinct of a new born baby is to cry. It is by crying that he takes his first breath in this world and begins to live as an individual human being! The first instinct of a newborn Christian is to pray. It is as natural as breathing and is the way that our new life in Christ is established and maintained. Prayer is connecting with God, the God and Father of our Lord Jesus Christ. Many of the world's religions engage in prayer but Christian prayer is different. Our relationship with God through the sacrifice of Jesus on the cross grows deeper as we pray. The Christian prays in the name of his Saviour Jesus! The Christian who neglects prayer is committing spiritual suicide! If you can imagine yourself living on your own in lodgings. There is no communication, meals are eaten in silence, no family life, no warmth and affection one feels completely alone in a hostile world. The person without prayer is like that solitary person! Jesus revealed that God was like a Father. He is the mighty creator and controller of the Universe, the one who flung the stars into space, and yet he is tender, concerned and compassionate-the perfect father. He is waiting to hear our cry, and anxious to supply our needs. His blessing towards us is only limited by our willingness to ask and receive from Him.

How then should the new Christian pray? The disciples of Jesus came to Jesus with a similar question. We read that «One day Jesus was praying in a certain place. When he had finished, one of his disciples said to him 'Lord teach us to pray just as John taught his disciples.' » (Luke 11:1) Jesus replied with these words which we call the Lord's Prayer: a model prayer for the Christian rather than a form of words to be repeated endlessly.

« Father, may your Holy Name be honoured » vs. 2 We are to address God as Father, but also to recognize His greatness, and his holiness.

« May your Kingdom come » vs.2   We recognise that we have been born again into the Kingdom of God but the rule and reign of God is yet to come. We pray that the Kingdom will come in all its fullness and that King Jesus will return soon! The Christian is engaged in promoting God's Kingdom by his words and his life style. We want to see the Kingdom of God come and his rule begin in the hearts and lives of all people.

«Give us each day our daily bread » vs. 3. In the west because of an abundance of food many Christians have spiritualised this petition! We are not as directly affected by the failure of the harvest through drought, famine, and wars as are people in the third world! Nevertheless it is right to pray for God's provision and to thank Him for all he has provided. It is good to pray before a meal. We note that before Jesus ate a meal he gave thanks to God. « When he was at the table with them, he took bread, gave thanks, broke it and began to give it to them » (Luke 24:30). Having enough food to eat is vital for every human being. If this petition in the prayer reminds us to seek spiritual food, 'the word of God' that is also good. Many Christians have lived by faith and relied entirely on God's provision. It is true where God guides He provides, He does not let his servants down. I am personally grateful to God for his provision in my life. That provision was particularly noticeable when I was training for the ministry.(I would emphasise here that the Lord will meet our **needs** but not necessarily satisfy our acquisitive nature!) Paul writes to Timothy « Command those who are rich in this present world not to be arrogant nor to put their hope in wealth, which is so uncertain, but to put their hope in God, who richly provides us with everything for our enjoyment. » (I Timothy 6:17) God loves us and knows our needs.

«Forgive us our sins, for we also forgive everyone who sins against us » vs. vs4 All Christians have received God's forgiveness. His love for each one of us is unconditional. Matthew adds some further words of Jesus « for if you forgive men when they sin against you, your heavenly Father will also forgive you. But if you do not forgive men their sins, your Father will not forgive your sins ». (Matthew 6:14-15) All of us are sinners saved by grace and are in need of God's forgiveness. All of us need to make prayers of confession. As John says in his letter « If we claim to be without sin , we deceive ourselves and the truth is not in us. If we confess our sins, he is faithful and just and will forgive us our sins and purify us from all unrighteousness. » (1 John 1:8-9)

«Lead us not into temptation » vs. 4 There are often times in a Christian's life when temptations are very evident. I myself find it helpful to pray for inner strength at such times. If you are weak willed, ask God to strengthen you so that you will be able to resist the tempter!

«But deliver us from the evil one » (Matthew 6: 13) It is right for us to pray for protection and to claim the benefits of Jesus' victory by his death upon the cross,over the evil one Satan. All true disciples of Jesus are engaged in spiritual warfare . Satan likes Christians who have stopped making any progress because he knows he's winning. In those times when our lives seem to have come to a spiritual standstill, our prayers are not only for protection but for deliverance from the evil one. We pray **in the name of Jesus** using the authority that Jesus has given to us to banish demonic forces that may be oppressing us.

In Mathew's gospel the prayer ends with « deliver us from the evil one »(Matthew 6:13) and then emphasises the importance of forgiving others that we might receive the Father's forgiveness. In later manuscripts, the prayer ends with the affirmation that God's Kingdom has arrived and that his power is available and we are to give Him all the glory.

Christians are to persist in prayer and not give up. Jesus illustrated this by telling two parables. « Suppose one of you has a friend, and he goes to him at midnight and says 'Friend, lend me three loaves of bread, because a friend of mine on a journey has come to me and I have nothing to set before him' Then the one inside answers 'Don't bother me. The door is already locked, and my children are with me in bed. I can't get up and give you anything.' I tell you, though he will not get up and give him the bread because he is his friend, yet because of the man's persistence he will get up and give him as much as he needs. So I say to you: 'Ask and it will be given to you: seek and you will find: knock and the door will be opened to you. For everyone who asks receives; he who seeks finds; and to him who knocks the door will be opened' » (Luke 11:3-13) In the east many people travelled at night to avoid the heat of the sun. In this story the man had arrived towards midnight at his friend's house. Hospitality was a sacred duty, but he had no bread. Normally one only baked enough for the day. As he had none he went to borrow three loaves from a neighbour! The neighbour was reluctant to get up because of the sleeping arrangements! Normally in an ordinary person's house of that period there was one room, with a sleeping area raised about 30 centimetres above the rest of the mud floor. Each night the whole family slept there on reed mats, huddled around the charcoal fire. The lower part of the room would be full of animals as it was the custom to bring inside, hens, cocks, goats , sheep, and dogs! If the man got up to help his friend in order for him to open the door all the children and all the animals would be disturbed. However, everyone would have been awakened by the man's persistent knocking, so eventually the neighbour got up and gave him what he needed! The word in the original Greek for « ask » means « keep on asking! » We are to persevere in our praying. We live in an instant age where if you put a coin in a machine, or press a button, there is an immediate response! In our praying we have to be prepared to keep on praying until we receive God's answer. The second parable Jesus told was to show his disciples that they should always pray and not give up. He tells a story of a widow petitioning for her rights from an unjust judge! (Luke 18:1-8) Her persistence brought its reward! Keep praying do not give up until you receive an answer.

Jesus' teaching on prayer makes it plain that God our Father gives us good gifts. He will not answer our prayers in a way that will harm us! « Which of you fathers, if your son asks for a fish, will give him a snake instead? Or if he asks for an egg will give him a scorpion? If you then, though you are evil, know how to give good gifts to your children, how much more will your Father in heaven give the Holy Spirit to those who ask him! » (Luke 11:11-13). When we pray we are praying to a good God, our heavenly Father, who loves us and will not hurt us! He is not a God who is waiting with a big stick to vent his wrath upon us when we fail and fall into sin. God sent His son to take the punishment for our sins, so that we might be set free from guilt and receive the gift of eternal life. We recognise God's goodness.In Africa when a pastor says to the gathered people 'God is good' they will reply in unison, with one accord 'All the time'.

When we pray to God our Father we must be ourselves! Jesus condemned hypocrisy and self exaltation! He told a parable of two men going to the temple to pray «To some who were confident of their own righteousness and looked down on everybody else, Jesus told this parable: Two men went up to the Temple to pray, one a Pharisee and the other a tax collector. The Pharisee stood up and prayed about himself 'God I thank you that I am not like all other men - robbers, evildoers, adulterers - or like this tax collector; I fast twice a week and give a tenth of all I get.' But the tax collector stood at a distance. He would not even look up to heaven, but beat his breast and said 'God have mercy on me a sinner' I tell you that this man, rather than the other, went home justified before God. For everyone who exalts himself will be humbled, and he who humbles himself will be exalted ». (Luke 18:9-14) This parable helps us to pray without pretending! The Pharisees were a strict religious sect of Judaism, devoting a great deal of time to prayer and fasting! The Pharisee paraded his « good works » saying « What a spiritual person I am! » He had too good an opinion of himself and too bad an opinion of the tax collector. Tax collectors were generally hated by the Jews, because they worked for the Romans and cheated their own people! They were called traitors and sinners. The tax collector recognised his own sinfulness and pleaded with God to have mercy on him. He went home believing that God had heard and answered his prayer. This parable helps us to see that we should approach God with a humble heart, to recognise our weakness and sinfulness, and to ask for God's forgiveness. God loves us and knows all about us and is not deceived by our outward appearance. The word of the Lord to Samuel the prophet when he went to Bethlehem to chose one of the sons of Jesse to be Israel's king was « Man looks on the outward appearance, but the Lord looks at the heart ». (1 Samuel 16 :7)

The new Christian needs not only perseverance but faith. When we pray we believe God hears our prayers and answers them. It does not take much faith to ask God to do something. Many of the prayers in the Bible are specific requests which I believe is an important part of Christian prayer. When my son was a youngster he wanted to try his hand at a fair ground shooting gallery. There was a cowboy scene with lots of targets to aim at. When you hit one of them a door opened, water flowed down a pipe, and music started to play. He watched others hit the targets but when he tried he just sprayed bullets all over the place and nothing happened! It is the same with our prayers. When our requests are specific, things happen, God answers our prayers but when we pray in general often nothing seems to happen. There is the wonderful example of Abraham praying for the people of Sodom. He interceded with God to spare the city. God said « If I find fifty righteous people in the city of Sodom, I will spare the whole place for their sake » Then Abraham spoke up again « Now I have been so bold as to speak to the Lord, though I am nothing but dust and ashes, what if the number of the righteous is five less than fifty people? » 'If I find forty-five there I will not destroy it.' Abraham pleads for Sodom on the basis of the number of righteous people, beginning at fifty people and reducing the number to ten. (Genesis 18) When we make specific requests our faith is tried and tested. James in his letter speaking of praying with faith says « But you must believe when you pray, and not doubt at all. Whoever doubts is like a wave in the sea that is driven and blown about by the wind. Such a person is a hypocrite, undecided in all he does, and he must not think he will receive anything from the Lord.» (James 1:6-7 T.E.V) Jesus prayed specifically and with faith that people might be healed and even raised from the dead. Before Jesus raised Lazarus from the dead, He told them to take away the stone, He looked up and said « Father I thank you that you that you have heard me. I knew that you always hear me, but I said this for the benefit of the people standing here, that they may believe that you sent me » Then he called in a loud voice « Lazarus come out! » The dead man came out, his hands and feet wrapped in strips of linen, and with a cloth around his face. Jesus said « Take off the grave clothes and let him go. » (John 11: 41-44) Nothing is too great or too small to share with our heavenly Father. John Newton writes

> *« Thou art coming to a king*
> *Large petitions with thee bring*
> *For his grace and power are such*
> *None can ever ask too much. »*

There are many different types of prayer. Let us look at the ones normally used by those who are just beginning their walk of faith. There is no set way to pray, it stems from our relationship with God our Father and each of us is free to talk to Him as we wish. Many people have used the word ACTS as a memory aid to give structure to their prayer time. A=Adoration, C = Confession T= Thanksgiving, S=Supplication.

1) Adoration. The Oxford dictionary defines the word adoration as divine worship and to love deeply. Richard Foster in his book on prayer says «Adoration is the spontaneous yearning of the heart , to worship, honour, magnify and bless God »
Prayers of adoration are the most selfless form of prayer. We focus on who God is and his goodness. We love God for Himself, for His very being! I remember being moved the first time I heard the song that asks the question « Do you love Jesus? » and the answer « Yes I love Jesus because he first loved me! » Prayers of adoration often involve singing a song as a spontaneous response to the wonder of God's creation. When I was a minister at a seaside town, I often took an early morning walk along the pebbled beach. As the sun rose and the waves crashed on the deserted shore, my heart would

respond by spontaneously singing and shouting praise to God. When I reflect on what God has done and is doing in my life and in my family I find myself giving thanks and adoration to Him.

2) Confession. When we come to God asking His forgiveness for those things that we know are wrong in our lives, we are making a prayer of confession. As His children we can directly ask our loving Father to forgive us our sins. We need no human confessor because Jesus has died for us, and for the whole world, taking our sins upon Himself. We receive His pardon and we begin again. When we ask for forgiveness we might use the ancient refrain « Kyrie, Eleison, » meaning « Lord have mercy » When we know that we have deliberately sinned and feel ashamed, we may feel we can only pray « Lord have mercy » The next step is to name our sins before God and repent. We acknowledge our lack of faith, our hardheartedness, and tell our heavenly Father what we have done, in thought, word, or deed. The next step is to receive God's forgiveness. Sometimes it helps to gaze upon the symbol of the cross and recognise again God's great love for all who have sinned and have fallen short. Paul writes to the Colossians «When you were dead in your sins and in the uncircumcision of your sinful nature, God made you alive with Christ. He forgave us all our sins, having cancelled the written code with its regulations, that was against us and stood opposed to us; he took it away nailing it to the cross. »(Colossians 2:13-14) It was Corrie ten Boom who used to say that God had taken all our sins and cast them into the depths of the ocean. They are all gone, they are no more! Then she would add « No Fishing » The last step is to obey the Lord. Embedded in the very act of repentance is obedience. We turn our lives around and live for Jesus. We try not to commit the same sins again and again. We need to ask the Holy Spirit to deliver us from habitual sin.

3) Thanksgiving. In our prayers of thanksgiving we give thanks to God for all that he has done for us. We give thanks to God, for our health our family and his provision. We also thank him for the church and our brothers and sisters in Christ .All through the book of Psalms the reader is urged to give thanks to the Lord. Many people take all the good things they have received for granted, the Christian takes those same things with gratitude to God. Sincere thanksgiving must always flow from the heart. Thank Him that He is always with us in every circumstance.

4) Supplication. The dictionary definition of the word is to petition humbly. In this form of prayer we pray for ourselves, for our needs or for guidance. We pray for our Church and all people in need especially the sick. We extend our prayers to friends, family, and those in our community. We pray for people who hold responsibility in our community that they will make wise decisions. Paul writing to the young leader Timothy says « I urge, then, first of all that requests, prayers of intercession and thanksgiving be made for everyone - for kings and all those in authority, that we may live peaceful and quiet lives in all godliness and holiness.» (1 Timothy 2:1-2) Paul urges prayer for those in authority because « God our Saviour wants all men to be saved and come to the knowledge of the truth. » In other words Christians are to pray for favourable conditions for the spread of the gospel.

Two other types of prayer that are important for all believers, are prayers of intercession, and the prayer of relinquishment.
1) Intercession . All Christians are called to be intercessors, someone who pleads on behalf of another. I was once asked to intercede on behalf of the son of a friend with the legal authorities. The son was being charged with conspiracy to murder his wife! There was evidence in the form of a letter to suggest that he was hiring a hit-man to kill her. I interceded on his behalf because husband and wife were now reconciled to one another and the incriminating letter was not a true representation of the facts. The legal authorities took note of my plea and the case against the young man was dropped. In intercessory prayer we pray to God on behalf of others. It is a completely unselfish form of prayer. We give of ourselves because of our love and concern for others. The story of how Israel defeated the Amalekites is a good example of the power of intercessory prayer. « The Amalekites came and attacked the Israelites at Rephidim; Moses said to Joshua 'Choose

some of our men and go out to fight the Amalekites. Tomorrow I will stand on top of the hill with the staff of God in my hands' So Joshua fought the Amalekites as Moses had ordered, and Moses, Aaron, and Hur went to the top of the hill. As long as Moses held up his hands, the Israelites were winning, but whenever he lowered his hands the Amalekites prevailed. When Moses hands grew tired, they took a stone and put it under him and he sat on it. Aaron and Hur held his hands up - one on one side, one on the other - so that his hands remained steady till sunset. So Joshua overcame the Amalakite army with the sword. » (Exodus 17:8-13) Joshua and his army won the physical battle that day, but behind the scenes the spiritual battle was won by Moses, Aaron and Hur. Each role was essential for victory. Joshua fought the battle. Moses was needed to intercede on behalf of the Israelites. Aaron and Hur were needed to assist Moses as he grew tired. When we intercede for others our feeble prayers are reinforced by the eternal intercessor, Jesus Christ. Paul assures us that « Christ Jesus who died - more than that, who was raised to life- is at the right hand of God and is also interceding for us. » (Romans 8:34) We pray in the name of Jesus and our Father hears us and answers our prayers.

2) Relinquishment There are times in our lives when situations arise that we are unable to change and we wonder why God is allowing this to happen to us. A person one loves is seriously ill, or in great pain, and our prayers seem to remain unanswered. Like Jesus in the Garden of Gethsemane we desire things to be different. He did not want to be crucified. « Father, if you are willing, take this cup from me; yet not my will but yours be done » An angel from heaven appeared to him and strengthened him. And being in anguish, he prayed more earnestly, and his sweat was like drops of blood falling to the ground. » (Luke 22:42-44) Jesus God's son despite a great struggle submitted his will, to the Father's will, and was strengthened by angels so was able to endure the agony of the crucifixion. Humanly speaking the whole thing was unjust. The most innocent man who ever lived was unfairly tried, flogged, and sentenced to the most cruel death by crucifixion. The key words of Jesus are « Not my will but yours be done ». The crucifixion was no accident but God's plan to redeem human beings that he had created. That was his intention from the beginning of time. There are times in our lives when it is necessary to give difficult situations that we cannot fully understand to the Lord. To understand that He knows the beginning and the end. We can only see a small part of the picture. We submit our will to the will of the Almighty. We relinquish the situation we face into his nail scarred hands, as we pray in his name, «Thy will be done ».

Every Christian is engaged in spiritual warfare . When we gave our heart to Jesus we enlisted in his army. We are engaged in a battle with the devil and all unrighteousness. Some Christians lose their spiritual fervour and go A.W.O.L (absent without leave) In any form of warfare it is important that we have the right strategic weapons! Christian warfare is no different. Paul in his letter to the Ephesians urges us to put on the armour of God with prayer. « Finally, be strong in the Lord and in his mighty power. Put on the full armour of God so that you can take your stand against the devil's schemes. For our struggle is not against flesh and blood, but against the rulers, against the authorities, against the powers of this dark world and against the spiritual forces of evil in the heavenly realms. Therefore put on the full armour of God, so that when the day of evil comes, you may be able to stand your ground, and after you have done everything to stand. Stand firm then, with the belt of truth buckled around your waist, with the breastplate of righteousness in place, and with your feet fitted with the readiness that comes from the gospel of peace. In addition to all this take up the shield of faith, with which you can extinguish all the flaming arrows of the evil one. Take the helmet of salvation and the sword of the Spirit, which is the word of God. And pray in the Spirit on all occasions with all kinds of prayers and requests. With this in mind, be alert and always keep on praying for all the saints » (Ephesians 6:10-18) The Christian must take his stand against all the devil's schemes. We are engaged in spiritual warfare, but we have God's armour so that we can stand our ground against the enemy. Make sure you put on that armour each day.

We put on the belt of truth. We remember that Jesus is « the way, the truth, and the life » (John 14:6) Jesus reveals the truth about God and true living. Just as a belt holds everything in place so Jesus holds our lives together.

The breastplate of righteousness covers and protects the soldiers heart! Jesus is our righteousness. When he was crucified a great exchange took place. Our sins were nailed to the cross and in exchange Jesus gave us the robe of His righteousness. Clothed in his righteousness as a breastplate we take our stand against all evil.

Our feet are fitted with readiness that comes from the gospel of peace. We are mobile for the Lord walking in his way and treading under foot all evil. When the seventy two disciples returned with joy from their mission saying even the demons submit to us in your name, Jesus replied « I saw Satan fall like lightening from heaven. I have given you authority to trample on snakes and scorpions and to overcome al the power of the enemy; nothing will harm you » (Luke 10: 18) We have that power and authority to tread under foot all the works of the evil one.

We take up the shield of faith so as to quench the flaming arrows of the evil one. The shield was made of thick soft wood and when flaming arrows hit it, the flames were extinguished, as they easily penetrated the soft wood. Our faith is like a shield. When Satan attacks us we know by faith that we have the victory in our Lord Jesus Christ.

The helmet of salvation protects our heads and therefore our minds. We have the assurance of full salvation.

The sword of the Spirit is the word of God. We overcome Satan's wiles by using scripture like a sword that cuts through all his deceit. We use the scriptures in a powerful way when we proclaim them out loud. Proclamation helps us to pull down the devil's strongholds. « The weapons we fight with are not the weapons of the world. On the contrary, they have divine power to demolish strongholds. We demolish arguments and every pretension that sets itself up against the knowledge of God, and we take captive every thought to make it obedient to Christ » (2 Corinthians 10:4-5) Proclamation can be like a victory shout at the battle of Jericho when God demolished the walls of that city (Joshua 6:5)

We also are commanded to use prayer as a weapon at all times and in all situations. We can stand firm wearing God's armour. We are victorious in the name of Jesus. There are many different prayers we can use but when engaged in spiritual warfare , we must claim the protection of the precious blood of Jesus and in His name bind the evil one. We are given authority by Jesus to bind and loose. « Whatever you bind on earth will be bound in heaven, and whatever you loose on earth will be loosed in heaven » (Matthew 16:19).

Jesus was very practical in his teaching on prayer. His disciples were not to make a public show of their praying. Prayer was to be to God the Father, not to impress men. « When you pray, go into your room, close the door and pray to your Father, who is unseen. Then your Father who sees what is done in secret, will reward you. And when you pray do not keep babbling like pagans, for they think they will be heard because of their many words. » (Matthew 6:6-7). It is helpful to have a set place to pray. « go into your room » Time needs to be set apart so that there are no distractions. «close the door». Close the door on everything that would hinder your praying. There is a discipline that needs to be applied if we are to remain faithful in prayer. Daniel in the Old Testament is a good example of a man with a disciplined prayer life.There was a conspiracy by the other administrators in Babylon to discredit Daniel. They persuaded the King to issue an edict that no one was to pray to any god but the king for the next thirty days. We read « Now when Daniel learned that the decree had been published, he went home to his upstairs room where the windows opened towards Jerusalem. Three times a day he got down on his knees and prayed giving thanks to his God, just as he had done before. » (Daniel 6:10). Daniel's prayer life besides being disciplined had followed a pattern. He prayed on his knees in his upstairs room as he had always done. The posture for our praying will depend upon personal preference. Sometimes we feel we must bow down before the Lord or prostrate ourselves before Him. There are some Christians who like to place an empty chair in front of them when they pray and speak to God the Father as though he were sitting in the chair! It is good to be relaxed when we come into our Father's presence. Jesus also warned his disciples not to keep babbling as the pagans do. The lesson for us is that it is not the number of words we say or how loud we say them but our simplicity, sincerity and faith. Many find it helpful to pray out loud in secret « so that the Father who sees what is done in secret will reward you.»

Throughout Jewish history, in the time of Jesus and throughout the history of the Christian Church people have fasted! Jesus again says that fasting should be done in secret not to receive the praise of men! (Matthew 6:16-18) When we fast and pray we intensify our requests to God our Father. Our prayer times can be greatly enhanced by fasting especially if we are going through a period of temptation, spiritual examination, or having to make an important decision. Some Christians fast on a set day, others when led by the Holy Spirit. It is important to distinguish between a slimming regime and fasting! When we fast the time we normally eat will be taken up by prayer, listening to God or reading the Bible.

There are several things that can aid us when we pray. Many Christians pray spontaneously with the help of the Holy Spirit. Others pray privately in tongues to help them become more spiritually aware and receptive to what God wants to say to them. There are others who find it easier to write prayers down on paper. When we want to communicate with a friend it is sometimes easier to say what you want by writing it down! Many Christians are helped by using the prayers of others, especially those of leaders of the Church in times gone by. They identify with the prayer and make it their own. Using prayers that are part of a liturgy have helped countless Christians through the ages. Another aid to prayer is to keep a « Prayer Diary. » On one half of the page the prayer request and date is written, on the other half God's answer. When God answers your prayers don't forget to say thank you! The Bible is probably the most useful aid to pray that we can have. By praying the words of scripture, in faith, we remind God of His promises and align our wills with His. Many times when the early Church met for prayer they quoted Psalms in their prayers. The believers prayed after Peter and John had been released from prison using the words of Psalm 2. They prayed « Sovereign Lord, you made the heaven and the earth and the sea and everything in them. You spoke by the Holy Spirit through the mouth of your servant David.

« ' Why do the nations rage and the people plot in vain?
The kings of the earth take their stand and the rulers gather
together against the Lord and against his Anointed One' »

They were interpreting what was happening around them and by the Holy Spirit were seeing that this prophecy was being fulfilled and they prayed accordingly. As we become more familiar with our Bible we are more able to use Scripture in our prayers.

It is never right to judge a person by the prayers they offer to God. Sometimes people make the mistake of thinking that God has only answered their prayer when He grants them what they have asked for! Prayers are answered according to the sovereign will of God revealed in the Bible! In our culture children are encouraged to write letters to Father Christmas telling him what presents they would like! We must be sure our prayers do not become a Christian wish list! God does not always answer our prayers in the manner that pleases us! Some things we might ask for might not be in our best interest. This is like a child wanting to drink a bright coloured liquid, which may be pretty but is harmful! The parent will say an emphatic no. Ruth Graham like many young woman prayed to the Lord for guidance as to the person she should marry. When she looked back on prayers that were not answered as she wanted, she says « I would have married the wrong man several times over » When seeking guidance it is important to discern God's will in a situation. Every day I remind myself when I pray « All things work together for good for those who love the Lord » (Romans 8:28) The climax of a Christian's life is allowing the will of God to have uninterrupted sway in all things. Many times I have come to a point in praying when I know that I have been heard and have to leave the answer to the Lord. At these times one experiences a peace given by the Holy Spirit. Many books refer to this as « Praying Through ». When this happens it is time to move on and pray for another person or situation. Jesus is making intercession for us and we can rest assured our prayers are answered, in one way or another.

Every new Christian should try to be part of a church group, meeting for prayer. Often Christians meet together to pray for a specific situation. There are several descriptions of the Church at prayer in the Acts of the Apostles. At the time that Peter miraculously escaped from prison the church at Jerusalem in the house of Mary the mother of John Mark were praying for his release, «Peter knocked at the outer entrance, and a servant girl named Rhoda came to answer the door. When she recognised Peter's voice, she was so overjoyed she ran back without opening it and exclaimed 'Peter is at the door!' 'You're out of your mind' they told her. When she kept insisting that it was so, they said 'It must be his angel' But Peter kept knocking and when they saw him, they were astonished. » (Acts 12: 12-16) This wonderful picture of God's people at prayer reaches it's climax as they realise that the Lord has answered their prayers! They were astonished that Peter was standing outside the door! Many times we pray together sincerely but our faith is lacking. We should pray fervently but this does not mean we have to shout. God is not deaf ! The advantage of agreeing together in prayer is that our Lord promises to be with us. « For where two or three come together in my name, there I am with them« (Matthew 18:20) Also agreement in prayer intensifies our requests. Many Churches organise prayer triplets. Three people who agree to pray together at a set time for a set subject. Triplets or couplets can also operate by telephone. Many Churches have « Nights of Prayer ». We notice that Jesus spent whole nights in prayer particularly when he had to make a decision such as choosing the twelve apostles. (Luke 6:12-16) A night of prayer for particular needs of a Church can lead to unimaginable blessings. Prayer meetings are also an integral part of evangelism and outreach.

Paul writes commending Christians to pray without ceasing. « Be joyful always: pray continually; give thanks in all circumstances, for this is God's will for you in Christ Jesus » (1 Thessalonians 5:16). Many Christians are puzzled by Paul's words. How can one be continually at prayer? Perhaps if you are a monk or a nun it might be possible but not for ordinary people in everyday situations It is possible, but only when you give your conscious life up to regular prayer times so that your unconscious life becomes saturated by prayer. You will continue to pray even if you are not conscious of it. People have even prayed as part of a dream because the indwelling Holy Spirit is part of the subconscious as well as the conscious. It is not necessary to verbalise all our prayers, what about silent retreats. There is a liberty in silence and the mind can be cleansed by the Holy Spirit! In John's revelation we read that when the seventh seal was opened « there was silence in heaven for about half and hour » (Revelation 8:1) Silent prayer, arrow prayers, (in a difficult situation) and praying in tongues are ways of praying continually. Many preachers are grateful for those who support them by praying in tongues as they proclaim the gospel. Christian leaders acknowledge that there is a weakness in the Church's life which stems from a lack of prayer and of an unawareness of the need to pray. Christians need to grow and become mature in their prayer life, I exhort you whether young or old in the faith to keep praying, to open up yourself to God's Holy Spirit and seek to have a closer intimacy with God.

Chapter 16 - Giving to the Lord

«In France we don't talk about money or religion » This was the advice given to me by a French friend when I first lived in France. Sometimes people feel that money should not be talked about in the Church. I know that on one occasion a couple were so upset that they never came to the Church again. They were by far the richest couple in the congregation! Jesus spoke a lot about money. In the sermon on the mount he teaches his disciples that they are not to lay up for themselves « treasures on earth but treasures in heaven » (Matthew 6: 19-24). Jesus makes the contrast between two treasures - two conditions,- light and darkness and two masters- earthly and heavenly, God and money. He says «You cannot serve God and money. » What comes first in **your** life God or money? For the disciple it must be God. Our **attitude** to money and possessions is of first importance.

Two parables recorded in Luke's gospel teach very clearly how money is **not to be used**. The parable of the « Rich man and Lazarus the poor beggar » (Luke 16:19-31) and the parable of the « Rich fool » (Luke 12:13-21) In the first of these stories there was a rich man who had everything money could buy! He lived in luxury every day of his life. At the gate of his fine house, was laid a beggar named Lazarus. He was covered with sores and was longing to eat what fell from the rich man's table. Even the dogs came to lick his sores! Lazarus died hungry and the angels carried him to Abraham's side. The rich man also died and went to hell where he was in torment. He looked up and saw Abraham in heaven with Lazarus by his side. He called to him « Father Abraham have pity on me and send Lazarus to dip the tip of his finger in water and cool my tongue because I am in agony in this fire » Abraham replied « Son remember in your lifetime you received your good things, while Lazarus received bad things, but now he is comforted here and you are in agony.» The story goes on to tell of the unbridgeable gap separating them and the request of the rich man to warn his family! The main point the parable is making is that the rich man in his days on earth did not even see the needs of poor Lazarus who had been laid at his gate. The rich man's money was not the problem it was that he **misused** it. Jesus teaches us to use our resources to help those in need. The Christian's eyes are to be open to see the plight of the poor and needy and to help meet those needs if possible. The new Christian has a new heart that is compassionate and kind and ready to share his goods.

The second parable is also about the misuse of money and possessions. It is the story of a rich fool. (Luke 12:13 -21). A person came to Jesus who was having trouble getting his fair share of an inheritance from his brother. There are many family squabbles over inheritances! Jesus refused to be an arbiter between them instead He warned him « Watch out! Be on your guard against all kinds of greed.» Our materialistic society has become increasingly greedy and this parable is especially relevant for our generation. He goes on to say« The ground of a certain rich man produced a good crop. He thought to himself 'What shall I do, I have no place to store my crops.' Then he said. 'this is what I'll do. I will tear down my barns and build bigger ones, and there I will store all my grain and my goods. And I'll say to myself. You have plenty of good things laid up for many years. Take life easy, eat, drink and be merry. But God said to Him. 'you fool! This very night your life will be demanded from you. Then who will get what you have prepared for yourself?' This is how it will be for anyone who stores up things for himself but is not rich towards God. » (Luke 12:16-21) We can see this person was using his money just to please himself and satisfy his greed. It is a warning to us not to live selfishly, but be good stewards of what God has given us and not be greedy!

Greed causes people to develop an insatiable appetite for money in order to obtain more and more possessions. The whole advertising industry relies on man's natural instinct to want more and more and to never be satisfied. Many people's lives are dominated by television. The first thing they do on entering their home is to turn on the TV no matter what the programme! The words and jingles of the advertisements enter into our subconscious and make us **believe** that we need more and more material possessions, trying to persuade us that it is only by having more and more that we will be happy. Many people seek a life of ease and security but discover that despite all they have they are not happy. In our affluent society there are more depressed people, more broken relationships than ever before. Consumerism has become a business philosophy and to a great extent has gone unchallenged. People are encouraged to « shop until they drop », or to use shopping as a kind of therapy! Money and possessions although necessary are not what we as Christians should build our lives upon. Paul in his letter to the Colossians equates greed with idolatry. (Colossians 3:5) Worshipping money and possessions is a form of idolatry and is breaking the commandment « You shall have no other gods before me; you shall not make for yourself an idol of anything in the heavens above or on the earth beneath or in the waters below. You shall not bow down to them or worship them for I your God am a jealous God » (Exodus 20: 3-4) The God and Father of our Lord Jesus Christ is the one true God and demands our exclusive worship. When we allow money and possessions to **dominate** our lives we are breaking His commandment.

We must not allow our possessions to possess us. We must not allow ourselves to love money so much that it takes over our lives! Many people's lives are selfish, built only on trying to make as much money as possible. I have a friend, who when ever he opens his mouth talks of money, either what he has made, or what he has lost! Money dominates his life. I once prayed with the wife of a millionaire who felt that her husband did not love her as he spent all his time either making money or protecting the money he had already made. Her husband's behaviour had made her turn to drink and she was becoming an alcoholic. Paul writes to Timothy that « the **love** of money is a root of all kinds of evil » (1 Timothy Ch 6 vs. 6-10) We came into the world with nothing and we shall leave it with nothing. As the Spanish proverb says « there are no pockets in shrouds! » Peter in his letter tells us that there were false teachers in the church causing a great deal of harm because « they were experts in greed - an accursed brood » (2 Peter 2:14). They were also pleasure loving with eyes full of adultery! « They have left the straight way and wandered off to follow the way of Balaam son of Beor, who loved the wages of wickedness » (2 Peter 2:15). A wise old Christian once said to me « Gerald, the biggest problem with our world today is greed! » Greedy Christians must repent and be satisfied with what the Lord has given them. The author of the book of Hebrews concludes with this exhortation to Christians « Keep your lives free from the love of money and be content with what you have, because God has said 'Never will I leave you; never will I forsake you.' » (Hebrews 13:5) Such teaching is unacceptable to many people in our world but for the Christian it is crucial.

At the time of writing this book much of Europe, and for that matter the world is suffering from an economic recession. Individuals, banks, and other commercial enterprises have run up enormous debt due to heavy borrowing. Politicians do not seem to have any answers and our whole economic system is out of control with individuals and whole nations amassing spiralling debt. The « Live now pay later » way of living is catching up with us. How should the Christian handle his money? In the matter of giving the disciple of Jesus is urged to give to those in need and to lend to those who ask without seeking a return on his money. Jesus told another parable about the final judgement that we all have to face. The great judge on the white throne will not be impressed by our pious words, but by our concrete actions. The parable of sheep and goats is not about earning our salvation by doing good works, but is about how the believer should behave towards fellow human beings especially other Christians. Those who have responded to the needs of the hungry and given them something to eat, invited strangers into their homes, provided clothing when needed; visited the sick and those in prison; will be blessed because in doing it « for one of the least of these brothers of mine, you did it for me » said Jesus (Matthew 25:31-46)

I recently read a modern parody of this parable.

« I was hungry, and you formed a committee to investigate my hunger.
I was homeless and you filed a report on my plight.
I was sick and you held a seminar on the situation of the underprivileged.
You have investigated all aspects of my plight.
And yet I am still hungry, homeless and sick ».

In today's western society, action to care for people's individual needs can often get lost in bureaucracy, but of course there must always be standards to be met, in 'health and safety' and the 'safe guarding of children and vulnerable people.' The Christian should be at the forefront in helping people who have fallen on hard times. Not judging them but loving them with Christ's love. Very often it is Christians who are at the centre of organisations to help the poor, through 'soup kitchens' 'food banks' or 'fund raising initiatives.' Christians must work according to the rules laid down by governing bodies and not against them. The Christian should not be put off by opposition, or weariness but should keep persevering in helping those in need.

The Christian is taught to give to God and not to count the cost. If our gift is to be acceptable to God it must have cost us something in terms of self denial. The **motive** behind our giving is all important. Some people broadcast how much they have given to charity or how well they have supported their local church, to obtain the approval of others. In the sermon on the mount Jesus teaches his disciples how they should give. « Be careful not to do your acts of righteousness before men, to be seen by them. If you do, you will have no reward from your Father in heaven. So when you give to the needy, do not announce it with trumpets, as the hypocrites do in the synagogues and on the streets, to be honoured by men. I tell you in truth, they have received their reward in full. But when you give to the needy, do not let your left hand know what your right hand is doing, so that your giving may be in secret. Then your Father, who sees what is done in secret, will reward you. » (Matthew 6:1-4) We should not be looking to see how much another is giving! The amount each gives is personal.

Our giving should be in proportion to what we are **able** to give. John Wesley the founder of the Methodist Church put aside the money he needed to keep himself and the rest he gave to the Lord. When the Lord increased the amount of money he received, he still kept the same amount for his personal needs, and gave all the increase to the Lord! He did this throughout his life. His motivation was to give back to the Lord what the Lord had given him and to be a good steward in the master's service. Jesus passed judgement on those who gave out of their abundance and pointed his disciples attention to a poor widow as she made her offering to God in the temple. « Jesus looked up and saw the rich putting their gifts into the temple treasury. He also saw a poor widow put in two very small copper coins. « I tell you the truth » he said « this poor widow has put in more than all the others. All these people gave their gifts out of their wealth: but she out of her poverty put in all she had to live on ».(Luke 21:1-4)

Jesus warns his disciples « Again I tell you that it is easier for a camel to go through the eye of a needle than for a rich man to enter the Kingdom of God » (Matthew 19:24) The picture he drew does not make a lot of sense to our western minds. The man of Jesus' time would have understood this simile in a different way. The camel is a large animal. In Israel the cities often had two gates, the main gate through which trade and traffic entered and beside it a low narrow gate used when the main gate was closed, locked and guarded at night. The gate was so small that it was difficult for a man to pass through it let alone a camel! This narrow gate was often called « the needle's eye ». Jesus said, that it is just as difficult for a rich man to enter God's kingdom as it is for a large camel to go through the little gate. If we would seriously be followers of Jesus and become his disciples we must count the cost and not be too attached to our money and possessions. This does not mean that to be a disciple of Jesus we should all take a vow of poverty! Jesus talked about the « eye of a needle » and the rich man entering the Kingdom of God in response to a rich young man who had wanted to follow him. This young man asked Jesus how he could obtain eternal life. Jesus replied «If you want to enter life obey the commandments » 'All these I have kept' the young man said 'what do I still lack?' » I believe that young man was sincerely searching for the Kingdom. There was something missing in his life. He had plenty of money, and the energy of youth. He was a moral man, he had probably studied the Jewish law at a Rabbinic school. Jesus looked into his, heart and loved him. « 'If you want to be perfect, go sell your possessions and give to the poor, and you will have treasures in heaven. Then come follow me' When the young man heard this he went away sad, because he had great wealth » (Matthew 19:-22). He was not being called to become destitute and friendless but to share with Jesus in the greatest project the world has ever known, the Kingdom of God, but his money, possessions and comforts came first in his life. He was unable to rearrange his priorities or his life -style. If we would follow Jesus, He must come first in our lives, above the making of money and accumulating needless possessions. The disciples of Jesus found this teaching hard just as we do today but all who would follow Jesus have to make choices, and all must count the cost.

Let us go deeper into the subject of money and giving. The Old Testament clearly teaches that we should tithe. God commanded Israel to give back to Him one tenth, (a tithe) of all that He had given them. This commandment was given to the Israelites as they prepared to enter the promised land, but long before this Jacob, grandson of Abraham had made a vow to give back to God a tenth of all God would give him (Deuteronomy 14:22) The story of the life of Jacob is both fascinating and informative. Jacob stole his brother Esau's birthright and at his mother's prompting, stole the blessing that was also reserved for the oldest son, from their father Isaac. He left home to go to his uncle Laban's house and to escape from his older brother who was determined to kill him. Alone on that journey he stopped for the night at Bethel. « Taking one of the stones there, he put it under his head and lay down to sleep; he had a dream in which he saw a stairway resting on the earth, with it's top reaching to heaven, and the angels of God were ascending and descending on it. There above it stood the Lord and he said 'I am the Lord the God of your father Abraham and the God of Isaac. I will give you and your descendants the land on which you are lying.' » The dream concluded with God saying «'All peoples on earth will be blessed through you and your offspring. I am with you and will watch over you wherever you go, and I will bring you back to this land. I will not leave you until I have done what I have promised you' » What a wonderful word of the Lord to Jacob when he was at the lowest point in his life. How reassuring to know that he would one day return home to his own land and his own people. « When Jacob awoke from his sleep, he thought, 'Surely the Lord is in this place and I was not aware of it' He was afraid and said 'How awesome is this place! This is none other than the house of God; this is the gate of heaven'. Early next morning Jacob took the stone he had been lying on and set it up as a pillar and poured oil on top of it and he named that place Bethel which means House of God . Jacob made the following vow. 'If God will be with me and will watch over me on this journey I am taking and will give me food to eat and clothes to wear so that I return safely to my father's house, then the Lord will be my God. This stone that I have set up as a pillar will be God's house, and **of all that you give me I will give you a tenth'** » (Genesis 28:10-22).

Jacob was renamed « Israel » by God. The practice of giving to God a tithe has continued ever since. As Christians we also must give God his due by giving back to Him a tenth of what He has given us. A simple way to illustrate this principle. An adult buys a large box of chocolates, a present for a child. The child is thrilled and takes the box of chocolates. He might react in one of two ways; grab the box of chocolates hastily rip off the cellophane wrapping run into another room and eat all the chocolates! We would think that the child was very selfish and ill-mannered to act in that way. The other way the child might react is to carefully un-wrap the box, open the lid and offer to the adult the first chocolate. We would commend that child's behaviour because he has given back to the giver of the chocolates, the first choice as a way of saying thank you. The Lord has blessed us in so many ways and so we say thank you to Him by bringing our tithe as an offering of thanksgiving. We give to God his due. The men of Israel were commanded by God to appear before Him three times a year. They were to celebrate three feasts in Jerusalem. The Feast of Unleavened Bread, the Feast of Weeks and the Feast of Tabernacles « No man should appear before the Lord empty- handed . Each of you must bring a gift in proportion to the way the Lord your God has blessed you ». (Deuteronomy 16:16-17) The law of Moses gives instruction on how to worship God. On entering the promised land the children of Israel are not to worship the gods of the peoples they have conquered. « You must not worship the Lord your God in their way. But you are to seek the place the Lord your God will chose from among all your tribes to put His Name there for His dwelling. To this place you must go: there bring your burnt offerings and sacrifices, your tithes and special gifts, and what you have vowed to give and your freewill offerings and the first born of your herds and flocks. There in the presence of the Lord your God, you and your families shall eat and shall rejoice in everything you have put your hand to, because the Lord your God has blessed you. » (Deuteronomy 12:4-7) The principal of giving God his due, of giving ten per cent of the annual produce of the land, was obligatory for the support of the temple and the priesthood. It has been carried over into Christianity especially for the support of the clergy and the work of the Kingdom of God. It is important that Christians are taught to tithe. Giving ten percent of your net income seems a difficult concept, but if you do God will bless you and prosper you.

At the end of the Old Testament period the prophet Malachi accuses the Jewish leaders and the people of 'robbing God' « Will a man rob God? » asks the prophet. The people ask « But how do we rob God? » The prophet replies « In tithes and offering. You are under a curse - the whole nation of you - because you are robbing me. Bring the whole tithe into the storehouse, that there may be food in my house. Test me in this says the Lord Almighty, and see if I will not throw open the floodgates of heaven and pour out so much blessing that you will not have room enough for it. » (Malachi

3 : 8-10) We do not give our tithe to the Lord to receive material rewards, but many who have given sacrificially for the work of the Kingdom have been richly blessed.. If a man honours God - God will honour him and bless him. The Lord provides for His work.

Many times in my life the Lord has provided for me and my family. God has answered prayers for provision in the most unexpected way. Many years ago we were on a journey with our two small children to my youngest brother's wedding. Our car broke down on the motorway and we had to be towed to a garage. The repairs were to cost £46.00 which we did not have, but my father advised us to go ahead and get it repaired as it was no good as it was. This we did. While we were waiting for the work to be done, we walked into the nearby town. We saw a church and wondered if we might be allowed to sit quietly out of the July sun and wait there with the children. We were met by the minister, who kindly invited us to his house, where he and his wife shared their midday meal with us. She provided a clean nappy for the baby as all our luggage was in the boot of the car and then she insisted that we took a siesta. Later after ascertaining that the work on the car was complete the minister drove us back to the garage. We then continued on our journey arriving very late in the evening in time for the wedding the next day. How great is our God! At that very moment he provided someone to take care of us in our time of need. A few days after we had returned home, we were sent a cheque for forty six pounds, by a man whom I hardly knew: the exact amount we needed to pay the garage bill. He had been told by the Lord to make us a special gift. He did not know why but he was obedient. Praise the Lord for His provision. (In those days forty six pounds was a lot of money probably equivalent to four or five hundred pounds nowadays!)

Often we are asked to give over and above the tithe with a free will offering. We read about the building of the temple by King Solomon and how the people gave their money and precious articles as a free will offering so that the Temple could be built. King David set the people an example by giving of his « personal treasure of gold and silver for the temple » (1 Chronicles 29:3).The

230

leaders followed the King's example and « the people rejoiced at the willing response of their leaders, for they had given freely and wholeheartedly to the Lord. » (1 Chronicles 29:9). We learn from the apostle Paul that, «God loves a cheerful giver » (2 Corinthians 9:7) and that the disciple should give for the work of the Church, the relief of famine and the care of widows and orphans.

Paul writes « On the first day of every week, each one of you should set aside a sum of money in keeping with his income. » (1 Corinthians 16:1-2) Each Sunday we too should set aside money to give to our Church for the work of the Kingdom. Paul commends the Macedonian Churches for their generosity; « Out of the most severe trial, their overflowing joy and their extreme poverty welled up in rich generosity. For I testify that they gave as much as they were able, and even beyond their ability. Entirely on their own, they urgently pleaded with us for the privilege of sharing in the service of the saints. And they did not do as we expected, but gave themselves first to the Lord and then to us in keeping with God's will. » (2 Corinthians 8:2-5) The Macedonian Churches provide us with a wonderful example of how to give. There is no reluctance to give. They themselves were under pressure of persecution. They were not rich in the things of this world but what they had they gave, holding nothing back. They had generous hearts because they had been so blessed by the gospel. Some friends who recently visited very poor Christians in Romania, told us of the Romanians generosity in wanting to share what little food they had with them, their visitors, because the Lord had so blessed them! The visitors were in tears as they remembered this kindness. The people gave sacrificially, not counting the cost but relying on the Lord to provide for them. The Churches were not putting aside money for next year or for the fabric fund! They had no fear for tomorrow believing that God would provide for the future if they were faithful to Him in the present. What a wonderful way to take the collection by first « Giving themselves to the Lord » and respecting their leaders, believing that they had discerned the will of God! Today in this whole area of giving people often rebel and challenge the authority of their leaders. Paul continues by saying that just as they excelled in other things the Church at Corinth should also « excel in this grace of giving » (2 Corinthians 8:7)

I believe that every Christian must give from the heart. It is the individual's responsibility to obey the Lord from a loving heart. This obedience refers just as much to our giving, as to any other area of our discipleship. As we have already noted we are to give cheerfully. When I consider God's love, and the change that He has brought about in my life, my heart overflows with love. That love must be translated into action. One of our actions is to give what we can afford to the Church and those in real need. We are called to be good stewards of what God has given us. We are not good stewards if we land ourselves in debt! Within the Church fellowship we are called to care for each other and to share each other's burdens. We see how the first Christians in the early Churches cared for one another. They shared with each other « All the believers were together and had everything in common. Selling their possessions and goods they gave to anyone as he had need.» (Acts 2:44-45) We read how « Joseph a Levite from Cyprus, whom the apostles called Barnabas (which means Son of Encouragement) sold a field he owned and brought the money and put it at the apostles' feet » (Acts 4:36-37) Barnabas from a generous heart held nothing back but gave all the proceeds of the sale of his land, to the leaders of the Church. In contrast there was a man named Ananias who also sold some property. « With his wife's full knowledge he kept back part of the money for himself, but brought the rest and put it at the apostles' feet ». Maybe he wanted to be like Barnabas. The problem was that Satan had so filled his heart that he lied to the Holy Spirit which resulted in his sudden death, and the death of his wife, consequently great fear seized the Church (Acts 5:1-10) We have to be totally honest before God with our finances.

We read of the Church's support of widows in the Jerusalem Church, and how the apostles were being drawn into disputes. « In those days when the number of disciples was increasing, the Grecian Jews among them complained against those of the Aramaic speaking community because their widows were being overlooked in the daily distribution of food». The Church responded to this problem by choosing seven men filled with the Holy Spirit and wisdom to attend to this matter so that the apostles were free to concentrate on the ministry of the word. (Acts 6:1-7). Just as Jesus fed the five thousand people the church has a responsibility to help feed the poor. «The Lord watches over the alien and sustains the fatherless and the widow but he frustrates the ways of the wicked» (Psalm 146 : 9) When I travelled and preached in Zambia, Africa, I became aware of the large number of orphans as a result of the AIDS epidemic. I was thrilled by the work the churches were doing in caring for, and supporting the fatherless. The Church has always been at the centre of providing aid to the very poor. All our giving whether for the work of the Church or for people in distress must be motivated by love. « If anyone has material possessions and sees his brother in need but has no pity on him, how can the love of God be in him? Dear children (believers in the Lord, children of God) let us not love with words or tongue but with actions and in truth » (1 John 3:17-18)

The world outside the church looks on and becomes disillusioned and angry when it sees the great wealth that some churches have amassed. This undermines the gospel and the message of the Kingdom. David Watson, evangelist, minister and author whose ministry touched many lives, wrote «The world is deaf to a church that has sold out to materialism» The church must not be concerned with the acquisition of money but with love. When people see evangelists on television appealing for money and becoming rich they turn away in disgust. What have they to do with Jesus who was born in a stable, had few possessions and nowhere to lay his head they ask? How the Church handles money is of great importance. I have known churches who at the end of each financial year gave away their surplus money! This is to be commended as being more in line with the teaching of Jesus than many other systems of church accounting. Other churches give away a tithe of a tithe. If a Church is heaping up riches on earth it will be lacking in treasures in heaven. This question of how we use our money is of the utmost importance. The new believer must as soon as possible after conversion decide about the way he gives. May the love of Christ in your hearts be stronger than the love of money and may it motivate all of your giving. We are not to worry about food, drink, clothes and all life's necessities « But seek first the Kingdom of God and his righteousness and all these things will be given to you as well. Therefore do not worry about tomorrow, for tomorrow will worry about itself. Each day has enough trouble of its own. » (Matthew 6:24-34)

Chapter 17 - Witness and Service

My wife and I were invited to dinner with our pastor and his wife. As we were ushered to the dining table I looked up to the ceiling at the light fitting. It was a yoke that had once been used by oxen for ploughing. The pastor saw me gazing at the light fitting and said that it remind him that he was called to serve. Jesus came to serve. His whole life was one of service to others. He fulfilled the prophecies of Isaiah concerning the promised Messiah. In particular he was understood by his followers to be the « Suffering Servant ». (Isaiah 53). The apostle Peter understood the mission of Jesus as fulfilling the Messianic prophecy of Isaiah. Jesus came from his Father in heaven as a servant who suffered for the sins of the world. « he himself bore our sins in his body on the tree, so that we might die to sins and live for righteousness; by his wounds you have been healed; for you were like sheep going astray, but now you have returned to the Shepherd and Overseer of your souls » (I Peter 2:24-25, Isaiah 53 :5-6 &12) and again the gospel records « Here is my servant whom I have chosen, the one I love, in whom I delight. I will put my Spirit on him and he will proclaim justice to the nations » (Matthew 12: 18 quoting from Isaiah 42:1-4) Jesus himself understood his ministry as one of serving others. James and John wanted to sit either side of Jesus in His glory   (Mark 10:35 -41) which caused great indignation among the other ten disciples. Jesus defined his ministry in terms of service. He said « For even the Son of Man did not come to be served but to serve, and give his life as a ransom for many. » (Mark 10:45) Paul writing to the Church at Philippi, urges them to follow the example of Christ's humility and become servants « Your attitude should be the same as that of Christ Jesus: who being in the very nature God, did not consider equality with God something to be grasped, but made himself nothing, taking the very nature of a servant, being made in human likeness. »

(Philippians 2:5-7)

It is by faith in Christ Jesus that we are saved, but we are saved for a purpose. We are in the words of the popular slogan **« saved to serve »**. One of the favourite hymns of many Christians is the « Servant King » which Graham Kendrick wrote in 1983. This hymn often creates such an atmosphere that people experience the Holy Spirit challenging them to offer themselves to serve.

The Chorus and the fourth verse in particular are inspiring.
    « This is our God,
    The Servant King
    He calls us now
    To follow Him,
    To bring our lives
    As a daily offering
    Of worship to
    The Servant King »

    « So let us learn
    How to serve,
    And in our lives enthrone Him;
    Each others needs
    To prefer,
    For it is Christ
    We're serving »

Simon Peter begins his letter with « Simon Peter **a servant** and Apostle of Jesus Christ » (2 Peter 1:1) Leaders are called to be servants, in fact all Christians are to be servants and it is important that new believers understand this truth. Often to be a servant means being humble and available to do the most menial of tasks. John, in his gospel, tells how Jesus gave his twelve disciples a demonstration of how they should serve one another. «The evening meal was being served, and the devil had already prompted Judas Iscariot son of Simon, to betray Jesus. Jesus knew that the Father had put all things under his power, and that he had come from God and was returning to God; so he got up from the meal, took off his outer clothing, and wrapped a towel around his waist. After that, he poured water into a basin and began to wash his disciple's feet, drying them with the towel that was wrapped around him. He came to Simon Peter, who said 'Lord are you going to wash my feet?' Jesus replied, 'You do not realise now what I am doing, but later you will understand' 'No' said Peter 'you shall never wash my feet' Jesus answered 'Unless I wash you, you have no part with me.' 'Then Lord' Simon Peter replied 'not just my feet but my hands and my head as well!'» (John 13: 2- 8) « When he had finished washing their feet, he put on his clothes and returned to his place. 'Do you understand what I have done for you?' he asked them. 'you call me Teacher and Lord and rightly so for that is what I am. Now that I your Lord and Teacher, have washed your feet, **you also should wash one another's feet. I have set you an example that you should do as I have done to you**. I tell you the truth, no servant is greater than his master, nor is a messenger greater than the one who sent him. Now that you know these things, **you will be blessed if you do them.'** » (John 13:12-17)

Let us look more closely at what this passage says to us. We realise that it was very necessary to wash one's feet before a meal in that culture. Normally one ate reclining on a bench with the feet of the person beside you near your head! People wore open sandals, so the dirt and muck from the road would soil their feet! This task of foot washing was normally done by a slave or a woman! In this instance the evening meal was being served and no one had been available to do this menial task! Only Jesus was willing to take a towel and wash his disciples' feet, in doing so He took the place of a household slave or servant. Jesus began to kneel at the feet of his disciples and wash them one by one. Simon Peter was not comfortable with Jesus washing his feet. He would, I think, have been much happier washing Jesus' feet! (There are many people who would rather serve others than allow someone to serve them!) Peter was maybe too proud to let Jesus wash his feet! Jesus was concerned that his disciples understood the significance of what he did and would follow his example and become each other's servant. They were to understand that as disciples of Jesus they were servants and not masters and were to be servants in the world! The disciples would be blessed if they obeyed and followed his example. We too, are to follow the example of Jesus being willing to give ourselves in service to others.

One of the most important qualities of the newly baptised Christian is to have a « servant heart » We know that we are called to follow our Lord's example of service but we find all sorts of excuses for not doing so. Many people want to serve on their own terms and leave others to do the more menial jobs. When opportunities arise to serve the Master a battle goes on in their hearts and minds! Sometimes it is pride that is the problem. Paul by the grace given him says to the Church at Rome « Do not think of yourself more highly than you ought, but rather think of yourself with sober judgement, in accordance with the measure of faith that God has given you. » (Romans 12:3) A servant heart is full of love for the Lord and for all people. The servant remembers that no one is outside the love of God and that Jesus died for all, that they might be saved. Some are by nature better servants than others. One of the gifts of the Holy Spirit is service. Peter tells believers « to live according to God in regard to the Spirit » « Each one should use whatever gift he has received to serve others, faithfully administering God's grace in it's various forms. If anyone speaks, he should do it as if speaking the very words of God. If anyone serves, he should do it with the strength God provides so that in all things God may be praised through Jesus Christ. To him be the glory and the power for ever and ever. Amen » (1 Peter 4:10-11) It is God who calls us and equips us to be able to serve. We serve not to pat ourselves on the back but to give glory to Him. There are many people who will never listen to the Gospel we proclaim but will be touched by our lives of service. Christians who care sacrificially and are always ready to help stand out in our selfish society. We should not underestimate the power of example. The way we live and serve maybe the only contact a person has with Jesus!

An elder in one of my Churches recalled how as a teenager she had been drawn to Christ as her Saviour and Lord by the kindness and caring of young Christians who had invited her to join them for a youth weekend. During her time with them she was touched by their service and love towards one another, she saw something very different in them. She had been brought up in a non-Christian family and this kind of caring was unfamiliar to her. Paul implies that all believers are « living letters » that may be read by unbelievers « You show that you are a letter from Christ, the result of our ministry, written not with ink but with the Spirit of the living God, not on tablets of stone but on tablets of human hearts » (2 Corinthians 3:3). Paul understood that our lives should mirror the life of Jesus. As has been said many times, in our generation where knowledge of the gospel and the contents of the Bible are unknown to many « The only gospel they will hear and the Bible that they will read is our lives as we serve the Lord each day »

The servant serves! There are many different spheres of service. The local Church as it seeks to fulfil it's purpose in the community, always provides opportunities for service. In many lively Churches they do not have enough willing people to fulfil the vision that they have received from the Lord! The key is to be willing to serve according to the gifts and abilities the Lord has given you. Take every opportunity to serve, the Church needs enthusiastic people. Sadly there are many lazy Christians as in the Church at Laodicea. Listed among the seven Churches of Asia, it is the lukewarm, self-satisfied Church. (Revelation 3:14-22). There can be however extremes in the area of servant-hood which hamper the work of the Church. There are people who will volunteer even if they do not have the gifts or abilities to do the job or are already doing too much. Such people lack wisdom and discernment and will eventually suffer from Christian burn out! Then there are those who are shy or timid, and have a poor self image and feel inadequate to serve. Such people must allow the Holy Spirit to minister to them and be encouraged by other mature Christians. There is a place for everyone in the local Church and everyone has a place! Followers of Jesus must **engage** in Kingdom work take responsibility, be reliable and be able to be corrected! We do not judge each other's service! Our Lord made it very clear to his disciples, He said «Do not judge, or you too will be judged. For in the same way you judge others you will be judged, and with the measure you use, it will be measured to you » (Matthew 7: 1-2) Leave all judging to the Lord! Don't be concerned with looking over your shoulder to see what others are doing.

There are many spheres for service in the wider Church. No Church stands on its own. We are all related to one another through Christ and the Holy Spirit. A believer might have a particular gift that is needed by another Church or group of Churches and may feel called to help there. Many believers may feel called to serve the Lord as missionaries or pastors in a local Church. The most important thing is to be able to distinguish between the « Call of God » and youthful enthusiasm. To serve as any sort of leader in the Church a person must have God's call on his/her life and receive confirmation of this from other mature Christians. There are many organizations that have been founded to help the Church in its mission. These have been called Para-Church groups and they are always looking for mature Christians they can employ either on a paid or voluntary basis.

Often Christians work in our secular society in the caring profession or education. They feel that they can best follow their Lord by serving in these situations. Their aim is to be good servants of Jesus Christ, their personalities and their actions speak louder than any words. I have met Christians in politics and many serve in this sphere applying Kingdom principles to their politics. There are a group of Christians in the British Parliament who meet regularly for prayer and Bible study. Wherever you work or live you are Christ's representative. The following prayer is used by the Methodist Church in its annual Covenant service. I think you may find it helpful.

> « I am no longer my own but yours.
> Your will, not mine be done in all things,

wherever you may place me,
in all that I do and in all that I may endure;
when there is work for me and when there is none;
when I am troubled and when I am at peace.
Your will be done when I am valued and when I am
disregarded;
when I find fulfilment and when it is lacking;
when I have all things, and when I have nothing.
I willingly offer all I have and am to serve you, as and where
you choose.
Glorious and blessed God, Father, Son and Holy Spirit,
you are mine and I am yours.
May it be so for ever.
Let this covenant now made on earth be fulfilled in heaven.
Amen »

If you have never prayed this prayer maybe now is a fitting moment to do so, or, if you have prayed it before then remind yourself of the commitment and search your heart to see if you are remaining true to it.

Every Christian should be able to speak a word for the Lord. The risen Lord commanded his disciples « Go and make disciples of all nations, baptising them in the name of the Father and of the Son and of the Holy Spirit, and teaching them to obey everything I have commanded you. And surely I will be with you always, to the very end of the age.» (Matthew 28:18-20) Every believer has a story to tell of what God has done in his/her life. We are to go and make disciples. We are called to be fishers of men. « As Jesus walked beside the sea of Galilee, he saw Simon and his brother Andrew casting a net into the lake, for they were fishermen. « Come follow me » Jesus said, « and I will make you fishers of men. At once they left their nets and followed him » (Mark 1:16-18) This simple command of Jesus, for Christians to be fishers of men, has been complicated by our reluctance to obey. Here is a cautionary tale which appeared in a Church growth magazine. It was written some years ago for the 'decade of evangelism'.

'Now it came to pass that a group existed who called themselves fishermen And lo there were many fish in the waters all around. In fact the whole area was surrounded by streams and lakes filled with fish. And the fish were very hungry. Week after week, month after month, year after year, those, who called themselves fishermen, met in meetings and talked about their call to go about fishing. Continually they searched for new and better methods of fishing. They sponsored costly nation-wide and world-wide congresses to discuss fishing and to promote fishing and to hear about all the ways of fishing, such as the new fishing equipment, fish calls and whether any new bait had been discovered.

These fishermen built large, beautiful buildings called « Fishing Headquarters ». The plea was that everyone should be a fishermen and everyone should fish. One thing they did not do however; they didn't fish!

All the fishermen seemed to agree that what was needed was a board which could challenge fishermen to be faithful in fishing. The Board was formed by those who had great vision and encouraged people to speak about fishing, to define fishing, and to promote the idea of fishing in far away streams and lakes where many other fish of different colours lived.

Large, elaborate, and expensive training centres were built whose purpose was to teach fishermen to fish. Those who taught had Doctorates in Fishology, but the teachers did not fish, they only taught fishing!

Some spent much time in study and travel to learn the history of fishing and to see far away places where the founding fathers did great fishing in centuries past. They lauded the faithful fishermen of years before who had handed down the idea of fishing. Many who felt the call to be fishermen responded. They were commissioned and sent to fish. And they went to foreign lands … to teach fishing.

Now it's true that many of the fishermen sacrificed a great deal and put up with all kinds of difficulties. Some lived near the water and bore the smell of dead fish every day. They received the ridicule of some who made fun of their fishing clubs. They anguished over those who were not committed enough to attend the weekly club meetings to talk about fishing.

The trouble was that the Master of fishing had said « Follow me and I will make you fishers of men » and they had not followed, they were not fishing.'

Mission and Evangelism are priorities in the life of every local Church. Every member of the Church is to be a witness for the Kingdom of God by acts of service and by the spoken word. We all have a story to tell and we should not be afraid to tell it. Many people have been converted through missionary outreach and very soon afterwards they have made a public profession of their new found faith. It is always good for a new Christian to tell his/her story, it's a way to start fishing for men and woman. I remember a group of American Christian ladies, singing a song on an aeroplane as they were returning home from a Christian convention. The song was very catchy and was entitled « It only takes a spark to set a fire going » The simplest word spoken for Jesus may be the spark to ignite faith in another person! Do not be afraid to witness for the Lord as you are led by the Holy Spirit and common sense! Do not deliberately break the laws of the land where Christian witness is forbidden. Witness by what you are and what you do and people will be drawn to you and ask you questions then you can share what Christ has done for you.

If you are asked to make a public testimony, prepare thoughtfully and prayerfully. The following pointers may help you.
1) Keep your testimony short or those listening will switch off
2) Keep it simple so that all will be able to understand.
3) Do not use religious language. If you say « I was washed in the blood of the Lamb » non Christian people will have no idea what

you mean neither will some Christians!

4)Tell those listening **a little** about yourself, who you are, what you do, your family etc. but beware of becoming too « I » centred.

5) Speak clearly about the time before you became a Christian. Do not overemphasise how sinful you were (That can give the devil a foothold)

6) Tell the story of how you came to believe in Jesus. How you received Him into your life. Tell how he saved you from your sins. Make it clear that you have been truly converted.

7) Tell of your new life with Jesus, the consequences and the difference it has made, with your family, friends, job. and social life.

8) Have an outline in your head, but trust in the Holy Spirit to give you the words to say. Trust in the Lord and be confident! This is a very important thing in your life.

9) If the situation seems hostile never become aggressive. Sometimes the people who most oppose the gospel become its biggest advocate. Saul of Tarsus for example!

10) Keep your testimony up to date. Do not major on something that happened thirty years ago but speak about the reality of God in your present life.

All of us who are disciples are called to be « Fishers of men ». Not only does a fisherman have to attract the fish but he has to land it! All people are different, and our approach will vary. Different bait for different kinds of fish! Paul writes « Be wise in the way you act towards outsiders, (non - Christians); make the most of every opportunity. Let your conversation be always full of grace, seasoned with salt, so that you may know how to answer everyone. » (Colossians 4:5-6).

All Christians should know how to lead others to the Lord. The story of Philip and the Ethiopian official is an excellent model for person to person evangelism. (Acts 8:26-40). Philip was directed by an angel (the messenger of the Lord) to take the desert road from Jerusalem to Gaza. On his journey he met an Ethiopian who was an important official, in charge of Queen Candace's treasury.

« This man had gone to Jerusalem to worship, and on his way home was sitting in his chariot reading the book of Isaiah the prophet. The Spirit told Philip « Go to the chariot and stay near it. » Then Philip ran up to the chariot and heard the man reading Isaiah the prophet. « Do you understand what you are reading? » Philip asked. « How can I » he said « unless someone explains it to me? » So he invited Philip to come up and sit with him. The eunuch was reading this passage of Scripture.

« He was led like a sheep to the slaughter,
And as a lamb before the shearer is silent,
So he did not open his mouth.
In his humiliation he was deprived of justice.
Who can speak of his descendants?
For his life was taken from the earth » (Isaiah 53:7-8)

The eunuch asked Philip, 'tell me, please, who is the prophet talking about, himself or someone else?' Then Philip began with that very passage of Scripture and told him the good news of Jesus. » (Acts 8:27-35)

As we look carefully at this story we notice that there are four points to help us in our person to person work.

1) Be sensitive - Philip was sensitive to where the spirit was leading. He was obedient, he followed the Spirits instructions.(Acts 8: 26 & 29 He was polite and stayed near the chariot, when he heard the man reading he asked the question "Do you understand?".

2) Take every opportunity Philip spotted his chance. The opportunity was there (vs30) We must take the opportunities that come our way, listen carefully and give the Holy Spirit a chance to speak to us. We must not be afraid of silence!

3) Start where people are. The Ethiopian was looking for answers (vs30-33). Philip answered his questions. We must start where people really are, be aware of the situation and put ourselves in their place. Many Christians find sharing their faith difficult, they are fearful.

4) When possible use scripture Philip shared the Good News using the Scriptures. (vs. 32) This is important if we are to lead someone to the Lord. We must use scripture in a reasonable way, to back up our explanations. Quoting unconnected texts one after another will more than likely scare someone away!

The Ethiopian responded to Philip's presentation of the gospel and asked for baptism. If your testimony leads to a person desiring to meet with Jesus, these following four simple steps will help you lead that person to the Lord. The same steps are useful if you are counselling someone who has responded to the preaching of the gospel.

A. Something to admit People must admit their need of God. They must admit that they have sinned and need to receive forgiveness. They must understand that all have sinned and sin separates us from God. Refer to (Romans 3:23) «All have sinned and fall short of the glory of God. » Whether we are at the top of a mountain or in the deepest valley we are unable to touch the stars! Whatever our situation we come a long way short of God's perfect standards shown to us in the Bible and supremely in the life and teaching of Jesus.

B Something to believe. Believe that Christ died for you. Jesus' death on the cross is not just an example of a good man dying but of God rescuing sinful humanity. Refer to (John 3 :16). « For God so loved the world that he gave his one and only Son, that whoever believes in him shall not perish but have eternal life » Imagine that you are trapped in a room with the door locked, and suddenly the door is flung open, someone is there to let you out. Jesus by shedding his blood on the cross has opened the door to eternal life. Use the scripture (Romans 6:23) « For the wages of sin is death, but the gift of God is eternal life in Christ Jesus our Lord » Only Christ can take away the barrier of sin which separates all human beings from God. We do not have to earn our forgiveness by trying to be good or do good things, we only have to believe in Jesus and receive his forgiveness as a free gift.

C Something to consider You must **chose** to allow Jesus to come first in your life.
« If anyone would come after me let him deny himself, and take up his cross and follow me »(Mark 8:34) We must be willing to say NO to sin and turn away from anything we know is wrong in our lives. We must say NO to self and be willing to let Jesus be Lord over every part of our life, home, work, money, time etc. We must be willing to be known as a Christian.

D Something to do Give your life to Jesus so that He can give His life to you by His Spirit coming to live within you. Share the Scripture (Revelation 3:20) « Here I am, I stand at the door and knock. If anyone hears my voice and opens the door, I will come in and eat with him and he with me » A person responds to the voice of Jesus by opening the door of his/her heart saying "Come into my heart Lord Jesus right now." Jesus hears and answers the prayer.

Leading a person in a prayer of acceptance.
If you feel that each step has been understood lead that person in a prayer. This or a similar prayer could be used. Ask if he/she is willing to pray this prayer out loud, repeating your words. Say **« Lord Jesus Christ I know that I am a sinner and I need your forgiveness. Thank you for dying on the cross for me to take away my sin. I am willing to turn from all that is wrong in my life. I am willing to put you first in my life. I give my life to you and ask you to come by your Spirit and live in me. Thank you Lord Jesus. Amen »**

Remember that this is a big step for someone to take, there may be tears, joy or a deep felt silence. Be sensitive, allow them to express themselves if they wish. Assure them that you will pray for them. If possible link them up with a contact to help them go forward in their new relationship with Jesus.

We make connections with human beings at different levels. God uses our service and our testimony to extend His Kingdom and build His Church. He also makes us what we are by his Holy Spirit. We are not what we were and we are not yet what we will be but something of Jesus maybe seen in us if we are truly born again by the Spirit. The Lord uses us to work out his purpose in the world. We connect not only by what we say and do, but by what we are. The words which follow from « Portrait of a Christian » by Beatrice Clelland sum up a great deal of what I have been trying to say in this chapter.

« Not merely in the words you say,
Not only in your deeds confessed,
But in the most unconscious way is Christ expressed.

Is it a calm and peaceful smile,
A Holy light upon your brow,
I felt his presence when you laughed just now.

For me it was not the truth you taught,
For you so clear, for me so dim.
But when you came to me you brought a sense of Him.

And from your eyes He beckons me,
And from your heart His love is shed.
I lose sight of you and see Christ instead. »

Chapter 18 - Equipped to Serve

To be a Christian is to be at **work** for the Lord Jesus Christ as well as being a follower. Sometimes a Christian is called to take up full time service for the Lord and become a minister a vicar, a priest or a missionary. Maybe this is how you are reacting right now. When the call is strongly felt then you can be sure that the Holy Spirit will guide you in the way forward, you do not have to strive but prayerfully trust in Him. When you are sure that this is a call you are prepared to answer wholeheartedly, then make enquires as to how this can come to fruition. Speak with your church leaders and let them help you to explore the right avenues and find ways that you may be fully equipped to enter into this ministry. The Lord knows you, your capacities, your weaknesses and he sees your potential. He does not make mistakes in whom He calls to serve Him. You will have to be equipped to serve, that may take years of training, but on the other hand the Lord will equip you by his Holy Spirit with the gifts we have already mentioned in earlier chapters. Although Paul was dramatically converted and it seems on first glance that he became a missionary immediately without any training or preparation, if we look closely at the scriptures we find in fact, he spent many years in training in Judaism before his spectacular meeting with Jesus. He went into Arabia and Damascus, and then met up with Peter in Jerusalem three years later (Galatians 1:14-17)

The question of being equipped, making preparation, and the opportunities to be grasped, are all in the Lord's hands. God equips us to do the work that He has called us to do. You can only serve to the degree that you are equipped and you must allow the Holy Spirit to put you in the right place and to open the right doors for effective service. In the Old Testament we read how God confronted people and called them to serve Him by taking on a specific task. God called Noah to build an ark, Abraham to live in a new land, Moses to set the Israelites free and lead them into the promised land. He called Jonah to go to the great city of Nineveh and preach against it. At first Jonah set off in the opposite direction from Nineveh! He called the prophets, Isaiah, Jeremiah, Amos and Hosea to warn His people Israel and Judah about the judgement that was to come upon them because they had forsaken Him, the one true God and were worshipping idols. In the New Testament he called John to preach that people should repent and prepare themselves for the coming of the Messiah. Jesus called fishermen, tax collectors, and a freedom fighter to follow him. They all responded. When the Church came into being as an agent for the Kingdom of God men and woman from all walks of life heard God calling them and gave themselves to serve Jesus and carry on doing the things that he had done. Today it is no different, God calls men and woman of all ages, social standings and nationalities, to continue the mission of Jesus and serve in His Church and in the world.

William Carey the founder of the Baptist Missionary Society came from humble beginnings but the Lord used him mightily. He worked as a cobbler in Northampton and felt called by God to be a missionary to India in 1793. Besides founding the Baptist Missionary Society and winning converts to our Lord, he translated the Bible into more than thirty languages. His motto was -

Expect Great things from God
Attempt great things for God

There is no limit to what God can do through a willing servant! Some new Christians are afraid to attempt to serve God in some particular sphere because they are afraid the they might make a mistake. The saying is true -
'A person who never made a mistake never made anything'

If you see an open door to serve the Lord and the Holy Spirit is prompting you, do not hesitate to offer yourself for the work God is calling you to do. We may not be called to be a minister or missionary but He commands us to influence society, members of our family, and the lives of those with whom we come into contact. Jesus explained the nature of Christian discipleship in terms of salt and light.

« You are the salt of the earth. But if the salt loses its saltiness, how can it be made salty again? It is no longer good for anything, except to be thrown out and trampled by men » (Matthew 5:13) Jesus called fishermen to be his disciples and they would have been familiar with the use of salt as a preservative. It has been estimated, when Jesus lived and worked in Galilee, that there were about 300 boats fishing from the lake, supplying the population of the city of Jerusalem. Fish was the staple diet for many and meat was only eaten on special days, such as the Sabbath or on the Day of Passover. Fish was preserved by rubbing salt into it and then was transported by donkey and cart to Jerusalem. There was of course no refrigeration in those days and the climate was hot so that the only way to preserve the fish was to salt it down! Some of that salt would have come from the area of the Dead sea. Salt, (sodium chloride), is very stable and does not decay or lose its saltiness. The salt from the Dead sea varied greatly in quality depending on the amount of impure substances it contained. Some of the salt came mixed with a white powder, possibly calcium carbonate or lime, such salt had lost its saltiness and it was thrown on the paths and donkey tracks. It was trampled under foot! Good pure salt then was a precious preservative, whereas contaminated salt was useless and thrown on the road.

In the Bible we read that babies were washed with salt at birth (Ezekiel 16:4) Food is tasteless without salt (Job 6:6). Salt was used in forming the covenant between God and His people. (Numbers 18:19 & 2 Chronicles 13:5) It was emblematic of fidelity and friendship among eastern nations. All offerings were offered with salt. It has the qualities of purifying and preserving and being antiseptic. The world that Jesus lived in was not idyllic as we often imagine it to have been. The New Testament makes it plain that there was much dishonesty and stealing, adultery and cruelty. His followers must be different. There must be a fundamental difference between Christians and non-Christians. Sometimes people have a veneer of Christianity and it is impossible to tell the difference between them and the people around them who do not claim to be Christian. It is difficult for Christians to penetrate and influence society as Jesus demanded if they are not radically different from their non-Christian neighbours. Just as the effectiveness of salt is conditional, depending upon the quality so the Christian who is not properly equipped will lose his saltiness, and fail to influence others. Jesus challenged his disciples with these words. « Salt is good, but if it loses its saltiness, how can you make it salty again? Have salt in yourselves, and be at peace with each other. » (Mark 9:50) We are to retain our saltiness having « salt in ourselves » only then will we be able to influence and change society, being an antiseptic in a corrupt world. We are also to be at peace with one another. We are to influence and help preserve good relationships with those with whom we come into contact.

Christians as salt affect society by their deeds as well as their words. There are many Christians who have influenced society in politics, sport and leisure. We think of people like Desmond Tutu and his opposition to apartheid, or Trevor Huddlestone who campaigned all his life against the same evil. His prayer for Africa has been used by many. Lesser known and just as courageous is Andrew White the vicar of St George's Church Baghdad and president of the 'Foundation of movement for Reconciliation in the Middle East'. Many are familiar with Jackie Pullinger who worked amongst the 'Triad' gangs, drug addicts and prostitutes in the notorious walled city in Hong Kong, where she founded the St Stephen's society, that provides rehabilitation homes for those with whom she worked. Christians in show business include, Dame Julie Dench, David Suchet, Bono from the band U2 and many more. All these have exerted influence on our society as a result of their faith. They acted as salt helping to stem the tide of evil that continues to corrupt our society. Christians like Mary Whitehouse spoke out strongly against pornography as did Ann Widecombe against the deterioration of family life. Salt is not to remain in the ornamental salt cellar, the church, but is to be an antiseptic in our wounded secular community. Many Christians condemn our secular society, saying « Things are getting worse and worse! » They tend to blame the non christian world throwing up their hands in despair when they should blame themselves for not being salty enough! Remember that Jesus came to save the world not condemn it!

Jesus left his disciples with no choice as to whether they would be salt. « You **are** the salt of the earth » he said. There are many ordinary Christians fulfilling their calling to be salt. I know a young mother in France who has set up a charity to support a school and orphanage in the Central African republic. A member of one of the Churches where I was minister had been a member of Parliament supporting a weekly prayer meeting taking the issues of the day to the Lord in prayer. There are many Christians leading the fight against poverty, by setting up food banks and furniture outlets » for the poor. Some Christians work voluntarily in charity shops to aid a hospice, or help the aged. Some volunteer to visit the sick in hospital or to visit criminals and young offenders in prison. Very often the Church is the originator of projects to help people who are struggling to find their way in life. Volunteers from several churches in a seaside town worked together to provide a hostel for homeless young people, helping them to become independent. I know Christians who themselves have been set free from drug addiction and a life of crime, and are now at work rescuing other men and woman who are in a similar position. There are Christians who share their faith with bikers, and befriend teenagers from broken families. Other Christians have set up projects to help people cope with debt, teaching them how to budget and use their money wisely. Many Christians help with school assemblies using resources such as «Open the Book ». Holiday clubs for children, preparing and serving meals for the handicapped, running clubs for the elderly and many more similar projects can be found all over our country these too are salt. There are countless ways that Christians can be salt at home, at work and in their leisure time. Jesus also taught that his disciples and followers were to be bright lights shining in a dark world. « You are the light of the world. A city on a hill cannot be hidden. Neither do people light a lamp and put it under a bowl. Instead they put it on its stand, and it gives light to everyone in the house. In the same way, let your light shine before men, that they may see your good deeds and praise your father in heaven » (Matthew 5:14-16) Christians are to shine in their surroundings with the light of Christ. Jesus commanded his disciples to be what he himself claimed to be. Jesus said « As long as I am in the world I am the light of the world » (John 9:5) The followers of Jesus are to be like Him. It is his light that should be shining through us. The radiance that shines from the disciple of Jesus, is not his/her own light, but is the light of the presence of Christ within the heart. There is a story told of a little boy who was taken to Church by his grandmother one sunny morning. They looked at the beautiful stained glass windows depicting the saints. « Who are they? » he asked, « They are saints » explained his grandmother. Later when the little boy went to school, his teacher asked « Does anyone know what a saint is? The little boy replied « Someone the light shines through », what a wonderful and apt description. In the New Testament all believers, those who had consecrated their lives to the Lord, were known as saints.

On a trip to Israel while I was standing beside the sea of Galilee a local guide pointed out the city of Saffed perched on the top of a high hill. That city can be seen from just about any point on the shores of the lake. He thought that maybe when Jesus spoke about a city on a hill that cannot be hidden, he possibly pointed in the direction of Saffed to make his point! Light dispels darkness and is seen. Christianity is meant to be seen. Jesus taught the same truth when he said « Neither do people light a lamp and put it under a bowl » (Matthew 5 15)   On visiting a village in Israel that was situated in Ephraim I entered a very ancient home. There was the raised sleeping area for the family enclosed by the space allotted to the domestic animals. The house was very dark indeed and was illuminated only by the light entering through a small round window and the open door. The only source of light after dark, at the time when Jesus lived, was a lamp in the shape of a gravy boat filled with olive oil with a wick floating in it. The lamps were not easily lit and if the family wanted to leave the house to visit a neighbour they did not snuff out the light but covered it with a ceramic bushel measure so as to minimize fire risk! When they returned the cover would be lifted and the light would continue to shine. We are light in a dark world and we are to let our light shine and not allow it to be hidden. Paul writes « Do everything without complaining or arguing so that you may become blameless and pure, children of God without fault in a crooked and depraved generation, in which you shine like stars in the universe - » (Philippians 2:14-15) Light dispels darkness. The darker it is the brighter the light shines. The Christian is not just to be visible in the Church but also in the world.

Jesus clarifies what he means by being light. When people see your « good deeds » they will « give glory to your Father who is in heaven » Good deeds or works is a general expression to cover everything that a Christian says or does because he/she is a follower of Christ. Jesus taught that being a light in the world meant

1) Doing good works. People must see your good works.

2) Light is a common symbol for truth. Tell the truth in every situation. We will not deal in half truths or white lies! What we are, what we say, and what we do, may influence people to become Christian. It will affect even the way we play games without cheating! Being a light will mean that we are honest in our dealings with other people.

3) Good works/deeds will include the words we speak. The Old Testament prophecy that God's servant would be a *'light to the nations'* is fulfilled not only in Christ but also in Christians who bear witness to Christ. Evangelism must be counted as one of the 'good works' by which our light shines and our heavenly Father is glorified.

4) Sometimes our actions speak louder than words! I know of a young lady who became a Christian because she saw something of the light of Christ in a group of Christians who were putting on a secular concert! The attitude and relationship among these people inspired her to discover what was special ,about them. She is now a preacher and leader in a local Church.

5) Following Jesus will affect our behaviour and how we relate to others.

6) Our light must shine in the way we regard people, what is our attitude to the person who serves us at the supermarket check out, or our attitude to other road users.

7) Just as runway lights guide an aeroplane when it lands in the dark,we must make clear the way for others. Although many lighthouses have been decommissioned there are still some that warn shipping of danger. Christians are to act as warning lights to others. We are to warn people of moral, social and spiritual danger. We do not warn people in anger, nor do we become irritated or critical, we do not condemn but warn people in love. We « Speak the truth in love ». Just as there is a fundamental difference between light and dark, the Christian is different from the non-Christian and the Church is different from the 'world'. In the believer's life and his impact on the world there is a battle between light and darkness. We don't always realise this so we must consciously seek to be lights.

Broadly speaking in the church community concerning the sphere of service there are three types of believers, those who want to do everything and do not want others to do anything, their service is often directly related to their self-esteem. They desire to impress others and earn 'brownie points' with God. There are also people in the Church who are quite happy to do nothing! Many times they will not become actively involved because they are afraid of failure, or being criticised by others. Then there are those who are not committed enough and have not surrendered their will to the Lord, they are looking for what the church will do for them not what they can do for the church; takers not givers. There are Christians who are working very hard getting nowhere, it's all too much for them and they give up. Our most important equipment is the person of the Holy Spirit. If we are relying on our own strength and are not full of the Spirit things get more and more difficult. Imagine trying to push a motor car up a steep hill, almost impossible. The answer is to start the engine! Imagine an aeroplane trying to take off without an engine. The steward tells the passengers to uncover the trap door beneath their feet and start running.! There is no way that they will be airborne! The Holy Spirit provides the power and the gifts for us to be able to serve the Lord. It is because of our need of the Spirit that Paul exhorts Christians to be full of the Spirit (Ephesians 5:18). The tense of the word 'be filled' in the original Greek means be filled and keep on being filled! To be filled we must be empty of self. I find it essential to remember that I have been crucified with Christ and ask the Father to fill me with the Holy Spirit at the start of each day.

Finally, we must be full of the Holy Spirit if we are to be effective disciples. The Holy Spirit equips the Christian to deal with every situation that has to be faced and every task he/she is called to carry out. Many Christians allow the living water (the Holy Spirit) to dry up! Jesus promised that the Holy Spirit would flow through a believer's life. « 'If a man is thirsty, let him come to me and drink. Whoever believes in me, as the scripture has said, streams of living water will flow from within him' By this he meant the Spirit, whom those who believed in Him were later to receive. Up to that time the Spirit had not been given, since Jesus had not yet been glorified. » (John 7:37-39) There is a river whose source is in the mountains of North Africa, it flows for many miles but never reaches the sea. The spiritual life of many Christians is like that river, starting well but never reaching its destination. Many fall away without reaching their full potential. If we are to serve the Lord to the best of our ability we must do it in the power of the Spirit. When we recognise that Jesus has risen from the dead, ascended into heaven, rules and reigns as King we can ask him to fill us with the Holy Spirit. When we ask in prayer, we must believe. We must not have any reservation that we can be filled by the Spirit. Just as a white flag or hands held aloft on the battle field are signs of surrender, so Jesus calls us to surrender our whole lives to Him. 'The Light of the World' is the title of a famous picture painted by Holman Hunt in 1854. It portrays Christ, thorn-crowned, and carrying a lantern, knocking at a closed door. When the artist showed the picture he had completed to some friends, one pointed out what seemed to be an omission. « You have put no handle on the door » he said. The artist replied, «**We** must open to the Light - the handle is on the inside. » Today, Jesus present in the power of the Holy Spirit, knocks at the door of our lives just as He knocked at the door of the lives of the lukewarm Christians in the Church in Laodicea. « Here I am! I stand at the door and knock If anyone hears my voice and opens the door, I will come in and eat with him, and he with me. » (Revelation 3:20) So dear friends open to Jesus let Him fill and influence your lives in every part and let His Holy Spirit transform your lives to His glory. « Let men see your good works and so glorify your Father in Heaven »